ENDORSEMENTS

Grant Berry is one of the newer voices and writers regarding the Church's call to understand the place of Israel in these last days. Grant takes a very biblical approach to the responsibility of the Gentile believers toward ministry to the Jew and to the nation of Israel, inclusive of how we view Jewish believers. This, in my mind, distinguishes him from other prophetic voices.

I have known Grant for over 25 years and can testify to his passion to explain G-d's covenant promised to both Jew and Gentile. I love Grant's commitment to see Messianic and Gentile believers come together as one family in Christ.

PASTOR DON WILKERSON
Cofounder and President of Brooklyn Teen Challenge

We are living in the greatest time ever in human history: the culmination of G-d's redemptive plan for mankind and the consummation of His kingdom on earth. As the world stage is rapidly being set for the return of Jesus Christ, it's urgent that we turn our attention to the biblical prophecies regarding Israel and the Church that have long eluded theologians and have been largely ignored by Bible preachers and teachers.

Grant Berry helps us take an important step toward understanding G-d's heart for the ultimate salvation of His people, Israel, and the restoration of His family between Jew and Gentile into One New Man. As the task of evangelizing the entire Gentile world is nearing completion, G-d has raised Grant up to introduce the Church to the missing, critical piece of the end-time puzzle, and her final quest in intercession and action.

REV. GLENN HARVISON
Lead Pastor, Harvest Time Church
Greenwich, Connecticut

Grant writes with clarity, conviction, and solid truth from a Messianic Jewish and kingdom perspective. A highly recommended read.

DANIEL JUSTER
Director, Tikkun International

Grant is a Jewish believer in Yeshua/Jesus, and he loves the Jewish people and the Church of G-d. He sees them in the Father's light as a spiritual family who are ultimately intricately connected. *The Ezekiel Generation* sheds light on the reconnection that he believes G-d wants to bring in these days, which will unite the Body of Christ with powerful end-time consequences. You might not agree with every point of theology, but his perspective on Church history and some of his ideas will challenge you. But please read this book prayerfully as I did and ask the L-rd to open your heart to how He wants you to connect more deeply with Him and His chosen people!

MITCH GLASER
President, Chosen People Ministries

The

EZEKIEL

GENERATION

The Father's Heart for Israel
and the Church in the LAST DAYS

GRANT BERRY

DESTINY IMAGE BOOKS BY GRANT BERRY

The New Covenant Prophecy

The

EZEKIEL

GENERATION

The Father's Heart for Israel
and the Church in the LAST DAYS

GRANT BERRY

DESTINY IMAGE® PUBLISHERS, INC.

P.O. Box 310, Shippensburg, PA 17257-0310

"Promoting Inspired Lives."

This book and all other Destiny Image, Revival Press, MercyPlace, Fresh Bread, Destiny Image Fiction, and Treasure House books are available at Christian bookstores and distributors worldwide.

For a U.S. bookstore nearest you, call 1-800-722-6774.

For more information on foreign distributors, call 717-532-3040.

Reach us on the Internet: www.destinyimage.com.

ISBN 13 TP: 978-0-7684-0360-2

ISBN 13 Ebook: 978-0-7684-8490-8

For Worldwide Distribution, Printed in the U.S.A.

5 6 7 8 / 17 16 15 14

DEDICATION

This book is dedicated to the remnant, who at this time are in great need of a louder voice amongst the Body of Christ. However, this is not just a remnant of natural Israel, but rather a remnant of all believers within the Church, both Jew and Gentile alike. These are they who have come to learn from the heart of G-d how the Father longs for His firstborn son to be rebirthed in the Spirit, how His covenants are to be established in the earth, and how significant they are to the entire family of G-d before Messiah returns.

Throughout this book I like to refer to these Gentile Christian followers as "Ruths" and "Corneliuses." These are men and women of G-d whose eyes have been unveiled by the Holy Spirit to understand the importance of Israel as revealed throughout the Scriptures, and whose hearts have been touched by the Father to connect with our firstborn brethren with a supernatural love that comes from above.

This remnant, although relatively small throughout the centuries, has always existed in the Body of Christ—from the prayers of the Puritans, who may have helped to fuel the birth of Zionism in the Spirit, to the numerous believers and followers of Christ who laid down their lives to help the Jewish people through Hitler's Germany, and finally to the many believers today who are praying for this transformation to take place in the Church.

As we approach this unique time in history, where G-d's family will be supernaturally united together, the cry of G-d is going throughout His Body to awaken us into G-d's end-time plan, as well as the new era that is to come upon us when Jesus establishes His kingdom on the earth.

It is to all of the cries and prayers of these saints that have gone up to G-d concerning Israel and the Church, and which I have personally felt on numerous occasions while writing this book, that *The Ezekiel Generation* is dedicated. My hope is that these prayers would not be in vain—that the Father's plans would be made known to His entire Body, to restore the Jewish people back into relationship with their G-d, and, ultimately, bring both Israel and the Church into their end-time destinies.

ACKNOWLEDGMENTS

Jesus promised a Counselor who would tell us about what is to come; and without the Holy Spirit's guidance, gentleness, and patience, this book would not have been written. In fact, it has been His handprint upon my life that has brought me to this point, to write this book with such a specific focus to help G-d's family find its destiny at this time.

Early on in my walk with the King, as I was fully absorbing all of the Christian theology I could possibly get my hands on, He gently instructed me through the Holy Spirit to become more dependent on Him for insight and revelation in His Word. Through dreams, visions, and prophetic pictures in intercession for Israel, along with day-to-day guidance and experience in Spirit and truth, He has carved this message of reconnection—G-d's family between Jew and Gentile finally coming together as one—deep into my heart. To the Father, the Son, and the Holy Spirit be the glory forever and ever, amen.

Special thanks to my family for their constant love and support; to those in the Messiah's House intercessory prayer group who have labored with me, especially in understanding the Holy Spirit's focus upon the Church as the key to Israel's spiritual awakening: Al Sanchirico, Kent and Josephine Johnson, Millie Torres, Jon Feinstein, Wilma Reyes, Susan Sevensky, Ruth Diaz, Bill Nugent, Frank Caporale, Angel Suarez, and Stephen and Claire Frieder.

Special thanks to the leadership in the Body who have helped to endorse this work: Brian Simmons, Don Wilkerson, Glenn Harvison, Dan Juster, Mitch Glazer, and Tod McDowell for his personal testimony. And to my dear friends: Don Finto for all of his personal support, to Al Sanchirico and Josephine Johnson for their insights, and to the Destiny Image team for editing and publishing this book.

G-D'S INSTRUCTIONS TO EZEKIEL CONCERNING ISRAEL

Then He said to me, "Prophesy to the breath; prophesy son of man, and say to it, 'This is what the Sovereign L-rd says: Come from the four winds, O breath, and breathe into these slain, that they may live.'" So I prophesied as He commanded me, and breath entered them; they came to life and stood up on their feet—a vast army.

Then He said to me: "Son of man, these bones are the whole house of Israel" (Ezekiel 37:9-11).

CONTENTS

FOREWORD

Grant Berry has given us fresh light on a needed topic—the distinct roles of Jews and Gentiles in the Body of Yeshua/Jesus, and how we work together in the kingdom of G-d! He gives great insights into this crucial topic that will be increasingly important the closer we get to the return of the Messiah. It is written in the fullness of the love of Christ yet addresses some delicate issues on both sides between the two groups, for the sake of G-d's healing and reconciliation at this time.

G-d has made us both one. But He has also given us functional differences as Jewish and Gentile believers that are crucial for us to see during these days. I'm convinced Grant's book will be used to give a roadmap to travel together as One New Man in the coming days!

Wonderful truths are contained in *The Ezekiel Generation*! I'm hearing the bones coming together, and I'm seeing a new army arise that celebrates the distinctions G-d has given each of us and how we need to see the firstborn of Israel in the family of G-d!

Thank you, Grant, for showing us the way! Read this book and be prepared for the dawning of a new day as Jews and Christians come together to expand the kingdom of G-d and glorify Yeshua!

Dr. Brian Simmons
U.S. Director, HIM

INTRODUCTION

Grant, a servant of Jesus Christ, called to help the Church spiritually reconnect with Israel in the end days: grace, mercy, and peace from G-d the Father and Christ Jesus our L-rd.

On a sunny winter day in 2010, on a beach in Connecticut off the Long Island Sound, I was on a prayer walk when the Holy Spirit clearly spoke to me about writing this book. At this time in my life, I was in a transition from a career path in the cosmetic industry into more of a ministry focus. With all that was going on in my life at that time (which was quite stressful), G-d said to me, "You are going to write a book to the Church, and you are to call it *The Father's Heart for Israel and the Church.*"

When He spoke these words to me, I immediately started to weep and felt the heavy burden of this call upon my heart. At the same time, however, I also felt tremendous gratitude because He knew I had been waiting many years to bring forth this message—a message He had placed deep within my heart.

Ironically, it was at this time that I felt the most inept moving forward. But as we know in our faith, it is when we are at our weakest point that His strength can truly work through us. This was certainly true for me at this time.

WRITING THIS BOOK

Early on in my walk with the G-d, as an intercessor for Israel, He started to put a burden in my heart and began to impart spiritual understanding to me that was not necessarily common to the Church. In the beginning stages, I often questioned myself in this regard. But as He started to mature me more in my faith and began to connect me with others who were also seeing similar things, my faith began to grow.

As I now complete this work, I have been a believer in Christ for 29 years and have spent most of my believing life in the Church (five of which have been in a Messianic congregation). I have always been involved in ministry along with my career as an entrepreneur, building up and selling a number of different businesses in the cosmetic industry—the most notable of which was a brand called Lord & Berry, where I named G-d as my business partner. In this company I developed a brand new concept, introducing and pioneering the lipstick pencil into the cosmetic world, which mushroomed from its launch. Lord & Berry was sold in over 84 countries, and with its success we were able to help finance the ministry efforts to awaken the Russian Jews.

In the early 1990s, I helped manage and oversee the Jewish ministry at Times Square Church in New York City under the Wilkerson brothers. From 1994–1997, I established a ministry in the former Soviet Union with two other leaders, Richard Davis and John Vigario, called Abraham's Promise. It was here that we reeducated the Russian Jews through a theatrical presentation of the Passover, where we explained its fulfillment through Yeshua/Jesus, seeing thousands come to faith. This whole experience changed my life as well as my perspective of Jewish evangelism, where I knew that it was only a matter of time before G-d would look to awaken the rest of my people in the West as well as those in Israel.

More recently, I lead a Messianic ministry in the Westchester area of New York, known as Messiah's House, which was founded in prayer. Messiah's House has a parachurch focus: Firstly, to reach out toward the Jewish community with the Gospel; secondly, to help equip the Church to be more effective in Jewish ministry; and, thirdly, to help unite the Body in prayer for Israel and the end days.

I am a Jewish believer who has a great love for the Church as well as for my Gentile believing family. In my theology, however, I am very much centered on the One New Man that the New Covenant introduces, where both Jew and Gentile dwell together in the Spirit of G-d (see Eph. 2:11-22). I am also focused on the unity of G-d's family between Jew and Christian, which has a central theme throughout this book.

I have considered this writing a holy work unto the L-rd and have not touched it once without offering my full body and spirit to the L-rd in prayer, that both His anointing and His Word would flow through me as I wrote. There have been numerous occasions and experiences where I have personally witnessed and felt His heart's cry, not only for His lost son, the Jews, but also for the unity of His entire family between Jew and Gentile; that as we draw down to the end of history before the L-rd's return, both groups would come into their unique destinies to glorify G-d upon the earth.

As that mysterious veil over the Jewish people begins to lift and more and more of them come to faith in Yeshua Ha-Mashiach/ Jesus Christ, the fulfillment of G-d's words to spiritually restore Israel in keeping His holy covenants now becomes a strategic plan upon the earth. This is a plan that we must not only fully understand, but one that also requires our full participation in fulfilling our own destiny within the Church, while helping awaken Israel in the Spirit. The end result of this is G-d's family finally being united, ultimately helping to usher in the L-rd's return. This, of course, is a huge consequence to consider and quite different from what we have been taught up to this point.

The Ezekiel Generation brings much of this understanding into the light in a way that helps us better prepare for the coming days. It deals with and addresses some very delicate and sensitive areas in the hope of introducing the additional healing and cleansing that is required for G-d's family to come together in the end times.

I started to write this book in January of 2011, and was planning to include some of my own testimony in it—parts that were relevant to the topic at hand. However, I kept writing about my own spiritual journey, which simply flowed out of me. It was at this point I inquired of the L-rd and asked Him about what was going on. I knew there was too much material written about my own life for this particular book.

One week later, the L-rd answered me as I was truly beginning to question its focus: "To the Jew first and then to the Gentile," the Holy Spirit whispered. In my spirit, I immediately knew what the L-rd meant. My ministry focus had always been called to this position, and I now knew that I was supposed to write two books—one positioned for the Jews and one positioned for the Church.

THE NEW COVENANT PROPHECY

In my first book, *The New Covenant Prophecy*, I wrote about all that Yeshua/Jesus has done in my life from my very first meeting with Him, continuing into the depths of my personal walk with G-d. I wrote about how He gave His life as the Paschal Lamb not only to redeem us from our sins but also to open the door to a New Covenant journey of faith in each of our lives where we would all finally have the opportunity to know G-d in a personal way.

As a Jew myself, I explained my personal spiritual journey in a way from my Jewish family could better relate to. I did this so that those of us who have not yet tasted the goodness of G-d would have the opportunity to be exposed to the New Covenant promise, which is intimacy with G-d (see Jer. 31:31-34).

In the same way, I have also written my previous book to give my Christian brethren a better understanding and perspective of how we Jews relate to the Gospel, inclusive of the barriers and challenges that every Jew has to face and overcome in their process to salvation.

THE EZEKIEL GENERATION

The Ezekiel Generation has been written with many of my personal insights and revelations from G-d about the reconnection of His family being essential to G-d's plan to reveal Himself during these days. Many of its messages have been carved upon my heart and spirit throughout my walk with the L-rd as a Jewish believer in the Church. And know that it has been written in a sea of love for both groups, because in these days it would greatly please our Father and His most beloved Son that we would unite in faith to see the return of our L-rd.

This book not only gives deep spiritual insights into G-d's plans for these days, but also addresses the significance of the reconnection between Israel and the Church in order for G-d to bring it about. It also provides greater clarity to the essential roles both Jews and Christians are to play in G-d's end-time plan so that He will ultimately be glorified in the earth.

In order for us to experience this reconnection, however, we must first be willing to address the areas that have caused us to become separated. I deal with these issues with the sole purpose of introducing G-d's healing touch that opens the door to a newness and fresh approach in G-d's plan—perhaps one we were not supposed to see until this time.

This is not just another story about Israel and the Church, but rather a challenge to us in G-d's Body, to both Jewish and Gentile believers alike, as to what we will do with this information, how it may actually change us in the process, and where we will go from here. It is written to provoke a reaction deep within the heart and soul of every believer, bringing forth G-d's revelation and spiritual understanding to complete the family of G-d in a crucial time for His kingdom upon the earth. And this, of course, is so that G-d would ultimately be glorified upon the earth (see Ezek. 36:22-24).

To begin the book, I would like to offer a prayer and ask you to come into agreement with me that its message would not only enlighten you, but also ignite your spirit into the plans of G-d for the end days.

> *Dear Heavenly Father, I come to You in the precious name of Jesus Christ, the Jewish Messiah. L-rd, I ask You to open my mind and my spirit to the message in this book, to show me if it is from You or not. I pray that You would enable me to hear and see its content from Your heart and mind so that I may understand Your purposes and Your will for these days—not just for me and the Church, L-rd, but also for the people of Israel and Your great desire to see Your family united in the kingdom of G-d.*

> *L-rd, despite our differences as Your children, help me to better understand this mystery between Israel and the Church. I pray that it would enable Your healing and cleansing to flow, to heal the divide between Jew and Gentile, so that Your plans would shine through all Your children, which will bring glory to Your kingdom upon the earth. In Jesus's precious name I pray, amen.*

A JEW AND A CHRISTIAN

In light of the fact that I am both a Jew as well as a believer, I consider myself part of both camps. As a Jew, I am part of Israel; and as a believer, I am also a part of the Church—the worldwide Body of believers throughout history, consisting of Catholics, Greek Orthodox, Protestants, and Messianic believers. Because of this, from time to time I take the first person when relating to both groups of people, which could otherwise be confusing.

And as in traditional Judaism, I never write out the full name of G-d or that of L-rd, always eliminating the middle vowel. As a Jewish believer, I like this tradition and with the liberty I have in the New Covenant, I have brought it into my faith as it quickly reminds me of the holiness of G-d as well as showing great respect to our Creator.

When I write to Jewish people, I use Jewish terms and descriptions; similarly, when I write to Christians, I use Christian terms. I fully acknowledge the apostle Paul's directive in His flexibility to promote the Gospel to both Jew and Gentile, becoming all things to all men so that I may win some (see 1 Cor. 9:19-23).

Please note that some concepts presented in this book are repeated several times. I have done this intentionally, not only to emphasize the main points, but also to shed light on these issues from different angles in order that we may see them in their entirety.

May G-d's presence and blessings be upon you as you read this book.

Part One

UNDERSTANDING THE MYSTERY BETWEEN ISRAEL AND THE CHURCH

1

JOSHUA'S BIRTH

HE WOULD BE BORN

The Roman clock sat high above the whitewashed wall, centered in an empty corridor with two wide doorways at each end of it. My view was from above, and I noticed the time on the clock, which read ten minutes to eleven. As I woke up, I knew the dream meant something but I didn't know what it was. So I prayed and asked the L-rd to shed light on it to give me spiritual understanding. It was Wednesday, March 21, 1990, the day my firstborn son was supposed to be born.

That date was given to him by the doctor who was to deliver him. The previous day I had been in my usual weekly prayer meeting for Israel with Diane Pearson in the basement of One Accord (the church I attended at the time), when the L-rd spoke a strange word to me about my son's birth. He said, "Joshua did not want to be born, but he would be born." I shared the word with Diane and the two of us asked the Holy Spirit for further direction.

By this time I was beginning to mature in my spiritual discernment in prayer and intercession, and I knew if I did not understand a word or direction from the L-rd in the Spirit, I would simply give it back to Him and wait. Often, in intercession, the L-rd can be quite mysterious and He likes to speak to us in puzzles and clues, as He also takes pleasure when we seek Him (see Prov. 25:2).

Of course, being the Creator of the universe, He definitely leans to the creative side. So when we release spiritual direction back to Him, the next piece is usually given to us so that we can gain the understanding He wants us to see for the next step. And that's exactly what Diane and I did.

"What do You mean, L-rd, that Joshua does not want to be born, but that he will be born?" I asked fully expecting an answer. It does not always happen like this, but on this particular occasion I sensed the L-rd's excitement as I asked. Instantly, I had a revelation and understanding in my spirit, that G-d was making a comparison between my firstborn son and His firstborn son, Israel.

What G-d was saying to us was that Israel did not want to be born. And while we did not get much more from that morning in intercession, I had a distinct word that I started to seek the L-rd about for additional understanding. Almost three years earlier when I had started dating my wife, Donna, the Holy Spirit had given me another word and told me that I was going to have a son and that we were to give him the name Joshua, which was quite specific.[1]

Little did Donna and I know what was ahead for us, but G-d obviously did. We were connected with an experienced and well-known English gynecologist by the name of Dr. Mary Wilson. We had been introduced through my brother Craig, who was doing some consulting for her on some pregnancy products. We didn't think much of it at the time, but Dr. Wilson was extremely specialized and only handled troubled births. She agreed to take Donna anyway because of my brother's connection with her.

Several days passed and still there were no signs of Joshua coming forth. Then, around 4 a.m. on Sunday morning, Donna's water finally broke. We called the doctor and proceeded directly to the maternity ward at St. Vincent's Hospital in Greenwich Village. At first, everything seemed to be fine; but it wasn't long before Dr. Wilson realized that Donna's cervix was not opening, and up to that point she had only dilated 2 centimeters.[2]

It had already been several hours since Donna's water broke, and so the doctor decided to put her on a hormone called Pitocin. It helps induce the labor and hopefully open the cervix so the baby can be born quickly. Donna was having rapid contractions at this time, which were coming every 60–90 seconds, equaling the same speed as the final phase of childbirth and are only supposed to last for an hour before the baby is delivered. But Donna had been on Pitocin for more than nine hours, the pain was intense and there was still no dilation, the cervix had not moved another millimeter.

The three of us were in the birthing room for most of the day. I must say that Dr. Wilson was absolutely fabulous and extremely calm through most of the labor and in light of the difficulties Donna was experiencing. She stayed with us most of the day, which is not usual these days with gynecologists.

Suddenly, Joshua's heartbeat dropped quite dramatically, and, for the first time, I felt the doctor's nervousness. "Dr. Wilson, would you mind if we said a prayer?" I asked. She quickly agreed and the three of us joined together, holding hands around Donna's bed as we prayed to G-d for wisdom and direction.

Immediately after that, Dr. Wilson decided to attempt to deliver the baby through a caesarean section. The anesthesiologist gave Donna a general anesthetic, and then took her into the operating room shortly after, which I was not allowed into for medical reasons. But there was a round window in the main door to the operating room in which I glued my curious and worried head so that I could at least get a glimpse of what was going on.

I was praying in tongues silently and had been since Joshua's heartbeat had dropped. In the Spirit I could sense a battle going on for Joshua's birth. I could feel the Spirit of G-d arising within me, and I could hardly contain myself. I was now praying out loud and was warring in the heavenlies. To be perfectly honest at this point, I really didn't care who heard or saw me since I knew my son's life was on the line.

As I looked through the window, I could not believe my eyes; Donna was stretched out on the operating table in the form of a cross, arms outstretched and strapped down. As I looked on, the spiritual battle intensified and I knew that something was trying to destroy Joshua. I could feel the tension and nervousness around Donna and our child as I continued to pray in the Spirit.

By now, Dr. Wilson had already cut Donna open and was rigorously trying to deliver Joshua, but both baby and mother were resisting too much and she could not get to Joshua in order to bring him out. Exasperated, the doctor pulled back to rethink the situation, and then decided to tell the anesthesiologist to give Donna additional dosage. Several minutes had passed as we all waited for the new dose to take effect, and I continued to pray without ceasing, feeling the intensity of the battle with every breath. The doctor then resumed her efforts to deliver Joshua. By now I could see almost the entire arm of the doctor inside my wife's womb, trying her utmost to pull Joshua out into the world.

This went on for several minutes as the struggle continued. Joshua did not want to be born, but he would be born. I could see the doctor trying to get a hold of his head in such a way that she could deliver him, but still the fight continued. Several minutes later the doctor wiggled her hand into place and pulled him out with all of her might. Joshua was born at 10:54 p.m. on March 25, 1990, the same time I had seen on the clock in the dream.

Joshua was washed and cleaned up, then immediately given to me. I worshiped and praised the L-rd, singing songs over him for the next couple of hours before Donna would wake up to greet him. What a traumatic ordeal for all concerned, and especially for Donna who had weathered the storm and suffered this rather unusual birth.

I stayed with Donna in the hospital through the night, and later the next day I went home for a couple of hours to freshen up. On the way out of the hospital, I took a different route that I was not familiar with and walked through the hallways that would take me out on the north side of the street. As I got close to the end, I could not believe my eyes as I found myself walking through the same doorways I had seen in my dream the previous Wednesday. And up on the white wall was the same clock that I had seen! As I saw it, my spirit jumped, the presence of G-d was all over me, and I knew that G-d was definitely trying to get my attention. There was a deeper message here He wanted to show me.

A PROPHETIC PICTURE

In the midst of all of the excitement of Joshua's birth and family visiting, G-d was in the process of imparting a prophetic picture to me about the Church regarding Israel's spiritual rebirth. I could feel it deep inside my spirit, especially after I left the same corridor I had seen in the dream, as well as having received the word about Joshua not wanting to be born. With what I had just experienced, at this point I did not need to be too spiritual to figure it out.

So I submitted it all back to G-d in prayer, seeking further direction from Him. I sensed that there was something sovereign to be given to us from above. Over the next 24 hours, the L-rd continued to impart His revelation to me through His Word. I already knew prior to his birth that Joshua represented Israel in the picture (see Exod. 4:22). In further prayer, G-d showed me that the doctor, who represented authority and whose outstretched arm actually represented the outstretched arm and hand of the L-rd in the story of the Passover (see Exod. 6:6; 13:9,14), now represented the L-rd spiritually giving birth to Israel and bringing them forth.

I knew then that Donna was never supposed to give birth naturally. She could have been on that medicine for days and it would not have made a difference because Joshua was not supposed to be born of natural means, but *only* by the mighty hand and outstretched arm of the L-rd. This is certainly true of Israel as well when it comes to them receiving the breath and Spirit of G-d. After that, I strongly felt that G-d would give Donna natural births for our other children so His message would also be confirmed. And this was true for both Jonathan and Madison.

The revelation continued, and a day or so later, as we were trying to put the pieces of the puzzle together, it suddenly occurred to us that there were a number of other symbols being given through this whole event. We then asked G-d who Donna represented in the story, and almost immediately He reminded us of Ephesians 5, where the wife is representative of the Church (see Eph. 5:25-27). Nearly every detail had some kind of spiritual insight and connection associated to it, almost as if the L-rd had planned out these details Himself. Now the rest of the picture was given to us.

THE DETAIL IN THE PORTRAIT

The clock on the wall in the dream reading ten minutes to eleven signified Romans 10–11, which focus the Gentile Church on Israel. The cervix not opening was an indication that Israel could not come forth through natural means, the way most Christians come to faith. The sudden loss in heartbeat, where we almost lost Joshua, is indicative of the near-death experience Israel will have to go through before they are fully awakened (see Rev. 16:16; Zech. 12). The three of us gathering for prayer after Joshua's heartbeat dropped is symbolic of the Church, represented by my wife, Jesus, represented by me (the husband), who sits at the Father's side interceding for us all, and the Father, represented by the doctor, who was the authority bringing Israel forth—all of which reflected the unity and order necessary to bring Israel to life.

The spiritual warfare I was feeling portrays Jesus's own fight and warfare He is engaged in against the enemy in the heavenly realm as He intercedes for Israel to come forth. My wife represented the Church, through whom G-d labored to bring forth His son, and was positioned on the operating table, which was in the shape of a cross, portraying the pain, labor, and sacrifice needed of them. And all of this was working together, rebirthing this little child that did not want to be born in the first place, but that must be born in order for Yeshua to return and take His natural place as King over all of the earth, thus fulfilling His covenants. Needless to say that this was a powerful picture!

THE PLAN OF G-D

So what was G-d was saying through this message? And why was He giving me this picture and all of the details along with it? Through Joshua's birth, the L-rd was imparting a prophetic message to us for the Church: it has a crucial role to play in the rebirthing of Israel in the Spirit, and that it must come into this in order to help G-d establish His kingdom upon the earth, which is quite different from its current understanding.

Despite Israel's current spiritual condition, that G-d would work the natural circumstances to bring Israel into place, so the breath of G-d will be released to awaken them and reconnect them to G-d as well as to us, His spiritual family (see Ezek. 37). He was showing me that G-d's covenants and promises to Israel must still come to pass in order to fulfill His holy Word (see Ezek. 36), that the Jewish people will look upon the One that we pierced and then suddenly realize what a tragic mistake we actually made, which was foretold by the prophet Zechariah (see Zech. 12:10). He showed me the prophetic picture so that the veil, which was sealed upon Israel's hearts through the prophet Isaiah (see Isa. 6:9-10), would be super-naturally lifted so that we could each know G-d for ourselves and finally be restored (see Jer. 31). *For just as Israel helped to give birth to the Church, now the Church would help to give birth back to Israel with the mercy it has received from G-d* (see Rom. 11:29-32).

Yet my people do not want to be spiritually rebirthed, to that I can attest. The veil and its sealing has so blinded and deaf-ened the Jewish people that most are indifferent as a result. And except for the grace of G-d, I would not be here either to tell this story, as the veil would not have been lifted from my heart when I used to think like the rest of the world. However, Israel will be reborn and the breath of G-d will be breathed into them once again. The holiness and the glory of the G-d of Abraham will still shine through them when He removes their godlessness and takes away the sins of Jacob (see Isa. 59:20).

G-d will bring about the correct circumstances and timing for this to happen because He has spoken it and He certainly can-not deny Himself or His promised word to always restore them. Israel is a covenant people, and they must be restored in order that G-d's own words and promises are fulfilled. As a result, G-d is now beginning to awaken the Church to the strategic role that we will play to help bring this about. For up until this point, many of us have not seen this connection. What an honor that He is actually bestowing upon us in the Church!

The Hebrew Scriptures are full of prophecies that speak of this time and action in Israel's history when they will return to G-d, and also of His overwhelming love for them as a heavenly Father. However, nowhere is this specific word clearer than in the book of Ezekiel. The prophecy promises both a physical restoration to the land for the Jewish people as well as a spiritual awakening. G-d is quite clear to point out why He is doing it: *"For the sake of My holy name"* (Ezek. 36:22); and indeed that my people should actually be ashamed—it was said that we are His people and yet we were dispersed because of idolatry, disobedience, and unbelief.

THE REBIRTH MUST COME THROUGH US

However, unlike most modern teachings, exciting books, and movies about Israel's restoration in the end times, this will not happen by itself or through G-d alone. This has major significance to us in the Church for Israel cannot be born without us! The main reason I believe G-d gave me this prophetic portrait in the first place is so we can properly understand the position and role the Church is to play in G-d's plan and the glory that He wants to bring through us.

He wants to show His glory through Israel in both awakening and restoring them into the kingdom and family of G-d so His word will be fulfilled, which must take place before Jesus can return (see Ezek. 36:22-23). But we in the Church also have a unique role to play because Israel, G-d's firstborn son, cannot be awakened without the breath of G-d that is to be released through the other children in G-d's family. We just don't know yet how intricately connected we really are!

Everyone present was involved in Joshua's birth to bring him forth, and, in this picture, the Father could not have delivered the child without the intercession and labor of Jesus and His Church—without the groom and the bride being actively involved. In this story, Israel came out of the Church's womb, and this picture shows the tremendous cooperation and unity needed to make this happen. Even as Joshua was born from his mother's womb, so Israel will be born through the cries of the Church—that intercession would come forth from her on their behalf. Indeed, the Church has received mercy as a result of Israel's blindness, and during this time and this hour may it begin to cry and push, just like a pregnant woman in labor, that the mighty hand and outstretched arm of the L-rd would bring Israel forth!

Without the Church's participation, however, both the Father and the Son could not bring their plan to fruition, and G-d's first-born would not have been born. Yet, he was born, because all who were involved accepted responsibility for their particular roles, finally coming into the sovereign plan of G-d to reawaken His firstborn (which, of course, I will speak much more about as we progress in this book).

In this picture, the Church's role is strategic and the burden of rebirth is fully shared by all of the parties involved, not just the Father and the Son, but the whole Body of Christ as well. This is quite different from what we are being taught currently, or what we are expecting to take place in the earth today.

Perhaps this is the greatest plan of G-d still yet to happen in the world before Jesus returns to the earth to reign as its sovereign King. Up until this point the Church has not yet fully understood its role and position to help rebirth Israel, to the end result that our L-rd can come back to the earth to take full dominion over it. But we will come into our role and position, just like Israel will, as I believe these changes are still to take place. The Word of G-d is quite clear about showing G-d's glory to the nations through Israel. So why is it that the Church does not yet fully comprehend its role in G-d's plan?

G-D LOOKS FOR AN INTERCESSOR

Not only will I fully answer this question in this book and lay out what I feel and think G-d is saying to us in this final hour we find ourselves in before Messiah returns, but I will also address some of the challenges and changes that we will need to make to help G-d bring this to pass. As we look through Scripture, it is evident that whenever G-d moves upon us or through us, He always looks for an intercessor, one who stands in the gap. From Abraham and Moses, all the way to Christ and beyond, G-d has always moved through people to effect His changes and plans amongst us. So why should the end be any different from the beginning?

For have we in the Church not received G-d's mercy as a result of Israel's disobedience? And is it not both fair and equitable of our Father, at this point in history, to now release that mercy back to them? For is this not the point the apostle Paul makes in Romans 11:30-31?

CONSIDER CAREFULLY

I am not just writing to outline all of the issues that are involved here between Israel and the Church nor for the changes that may be necessary for us to make in order to sign on with His end-time plan. Rather, it is to challenge each of us to participate in this plan if we believe it to be G-d's will. This book is written to address our current theology, causing us to look deeply into our own hearts, ensuring that we are moving into the direction of our Father's plan to glorify His Son.

You may say, "Who am I to make such bold statements but a common voice crying in the wilderness that our Father in heaven would be glorified, that His kingdom would come and that His will be done upon the earth as it is in heaven?" In His Body, are we not longing for truth, justice, and mercy to truly come into its full measure in the new millennial age that G-d has both covenanted and promised to all of His children, that His family would finally be brought to unity and reign together with Christ?

THE ROLES

While I personally believe and encourage Jewish believers in their Jewish identity, which I see as a critical place for us in the Church, I also believe that it comes out of the One New Man spirit that G-d has released to us in the New Covenant (see Eph. 2:11-22). For while both Jew and Gentile are equal in the Spirit, this does not necessarily eliminate the unique roles that each of us are to play along with the rest of Israel in the final days before Yeshua/Jesus returns.

It is actually here, where there is still a great deal of misunderstanding and confusion, as well as in a number of other areas, that I will seek to unravel in this book. As a result, I would ask you to personally pray before we go any further as much of the content has to do with spiritual issues that may begin in the mind but are ultimately issues of the heart and spirit. I pray that you would be open to hearing and receiving many of the thoughts and ideas in this book, and that you would bring them to prayer to seek His guidance and will over them.

As we know from Scripture, anything that is not of Him is like straw and hay that will be burned up as we stand before G-d (see 1 Cor. 3:12). So I want to encourage you to take everything I have written in this book to prayer and to test its spirit against the Word of G-d. For this message burns from deep within my heart and I now feel compelled to share it with my dear brethren in the Church, whom I have come to love as my own spiritual family.

ENDNOTES

1. Joshua is the English name for Yeshua and Jesus is His Greek name.
2. For a baby to be born, the cervix needs to be open approximately 10 centimeters.

2

A New Time and a New Era

If we want the fire, we need to reconnect the wire!

The Reconnection

Before we move on into the depths of the message of this book, I would like to give you a brief outline as to what reconnection may look like as this message is received into the very heart and spirit of our beings.

We are in a new day, a new time, and a new era. The world is getting darker and we are witnessing firsthand the fullness of the parable of the wheat and the tares before our eyes, reflected through sin and righteousness as the end-time harvest comes upon us. It is as if sin itself has to become utterly sinful in order that its judgment might come upon the world. This is one of the most exciting times to be alive upon the earth as a believer and follower of Christ, but at the same time it will also be extremely challenging.

The Bible refers to this time as the "last days." And, as we approach that time, which will also manifest the fullness of the Gentiles upon the earth, we also know that Israel's spiritual awakening is not far off (see Rom. 11:25-26). *Both of these events point to an unprecedented outpouring of G-d's Spirit and are intricately connected but may not have been seen as such before.*

For this reason, we must truly take a fresh look at these times to ensure that we are not ignorant to what is about to take place. G-d's final plan is intertwined in this mystery that exists between Israel and the Church, one that we must truly understand from deep within our spirits. This understanding cannot come through the Word of G-d alone, but it must come through the heart, which the Spirit desires to make known to us at this time.

WE ARE IN A TIME OF TRANSITION

With this in mind, we need to become more conscious of this movement of G-d's Spirit to awaken Israel—a movement that has already begun. He is transitioning solely from a Gentile Christian focus to once again including the firstborn of G-d's children, truly uniting His family in the Spirit of G-d, which has always been His heart's desire. But what will this look like? And will we need to make adjustments to help bring it about?

Before I go any further, I want every reader to know the intentions of my heart. First, I want to emphasize how extremely grateful I am to my Gentile believing family in helping me reconnect with my G-d, without whom I could not have been saved. Not only was it through the Body of Christ that I have learned of my salvation, but I also received the great teachings of learning to walk intimately with G-d, knowing His voice and discerning the direction of the Holy Spirit.

For I was brought into relationship with G-d through the Church, which is what the New Covenant is all about (see Jer. 31:31-34). In fact, I have come to love the other sheep in G-d's family as my very own, praying fervently that both Jewish and Gentile Christians would dwell together in unity, and would live in respect and understanding of our unique callings from within that unity that up to this point has not been properly understood.

As we enter this transition more fully, it will require greater sensitivity and flexibility from within the Church and its Gentile believing family. The same was required of the Jewish believers when the Gospel was first established, when the Jews pulled down every possible barrier in order that the Gentiles could be introduced to the faith. This was done after the Holy Spirit had confirmed to the Church that this was His directive, not just to awaken the Jews, but also now to make Himself known to the rest of the Gentile world.

Now that we are coming into the fullness of the Gentiles and G-d is shifting His attention to restore the unity in His family by awakening Israel, I would like to suggest that we should carefully think through some of the changes we need to make to help this transition take place.

Please note that this transition was not easy for the Jews, and despite the directive of the Holy Spirit, the apostles were met with great opposition from within their own camp. It was not easy for some of them and it may not be easy for some of us either. For a time, it seemed as if the house of G-d was divided over this issue, so please understand that we are not alone in this, but must seek G-d's directive here to know how to respond. It is a new day and a new era in the workings of G-d, one that will require great wisdom, love, and understanding to properly address. This may even be difficult for many of us to process; however, if it is of G-d, we must ensure that we are fully in line with it as well as giving it our complete and utter support.

We need, as a result, to be open to any new revelation that G-d may bring to us at this time to better position and equip ourselves for what is about to take place. I call this plan the "mercy plan," which I often refer to in this book, as I believe salvation for both Jew and Gentile is ultimately about G-d's mercy, especially as it refers to His end-time plan.

MANY HAVE ALREADY BELIEVED

Unlike untold numbers of Christians who have gone before us and who have held to G-d's Word—that He is not finished with Israel and that the Church has not replaced Israel in succession—we have already witnessed the happenstance of numerous prophetic Scriptures that have foretold of Israel's restoration to their land. Not only has G-d done this miraculously, but also these Scriptures are no longer prophetic as they have been fulfilled before our eyes.

Yet we are now living in a time when the final part of Israel's restoration is about to take place—their spiritual awakening. If we trust Scripture and the writings of the apostle Paul, we know that Israel's hardening is only temporary, and as we come into this time of the fullness of the Gentiles *all Israel will be saved"* (Rom. 11:26).

NOT UNTIL THEY SAY...

Jesus told us that He would not return until His Word had gone out into all the nations. And it is evident that a great deal of the Church is focused on these words of Christ, which compel us to preach the Word wherever possible; and is obviously good. However, Jesus also said that He would not return until the Jewish people say, *"Blessed is He who comes in the name of the L-rd"* (Matt. 23:39).

So how come there isn't similar emphasis in the Body to this aim? How will the people of Israel speak these words until their eyes have been opened? Therefore, their spiritual awakening is not only crucial to G-d, but it should also be crucial to us as well, for the L-rd does not return to establish His Davidic kingdom upon the earth until Israel is redeemed. This means that we do not receive our spiritual inheritance to rule and reign with Christ until they receive theirs (which is of utmost importance for us to understand), and it is His perfect plan to bring it all to pass (see Isa. 61:6-9; Rev. 2:26; 5:9-10).

UNDERSTANDING THEIR SIGNIFICANCE

Up until this point in time, however, we hardly see or hear about any spiritual connection between the people of Israel and the Church. It is almost as if G-d is going to deal separately with Israel and that we will have nothing to do with these events that must take place. Or at least this is what is being taught most of the time.

Many of us are praying for the peace of Jerusalem, but do we really know what we are praying for and how strategic Israel's spiritual awakening really is? Not only that, but up to this point we have not yet understood our connection to them as family and the great significance of the role that G-d has chosen for us to play in His mercy plan that will show His glory to the world. And there are reasons for this, which I will explain further.

As we approach the end, a great number of us sense a connection to the land of Israel, which is good. But we must not lose sight of what is still to take place. This is not only of vital significance to G-d but also to all of us in the Church.

We must understand the significance of Israel's spiritual awakening and the role G-d has chosen us to play as being absolutely crucial at this time. And we must be fully cognizant of their current condition while this is taking place. For not everything Israel does is righteous, and we should be careful what we are supporting with our prayers. For it is part of G-d's plan to use Israel's enemies to bring them to a breaking point, which is still to take place. And this is sometimes difficult for any of us to fully comprehend (see Habakkuk 1 and how G-d used Israel's enemies for His purposes).

As a result, I believe that with full awareness of this revelation, there will come the repositioning in our priorities that will drive the spiritual reconnection necessary between Israel and the Church in the family of G-d during this time. By G-d's design, His children are intricately linked to one another, and none of G-d's sheep can come into their own end-time destinies without each other. It is ultimately this mercy plan that will bring about the unity in G-d's family to finally usher in Christ's return.

SUMMARIZING THE RECONNECTION

The reconnection fully recognizes these issues to be tantamount at this time. So what does it look like? The reconnection is a Church that will become more open to this transition between Jew and Gentile. It is a Church that believes G-d's promises and holy covenants with Israel are still yet to take place, through their spiritual awakening. It is a Church that will come into agreement with His word to show His holiness through Israel before Jesus returns.

As a result, the reconnection is a Church that puts Israel's spiritual awakening into first gear, as a top priority, without exalting them in the flesh. It is that we understand G-d's kingdom principles, to the Jew first and then to the Gentile, and in applying this principal through Christ with the changes it will bring, will help to usher in the end-time power and revival the Church is seeking.

It is a Church that has been willing to look at its past, its ancestry and bloodline, without any condemnation in order to break off any negative spiritual influence, receiving healing in how it has acted toward Israel and the Jewish people.

The reconnection is a Church that has spiritually reconnected to its firstborn brethren through the Father's heart and love for His complete family so that it can now be used to help bring about G-d's end-time plan. It is a Church that recognizes that the mercy and grace of G-d is greater than anything the devil can throw at it to keep it from its destiny.

It is a Church that fully embraces the unity between Jewish and Gentile believers in the One New Man of the Spirit of G-d. It is a church that fully recognizes and blesses the unique and distinct roles that both groups, as well as the rest of Israel, are still to play out in order for the kingdom to come upon the earth. And in so doing, it is a Church that once again learns how to communicate the Gospel back to Israel in a way that connects them to their Jewish roots and heritage.

The reconnection is a Church that looks to reconnect to Israel in the same manner in which the apostles fostered unity between the two groups and yet presented Christianity as a Jewish concept, especially when sharing the faith with Jewish people. It is a Church that not only comes to fully understand the mercy plan of G-d but one that completely embraces it along with its own unique role to help give spiritual birth to Israel through prayer and intercession.

The reconnection is a Church whose leadership fully embraces G-d's mercy plan and repositions itself not only to be receptive to it but also to give it its full support.

HANG ONTO YOUR SEAT!

If you're interested in what you're reading, this is but a small taste of what is to come in your new understanding of this most crucial time for the Church in human history. As you read on, you will discover the many issues that surround this reconnection and what G-d wants us to address to help us get into the place and position, so He can actually bring it to pass. He longs for us to come into a new and fresh understanding that better equips us for this incredible time in history, that our generation or the ones that tarry before the L-rd's return, may witness the actual return of Yeshua/Jesus to establish His kingdom amongst us. What an honor indeed!

3

G-d's Plan for Israel—G-d's Plan for Us

We have already entered into the beginning period of G-d's plan to awaken Israel. However, so often when G-d's end-time plan for Israel is spoken about or taught from a Jewish perspective, the rest of us may begin to think, *Well, what about me, L-rd? Where do I fit into all of this? And how come Israel is so important? I'm Your child too!*

As a result, I have chosen to focus on the Church's position at first from a more Gentile Christian perspective in order to explain in greater depth how He will bring us together so we can all find a greater comfort level in G-d's end-time plan. Just like Israel, the Church has a unique role to play to glorify our Father throughout the earth, which we have already seen through Joshua's birth, so that Jesus can ultimately return and take full dominion over His creation. There is a major connection here that we truly need to better understand.

In fact, we will see that without us in the Church, G-d's end-time plan cannot come to fruition. We will begin to see that indeed we are the missing link the Father and Son are waiting for, that we will come into our end-time role to help finish the job, experience Israel's rebirth, and, ultimately, the return of the L-rd.

When one speaks about Israel and the role that they have still yet to play, and how we need to focus on them, he or she can often be accused of being a Judaizer in the Church. This is because there is so much misunderstanding and confusion when it comes to these issues. In the Church, we have tended to focus on Israel more as just another group or nationality, when instead they must be seen as a covenant people. This switches the focus back on G-d in light of His promises to restore them through His holy Word.

To be quite frank, the devil has been all all over these issues between Israel and the Church since the Gospel began, and he will continue to sow his deceptions until he is fully and properly exposed. Even then, there will still be division amongst us relative to Israel and the Jewish people until the L-rd returns. But as we approach the last days, our reconnection to His firstborn will become vital to our spiritual wellness and condition, for without it we may suffer great loss.

Just for the record, Judaizers in the apostle Paul's day (whom he was having to contend with in the first century) were Jews who wanted Gentile believers to not only go back to the law but also find their salvation through it. Thank G-d that the apostles (along with many of the initial believers) fought vigorously against this, costing them personal suffering to boot.

ONLY ONE WAY TO SALVATION

Before I go any further in bringing additional clarification to the different roles between Jewish and Gentile believers, I want to clearly point out my beliefs. I believe that Jesus's death and resurrection has bought everyone the right to be part of the New Covenant. He laid down His life, which caused the veil of the temple to be torn in two, allowing access to G-d. This was to carry us into a better covenant, bringing each of us into personal intimacy with our own Creator, who is the G-d of Israel (see Luke 23:45; Heb. 10:19-20). He opened the doors of heaven to all of His children so that the Gentile world could also find redemption at this point in time, which was obviously according to His plan. It was to bring both Jew and Gentile into the One New Man where there would no longer be any division between us.

As a result, I now willingly share and embrace all of my Gentile Christian brethren as joint-heirs in our Father's kingdom, which His most magnificent Son has given to us all to share. I am also truly thankful and grateful for the rest of my spiritual family—were it not for them, I would not be in the kingdom today. I was personally aroused to jealousy by a Christian who loved G-d *and* the Jewish people (see Rom. 11:14). However, as Gentile believers we must also willingly embrace our Jewish brothers back into their own vine, which up to this point, has been a challenge for us.

THE BATON HAS BEEN PASSED, BUT NOW IT MUST BE SHARED

It pleased G-d in wanting to reach the Gentile world to pass the baton from Israel to the Church, which it has faithfully carried it despite its humanity and treatment toward Israel through the centuries. But now, in order for Israel to be restored, the baton must be passed back to her, except this time it will be shared by both groups, both Jew and Gentile alike, finally bringing unity to G-d's spiritual family.

G-d earnestly desires His family to be united during these days. But as we will see, there are still different paths for each of us to follow in order that the oneness may be achieved.

ONE G-D, ONE FAMILY, BUT TWO DISTINCT ROLES

For the sake of unity in the family of G-d, try to think of Israel as the firstborn brethren and Gentile believers as the other children in G-d's family whom He dearly loves just as much and with equal rights. He longs for us to be united as one under His love. Jesus makes this clear to us in John 17, where we can see His heart crying out for His spiritual family to become one. Right before He enters the garden of Gethsemane to take on the sins of the world, where He would sweat blood and endure the greatest struggle of His mission, He prayed this prayer of unity for His children:

> *My prayer is not for them alone. I pray also for those who will believe in Me through their message, that all of them may be one, Father, just as You are in Me and I am in You. May they also be in Us so that the world may believe that You have sent Me. I have given them the glory that You gave Me, that they may be one as We are one—I in them and You in Me. May they be brought to complete unity to let the world know that You sent Me and have loved them even as You have loved Me* (John 17:20-23).

This prayer is not just about unity in the body, but also refers to the Gentiles that would believe in Jesus's message through His Jewish disciples—that we would all become one, not only with the Father and the Son, but also with each other. This would fulfill His desire for His spiritual family whom He is longing to unite. Looking at it more from this perspective can begin to shed more light on our Father's heart and how He views His family how He views His family whom He is deeply committed to, both Jew and Gentile alike.

PROMISES ESTABLISHED WITH ISRAEL ARE NOW SHARED WITH US

We know that the promises were given to Israel, for the apostle Paul says in Romans:

> *Theirs is the adoption of sons; theirs the divine glory, the covenants, the receiving of the law, the temple worship and the promises. Theirs are the patriarchs, and from them is traced the human ancestry of Christ, who is G-d over all, forever praised! Amen* (Romans 9:4-5).

However, we also know from Scripture that another one of His divine mysteries (see Col. 1:26-27) is how the Gentile world was to be birthed into G-d's promises and covenants through Christ. Through the Gospel, Gentile believers also became heirs and were grafted into Israel as a commonwealth people, members together of one body and sharers together in the promises of Yeshua Hamashiach, Jesus Christ (see Eph. 3:6). In the temple courts, on the holiday of Hanukkah, Jesus told the Pharisees, *"I have other sheep that are not of this sheep pen. I must bring them also. They too will listen to My voice, and there shall be one flock and one shepherd"* (John 10:16), which up to this point Israel never really understood.

But both groups must enter the New Covenant to be born of G-d's Spirit, which was given to Israel first although most of them rejected it. There are no exceptions to this, which the apostle Paul has made clear to us in his teachings to the Roman church. While Gentile believers came after Christ, for the most part they have received the New Covenant before the Jews, but they are still grafted into the olive tree of Israel. And, as a result, G-d's other sheep inherit His promises.

For in Christ Jesus we are all new creations, to the Jew first and then to the Gentile (see 2 Cor. 5:17; Rom. 1:16). As a result of this, we are not only equal, but in reality we become part of G-d's spiritual family when we believe in His message. In this light, shouldn't this beckon a desire in us to see the other members of our family spiritually restored? But this has not often been the case. And the separation between us as Jews and Christians requires a great deal of healing and restoration, which is also G-d's heart for us.

This does not mean that we replace the people of Israel just because we embraced the New Covenant before them. Heaven forbid! For Scripture tells us, *"But as far as election is concerned, they are loved on account of the patriarchs, for G-d's gifts and His call are irrevocable"* (Rom. 11:28-29). And for purposes that may be difficult for any of us to understand, Israel has received a hardening but is to still come in at the end (see Rom. 11:25-26). And Jesus said, *"But many who are first will be last, and many who are last will be first"* (Matt. 19:30).

WHAT IS THE ONE NEW MAN?

In this context, let us try to understand what the One New Man is as well as the equality we all have together now in His family. But let us also shed light on any uniqueness there may be in each group in view of our callings. For while we are completely equal in the Spirit, this does not eliminate our unique roles as Jews and Gentiles nor alter how G-d views the kingdom between the two groups. In fact, there are significant reasons why we must gain a better understanding of these days we find ourselves living in. *For up to this point, many in the Church have not properly understood this and have seen the One New Man eliminating any differences between the two.* But with all my heart, I believe this not to be the case.

The apostle Paul writes about the One New Man to the church in Ephesus. He says:

For He Himself is our peace, who has made the two one and has destroyed the barrier, the dividing wall of hostility, by abolishing in His flesh the law with its commandments and regulations. His purpose was to create in Himself one new man out of the two, thus making peace, and in this one body to reconcile both of them to G-d through the cross, by which He put to death their hostility. He came and preached peace to you who were far away and peace to those who were near. For through Him we both have access to the Father by one Spirit (Ephesians 2:14-18).

Jesus established a spiritual path for both Jew and Gentile to follow that brings both of us into a new place in the Spirit and family of G-d. One Father, one Son, one Holy Spirit, and G-d's Jewish sons and daughters and G-d's Gentile sons and daughters—one family under one G-d, one spiritual Israel. We are called to be one Church whose foundation has been built on the Hebraic roots of the Jewish apostles and prophets, with Christ Jesus as the chief cornerstone (see Eph. 2:20).

For it is here that we can become one as His sacrifice destroyed the barrier of the old system of the law, which had to be given first so that sin was properly brought into account (see Rom. 7:7-13). This has enabled both of us to come into a new heavenly place, the holy, spiritual family of G-d, to the Jew as His firstborn and to the Gentile, who are the rest of His children in His family.

We must first fully understand that we are now citizens of Israel and are therefore equal to one another. The apostle Paul relates this to us in Ephesians, where he refers to our former lives being separated from G-d and excluded from Israel's commonwealth (see Eph. 2:12).

ONE NEW MAN: DIFFERENT ROLES

It is important to point out that all of G-d's children are chosen and can come into the same covenants that were given to Israel and established by G-d. For while our Father in heaven longs for the day of our reconciliation, our paths have been quite different even though they end up at the same point. For just like Israel, we believers are also a *"chosen people, a royal priesthood, a holy nation"* (1 Pet. 2:9). However, salvation is from the Jews and not the other way around (see John 4:22).

Let's also take a look at the letter to the Galatians:

> *You are all sons of G-d through faith in Christ Jesus, for all of you who were baptized into Christ have clothed yourselves with Christ. There is neither Jew nor Greek, slave nor free, male nor female, for you are all one in Christ Jesus. If you belong to Christ, then you are Abraham's seed, and heirs according to the promise* (Galatians 3:26-29).

Here the apostle Paul clearly points out that there is now no difference between us in the Spirit of G-d, for there is one Body and one Spirit. And it is evident that he had to work hard in his new ministry to make this clear to the Body of Christ, and especially to the Gentile believers, in light of Israel's rich heritage and background in the faith. As one could imagine, this reality was difficult for Gentile believers to fathom when the Church first began.

However, G-d never meant to eliminate the distinctions and callings among us, which some in the Church have greatly misunderstood. That's why the above Scripture is good, because the apostle Paul also points out that there is no spiritual difference between a man and woman, and yet we all know how different the roles are in our world between men and women, husbands and wives.

While we all have spiritual equality, this does not mean we are all the same in every way. And this is definitely true of Israel and the Church. For from within our oneness, we still have unique roles to play in the kingdom of G-d that are essential for all of us to understand and greatly support.

While we have equality, we also have come into Israel's covenants and promises, not vice versa. How is it that most in the Church still expect the Jews to conform to all of the Gentile traditions, becoming like them when they believe in Christ? There is misunderstanding here because we have not yet properly understood the distinctions and calls upon each of us that our Father makes in His kingdom. We expect the Jewish believers to operate and think completely like the Gentiles.

But now that we are in the time of Israel's awakening, we must be willing to face these issues and make the necessary adjustments so that our Jewish brethren may be blessed in their heritage, which now also belongs to us. For did not Jesus say that He will not return until Israel says, *"Blessed is He who comes in the name of the L-rd"* (Matt. 23:39)? And wouldn't they have to be redeemed first, before they make this proclamation? So who is going to reach them?

When we think about it for a moment in this light, could it be that the majority of the Church has become like the Judaizers, thinking that Jews coming into the faith must now become Gentiles following Church traditions? It's funny how things can work out when the tables are turned. But may it never be! And if this is indeed the case, like the first disciples we must all work hard to bring this to light and help change it. For Jewish believers greatly need all the support they can get, and to that I can personally testify.

KINGDOM POSITIONING

In fact, we need to come into a greater understanding of how G-d views the kingdom in this light. Even though there is truly only a remnant of Jews left upon the earth, the kingdom has an order to it—to the Jew first and then the Gentile (see Rom. 1:16; 2:9-10; Acts 13:46). This should also be reflected in the Church like in the days of the apostles and the prophets, whose foundation we live upon (see Eph. 2:20).

For while Jesus came to Israel first as it was not yet time for His Gospel to go out to the whole world, this position has never changed. Jesus came as a Jew, He died as a Jew, He was raised as a Jew, and He will return as a Jew. Will He not be called *"the Lion of the tribe of Judah, the Root of David"* (Rev. 5:5)?

This same position was also reflected through the apostle Paul, who was specifically called to the Gentiles. But he always went to the Jews first to fulfill protocol. This distinction will never go away, just like it won't in any of our natural families. For Joshua will always be the firstborn in my immediate family, just like Israel is G-d's firstborn son. Israel is forever marked and even carved upon the gates and foundations of the new heaven and earth, where the names of the 12 tribes of Israel and the 12 Jewish apostles shall be written forever (see Rev. 21:12,14).

Gentile believers have been grafted into a Jewish vine, which is intrinsically linked to its apostolic heritage and is Hebraic at its roots. And while the New Covenant does not take us back to the law, this does not and should not disconnect us from the richness of our past, which was natural for the apostles because they were all Jewish.

For there are significant reasons why G-d planned it this way, which we may not fully understand until it is complete. While most of Israel is still veiled, He still has a distinctive role for them to play in order that His unconditional covenants and His holy Word can be fulfilled. For G-d cannot deny Himself. As a result, the Church cannot come into its own spiritual destiny until Israel also comes into theirs; so we are intricately connected and need to see ourselves as such, which is quite different from what we have been taught up to this point.

G-d's Family—A Complete Circle

We need to try and view ourselves as a spiritual family, and, for example's sake, try to think of this family in the kingdom of G-d like a circle: Israel is in one half and the Church in the other. Israel was placed into the circle first, but was later removed through unbelief (see Rom. 11:20) so that the other half could be filled with the rest of G-d's family. In view of Israel's rejection and hardening (see Rom. 11:25), they have been temporarily brought out of their half while the Gentile side is in process of being filled. Except, from G-d's point of view, as a heavenly Father who loves all of His children dearly and equally, the two have not really ever fully coexisted in the circle and family of G-d.

One of the main goals of this book is to show how G-d desires both groups to be properly connected at this time. This is now of great significance to G-d as Israel's awakening has already begun and His most precious Body needs to respond to it so that His family circle can be completed. For what does the apostle Paul say in Romans 11 about this, but that their fullness will bring greater richness (see Rom. 11:12) and their reconciliation will bring resurrection power (see Rom. 11:15), life from the dead.

Could the Last Great Outpouring Be Connected Here?

Could it be that the last great outpouring of G-d's Spirit will only come upon us when we in the Church fully embrace our role to help the Father rebirth His firstborn in order to restore them? In fact, could our position toward the Jewish people be the missing piece in the puzzle? Could our connection to Israel be the golden key that opens the door to resurrection power (see Rom. 11:15)? *If we really want the fire, we have to first reconnect the wire!* Could our separation from the Jewishness of the Gospel and our spiritual reconnection toward our firstborn brethren be holding us back from the power we are so hungry and thirsty for in our lost and dying world?

I say all of that to say this: G-d loves His family and longs for the time as a spiritual Father when all of us (Jewish and Gentile believers) can dwell together in unity, which is His ultimate goal. For He has indeed chosen our firstborn brethren despite themselves, to both show and reflect His glory before He returns. This is all in light of His unconditional covenants toward them. Despite His chastening of them as a result of their own rejection, He has always planned to restore them because they will always be His children.

Take a look at these Scriptures for a better understanding of the connection here:

> *This is what the L-rd says: "Only if the heavens can be measured and the foundations of the earth below be searched out will I reject all the descendants of Israel because of all they have done..."* (Jeremiah 31:37).

And again:

> *I said I would scatter them and blot out their memory from mankind, but I dreaded the taunt of the enemy, lest the adversary misunderstand and say, "Our hand has triumphed; the L-rd has not done all this"* (Deuteronomy 32:26-27).

Even though they have not yet been spiritually cleansed before returning to the land, which is difficult for us to fathom but is in accordance to the timing in His Word, we must get behind this rebirthing as much as possible in order that our Father's end-time plans are fulfilled. For Jesus will not return until the Jews are reborn and are grafted back into G-d's spiritual family.

When we start talking about Israel's uniqueness, however, people start to get a little uncomfortable. There are of course reasons for this, of which I will get into further detail in future chapters. But could it be, as Gentile believers, that we have still not properly understood our unique role in G-d's final plans for His Son's return? *For in reality, the Church's role is just as significant to Him as Israel's.* Without each other we cannot complete the plan of G-d, because to G-d we are already intricately connected. But when we look at these roles in closer detail and the paths we both have to walk upon to fulfill our end-time destinies, we see that our inheritance is actually extremely similar. This is important for us to understand and know that we have equality in G-d with our Jewish brethren as they are restored.

IS OUR SPIRITUAL INHERITANCE CONNECTED?

Let's take a deeper look into that inheritance, which is necessary for us to come into a better understanding of G-d's family as well as to feel more comfortable as G-d reestablishes Israel and that, without a doubt, carries huge significance in the last days. For, if what I am writing is correct, it will require both action and change on the part of all believers, both Jews and Gentiles alike, to come to pass.

THE DIFFERENCES BETWEEN US

In the end, there are only two words that appropriately describe the differences in the inheritances between Jewish and Gentile believers. The first is *position*, which I have already briefly touched on as it relates to G-d's spiritual family in the kingdom, to the Jew first.

The second word is *location*. I have been a Jewish businessman most of my adult life. What if I came up to you one day and said with a heavy Jewish accent, "Do I have a real estate deal for you!" Then I went on to describe how I only wanted a piece of land a little bit larger than the state of New Jersey or the country of Wales, and I was willing to exchange the rest of the world for it. What would you say? Would it be a fair exchange: you take the entire world and I'll take something the size of New Jersey?

This is exactly what G-d will give to His Gentile children when Jesus comes. When He returns to establish His kingdom upon the earth, the land of Israel will go to His firstborn and the rest of the world will go to His other children in the Church. How do I know this? It is because Scripture tells us this is so.

PRIESTLY ROLES

The Word of G-d tells us that the people of Israel have a spiritual role that, for the most part, they are still yet to fulfill: *"Although the whole world is Mine, you will be for Me a kingdom of priests and a holy nation,"* G-d says (Exod. 19:5-6). While they may have performed a priestly role under the Old Covenant, Scripture is clear about Israel's future role as a nation of priests (see Isa. 61:6-7; 66:21; Jer. 3:17-18) who will reign with Christ:

> *And you will be called priests of the L-rd, and you will be named ministers of our G-d. You will feed on the wealth of the nations and in their riches you will boast. Instead of their shame My people will receive a double portion, and instead of their disgrace they will rejoice in their inheritance* (Isaiah 61:6-7).

This priestly role is not unique to Israel, however, for what does Jesus promise to all those who persevere to the end but the same authority to rule the nations: *"To him who overcomes and does My will to the end, I will give authority over the nations"* (Rev. 2:26).

And they will perform this calling as a nation of priests who reign alongside Israel and who also have the same priestly calling: *"And with Your blood You purchased men from G-d from every tribe and language and people and nation. You have made them to be a kingdom of priests to serve our G-d, and they will reign on the earth"* (Rev. 5:9-10).

The only difference here is location—*where* we will actually serve—for we are now all co-heirs with Christ. The Jews are called to a unique piece of real estate in the Middle East, which is called Israel, that has been covenanted to them (see Gen. 15:18). And Gentile believers, the rest of G-d's children, are called to the rest of the world. *But what is significant is that we will both reign together as a nation of priests in the different parts of the world to which He has called us.* And this makes sense in light of the many differences between us in our national identities, which seems to continue into the millennial reign of Christ on the earth (see Rev. 20; Zech. 8:2-23).

HE LOVES THE NATIONS

G-d is incredibly happy with the way He has created us all, along with the diversity among us throughout the many nations of the earth. He takes great pleasure in all of it and loves us all the same way—our different foods and cultures, and all of our differences as people. So if He created you as a Jew, great; and if He created you as a Greek, that is great too! The key is that we all need to be secure in who He has made us to be and love one another for all of the different gifts He has given us.

While there is definitely a spiritual reconnection ahead of us in this journey, this does not necessarily mean that He wants us to become anything different from the way He created each of us in the first place. He has made His family up of both Jew and Gentile, and we should be at complete peace with His creation as well as His choices. It certainly helps, however, to know that He treats us all with fairness and equality that is essential to our well-being. What else would we expect from a most loving and caring heavenly Father and His most magnificent Son who gave His life so that we could call Him friend?

G-D'S MERCY PLAN

However, did we not receive mercy as a result of Israel's disobedience? The apostle Paul writes to the Romans:

> *Just as you who were at one time disobedient to G-d have now received mercy as a result of their disobedience, so they too have now become disobedient in order that they too may now receive mercy as a result of G-d's mercy to you. For G-d has bound all men over to disobedience so that He may have mercy on them all* (Romans 11:30-32).

The greatest difference in our roles, therefore, is that G-d has called us in the Church to release His mercy back to Israel to help bring them to life and to reconnect them to the vine. Without our love and intercession for them, they cannot be grafted back into the olive tree, because this is His end-time mercy plan for us all. This is why it is so important for us to hear this message with our hearts and spirits. For just as they are the key to unlock the power of G-d upon the world through their restoration, we in the Church unlock the key to their salvation in order to help bring about G-d's end-time plan. We so greatly need each other more than we will ever know, which is ultimately His design to bring us together, so we can both serve Him upon the earth.

MANKIND'S HUMANITY

G-d knew Israel would be disobedient to the Old Covenant and forewarned them of the blessings and curses that would occur according to their obedience or lack thereof (see Deut. 28–32). There was no way in *humankind's humanity* (which includes the rest of us) that they had strength to be fully obedient to the law. Therefore, they were given over to disobedience and the consequences that the law required. So we in the Church and, in particular, our ancestry, were given a mandate to love the Jews despite their rejection of the Gospel.

But in our humanity we have also failed to love them on account of the patriarchs (see Rom. 11:28). Ultimately, this has resulted in the spiritual story of reconnection, that the full mercy plan of G-d would be shown to us all. For we cannot love Israel in our own strength. How can we love someone who constantly rejects us? Because of this, we are in desperate need of the Father's heart and His love for His firstborn children in order that, through us, they would receive His mercy and be spiritually reborn. This is why the apostle Paul writes, *"And how can they hear without someone preaching to them? And how can they preach unless they are sent? As it is written, 'How beautiful are the feet of those who bring good news!'"* (Rom. 10:14-15).

"Have we missed something rather important and significant here?" you may be asking. Are your eyebrows raising yet? Am I beginning to cause you to be more curious? And are you beginning to feel more empowered? Hang on, for this spiritual journey is just beginning!

It is important to our Father in heaven that we know how much He really loves us and has chosen us from the Gentile world to be part of His spiritual family. This is not only to share in His covenants, but also to share in all of its inheritance too (see Heb. 6:12).

HAVE WE MISUNDERSTOOD?

The missing link up to this point is how we in the Church have misunderstood the plight of our older spiritual brother, G-d's firstborn sons and daughters, the Jewish people and the children of Israel. For G-d was never meant to be for the Jews alone. And just like now, He is not meant only for Gentile believers. G-d longs for His spiritual family to be reunited once again. So the biggest question I am going to ask of you in this book is, "Are you willing to help Him make this happen?"

4

THE LAST SHALL BE FIRST AND THE FIRST SHALL BE LAST

THE ISRAEL PIECE

Since we have now hopefully gained a better understanding as to the Church's position in the plans of G-d to help redeem the earth, we are now ready to embark on a historical spiritual journey in order for us to be aware of our past as well as the call of G-d upon the other half of our spiritual family, Israel.

For just as the apostle Paul instructed us that we should not be ignorant to this mystery (see Rom. 11:25), we will also begin to recognize how in fact our eyes need to be opened to G-d's final plan to reveal His glory in the earth. We will also discover that while Israel is not the only matter He is working on, its significance is of tantamount importance in all that we do. Therefore, we must have its primary position among us first in order for His fullness to be released upon us, reflecting the kingdom positioning principle that I have already discussed briefly in the previous chapter in reestablishing the Church to its apostolic roots.

Could Israel and our position toward them be the *key* that begins to open the door to the additional power that we in the Church are seeking from G-d for true world revival and awakening to break out? For is this not indeed what G-d has promised as we begin to take a deeper look into these matters? And if this is the case, don't you think we should give it our utmost attention?

My dear friend, Don Finto, one of the main voices G-d has raised up in the American Church to trumpet this cause of reconnection between Israel and the Church, and who has written two great books on the subject,[1] often refers to this as the "Israel piece." Indeed, as we read on, it will become more apparent that if we do not yet have the Israel piece deep within our spirits, we will need to get it.

If it is so significant, then how come up until this point most of us in the Church have not yet recognized perhaps the greatest piece in the puzzle of the end-time Gospel that is a catalyst to ignite the rest? For while there is already a remnant in the Body that has this revelation, this movement and awakening to Israel's position is still in its infancy. And now is the time for it to come into much greater light so that our Father in heaven may achieve His purposes and plans among us.

A Personal Story

While I was writing this book, I was in Baltimore at one of my son's soccer tournaments. As I was on a prayer walk early one morning, there was a beautiful fog all around. As the sun was rising, the mist brilliantly veiled it, and as I looked on the L-rd spoke to me, "Grant, they cannot see what I am showing you, but they will see." As I finished my walk and went to watch Jonathan play, the mist was beginning to lift, so they started to play in the fog. However, ten minutes into the game I could not believe my eyes. The air and all the sky around us were the clearest I have ever seen, as in one of those brilliantly lit sunny days; but this was even more intense.

Then one of the soccer mum's turned to us all and said in absolute amazement, "Can you believe how clear it is?" As she spoke, I felt the Holy Spirit all over me, confirming His word to me about this message. I cannot fully explain this, *but for some significant reason we in the Church were not supposed to see this reconnection up until this point in time.* However, it is now upon us, and now that we are in a time of transition between Israel and the Church, we must take it seriously. Otherwise, if we fail to do this, we could miss G-d's will and purpose for us in this hugely important hour.

WE MUST SEE THIS CLEARLY

There are many in the Body of Christ who earnestly have a love for Israel in light of G-d's Word. Yet, our current theology, along with its many different views on this subject, still separates many of us from the unique role we are yet to play. There are many reasons why we have not fully seen this, and I promise you that as you read on you will gain a much greater and deeper understanding of these issues. But the greatest question that needs to be asked is, "What will you actually do with this information if you end up agreeing with it? And how will you allow it to both challenge and change you?" I hope now that I have sufficiently whetted your appetite for more, and you are now ready to join me in the unraveling of this mystery between Israel and the Church.

I don't think there is a better Scripture than from the title of this chapter—*"So the last will be first, and the first will be last"* (Matt. 20:16)—that better relates to the spiritual ingathering of the Jews and the Gentiles regarding the New Covenant. Even though sometimes when reading these scriptural references from the Gospels, one has to read between the lines to gain this inference. However, there is no question that Israel was chosen first and the rest of the believing world was called later. Just like there has been no question either, that aside from a remnant of Israel who actually founded the Church, Gentile believers as a whole have now come into the New Covenant first before the Jews did. As we will see through Scripture, the rest of Israel actually comes in toward the end.

Don't ask me why G-d has done it this way, in calling the Jews back to the land before He would breathe His Spirit upon them, so their character might be more holy. But in the parable of the workers in the vineyard, Jesus clearly points out that the owner of the vineyard has the right to do whatever He wants with His own money (see Matt. 20:1-16). If G-d is sovereign, which He most definitely is, He can do as He chooses. For who are we in the scheme of things to question the Almighty anyway? Is He not the potter and are we not the clay (see Rom. 9:20-21)?

As His child, I am very pleased to follow Him. His love for me is like no other. I have entrusted Him with my life and He is certainly worthy of it. As much as I can fellowship with Him as my best friend, I certainly respect that He is the boss and I am so glad for His leadership and guidance in my life.

For if the Gentile believing world now holds the baton of G-d regarding the Gospel because it has mostly received the New Covenant first, which it has actually carried for the past 1,900 years, then perhaps we in the Church also have a greater responsibility to help our Father bring His end-time plan about, don't you think?

REPLACEMENT THEOLOGY

Before we go further, we must gain a better understanding in our theology of what and who is meant when using the name *Israel* in Scripture. There are some who actually believe that the Church has replaced Israel, known as "replacement theology." While it is certainly true that we can look back into the Hebrew Scriptures and spiritualize the experiences of physical Israel as it relates to our own walk in the Spirit of G-d in the New Covenant, this does not mean that we can fully replace physical Israel with the Church. But often when listening to certain sermons in the Church at large, one can begin to wonder!

A typical definition of replacement theology can be paraphrased as such: "Israel has been replaced by the Christian Church, so the promises and prominent position once held by G-d's chosen people are now held exclusively by the Church."[2] Adherents of replacement theology believe the Jews are no longer G-d's chosen people, and G-d does not have specific future plans for the nation of Israel. It further teaches that the many promises made to Israel in the Bible are fulfilled in the Christian Church, not in Israel per se. So the prophecies in Scripture concerning the blessing and restoration of Israel to the Promised Land are "spiritualized" or "allegorized" into promises of G-d's blessing for the church.[3]

The name *Israel* is referred to 2,500 times in the Old Testament and 79 times in the New Testament. And in each case it refers only to the physical nation of Israel, the Jewish people.[4] In addition, there are only two potential references to Israel in the entire Word of G-d that could possibly also refer to G-d's spiritual family in the Church. Even here, though, these Scripture references (found in Romans 9:6 and Galatians 6:16) could also be making references to Jewish believers who made up the remnant of Israel in the first century. Many of today's theologians are actually split on their interpretations here, with both of these passages, believing in one or the other.

WE ARE A COMMONWEALTH OF ISRAEL

However, it is of great importance to point out that even if these two references include all believers, the Church has become a part of Israel and has definitely not replaced it. And it is only when the two come together that we will have the unity in the Body of Christ Jesus called us to. This is because through the Church Jesus has made His Gentile believing Body to be a part of Israel.

The apostle Paul actually clarifies this in his epistle to the Ephesians when he refers to the Church as a commonwealth of Israel, which makes perfect sense: *That at that time ye were without Christ, being aliens from the commonwealth of Israel, and strangers from the covenants of promise…"* (Eph. 2:12 KJV). For we have been grafted into their vine, their covenants, and their promises, and we must never forget our humble beginnings as a wild olive tree (see Rom. 11:22-24), even though Israel has been temporarily broken off because of unbelief (see Rom. 11:17-21).

Aside from spiritually relating to Israel through our own experience when Scripture so clearly points to one group of people, we should never look to replace them with anything else, otherwise we will be misled. There are still many in the Church, however, who do not actually believe this and indeed think that the Church has replaced Israel. This has resulted in that when we look at scriptural references that relate directly to Israel only the Church can be seen. May this never be and may this deception be fully exposed to bring us into repentance before it is too late.

Derek Prince, an English preacher who has loved the Jewish people and who has understood their calling, puts it best when he emphasized that Israel is a unique people and there is no one else in the whole earth like them.[5] Then he went on to quote First Chronicles 17:21-22:

> *And who is like Your people Israel—the one nation on earth whose G-d went out to redeem a people for Himself, and to make a name for Yourself, and to perform great and awesome wonders by driving out nations from before*

Your people, whom You redeemed from Egypt? You made
Your people Israel Your very own forever, and You, O
L-rd, have become their G-d.

Derek Prince went on to talk about how G-d adopted them and called them out as a kingdom of priests and a holy nation with a unique calling, which is still to be fulfilled. There has been no other nation whom G-d has ever spoken these words before or since. He gave them all of the covenants and His divine glory and the supernatural presence of G-d rested with them as long as they were obedient to Him. The giving of law, the priestly services of G-d, and the promises, were given only to Israel (see Rom. 9:5).

For the Savior of the world did not come through any other people, as He says, *"For salvation is from the Jews"* (John 4:22). Jesus was Jewish, and to fulfill G-d's plan for mankind He had to come through Israel. Not only that, but He will also return through them as well and He has never given up His Jewish identity. So why should we when we convert to Christianity? For when He returns, He will be known as the Lion of the tribe of Judah, the Root of David, and He will sit on a Jewish throne, known as the Seat of David. Judah was the name of one of the sons of Jacob and is also where the word *Jew* comes from.

To be perfectly honest with you, everything we have in the Church comes from Israel. Every spiritual blessing and all of our inheritance comes from G-d through them. Without Israel, there would be no patriarchs, no prophets, no apostles, no Bible, and no Savior. How much salvation would we have without these five things? In fact, when we are baptized in the name of the Father and the Son and the Holy Spirit, are we not immediately connected to the promises and covenants of Israel and do we not become children of Abraham (see Rom. 4:16-17)? G-d designed salvation to come from Israel, and we must never forget this as our connection to them counts down to Jesus's return and is more crucial than we may realize!

For G-d had His reasons for revealing Himself to mankind through Israel, being born first to demonstrate the plans of G-d. In my previous book about my Jewish testimony, *The New Covenant Prophecy*,[6] I bring attention to a wonderful teaching by another Jewish believer, Arnold Fruchtenbaum, called the Covenants, which can be easily accessed on the Internet. As we continue, we will recognize how significant these covenants are to G-d in understanding the end times and how they must be fulfilled in order for Jesus to return to the earth.

UNDERSTANDING THE DISPENSATIONS OF G-D TO BETTER UNDERSTAND ISRAEL'S ROLE

Let us look at G-d's past plans and covenants through His dispensations in order for us to gain a better understanding of Israel's calling, as well as our own, within the plans of G-d for the entire world. *Webster's Dictionary* defines the word *dispensation* as follows: "The order of events under divine authority." And G-d has certainly ordered a number of systems or plans in order to reveal Himself to man. So let's take a look at a few of these.

ADAM AND EVE

We all know the beginning, the story of Adam and Eve. It was their sin and disobedience that caused them to be cast out of G-d's presence. Right from the beginning, we are struck with the knowledge that the G-d of humankind is holy, and through these acts we see that nothing sinful or disobedient may enter or come into the presence of G-d.

It is important to note that we were not created this way in the beginning. But rather through disobedience we chose this journey for humankind and were also deceived into it by a rather crafty devil, who stole the dominion of the world from us.

G-d would now have to make a path back for us to be able to return to Him and find redemption. And we would also have to understand what caused us to become separated from G-d in the first place. Right from the beginning, we see that despite G-d's love, compassion, and provision for us, His character will not be compromised for our humanity, which is something the world simply does not really comprehend. This is fundamental to our understanding in the modern day, where we now see His Word being challenged because of mankind's own weaknesses and frailties. For the L-rd our G-d is a holy G-d and a consuming fire, and nothing sinful can enter His presence. However, we are also struck with G-d's concern and love for His creation and His family as a loving spiritual Father.

NOAH

After this there were people who sought G-d on the face of the earth, but the Bible tells us that G-d was grieved He had made humans because man's heart was desperately wicked and sinful (see Gen. 6:6).

G-d then touched the life of Noah and started over after the flood. Here again we see His wrath toward sin and His love and compassion with Noah for humankind to continue. G-d covenanted with Noah and the rainbow was given as a sign of a new beginning, that a flood would never again destroy the world.

Note here Noah's obedience and faith in G-d.

OUR JEWISH PATRIARCHS: ABRAHAM, ISAAC, AND JACOB

The world multiplied again and from one of Noah's sons, Shem, came a man by the name of Abram, who was called out by G-d.

When you think about it, Abram was actually the first Gentile convert. He was the father of all who believe, and G-d made a number of covenants with him throughout his years on the earth. He was also the first Jew, a Semite.

While G-d covenanted the land and a multitude of both physical and spiritual descendants, it was actually Abram's faith that was credited to him as righteousness (see Gen. 15:6). Here we see the blessing of G-d tied into faith and obedience once again, which would actually lay the foundation for the kingdom of G-d.

When G-d Makes a Covenant It Will Happen, or It Will Come to Pass

G-d made several other promises to Abraham, one of which is that his descendants would inhabit the land. He also promised that through Abraham's seed all peoples of the earth would be blessed.

We have already established that G-d is holy. And we also know that if He covenants and promises, His word will come true and He will bring it to pass. He was the One who established the covenants with us in the first place, not the other way around.

This is a significant point here, as it was G-d who made these promises to His people. *They were unconditional covenants, which means that it is up to G-d to bring them to pass.* This is indeed vital to us in the Church in the last days as we will see the G-d of Israel glorified through His own words, covenants, and promises given back to Israel, which must take place before Jesus can return (see Ezek. 36:22).

Shouldn't it be a little easier for us at this time in history, since the first part of Ezekiel's prophecy with the restoration of Israel to the land as well as numerous other prophecies have already been fulfilled? Before our very eyes we have witnessed the miraculous return of over 5 million Jewish people from over 100 nations throughout the earth over the past 50 years. Is this not proof that

G-d will bring His word to pass concerning Israel? Does this not truly throw the concept of replacement theology out the window?

Yeshua: The Isaac of G-d

It is also through the life of Abraham that we ultimately see the Gospel message and understand our need for redemption. G-d tested Abraham with the sacrifice of Isaac, and it is through this story that we see the love of G-d, though He actually spared Isaac, showed us what He would have to do to redeem us through His own Son (see Gen. 22:1-19). The offering of Isaac was a prophetic picture of Jesus on the cross as a sacrifice for our sins, who became the Isaac of G-d.

Sarah was way beyond her years for childbirth, and yet the child of promise was born to her through Abraham's seed. It was through Isaac that all of G-d's children would be born (see Rom. 9:7). So through Abraham, who is the father of us all, we see G-d's promises fulfilled both to Jews and Gentiles alike, yet with different callings and purposes—as the apostle Paul has pointed out, this was to the Jew first and then to the Gentile (see Rom. 1:16).

But why does G-d differentiate between the two? It's because Israel was called first, and, as we will see, they were called into a different path and journey compared to the rest of the world, who were not called until the Gospel was given—this is a major difference between the two brethren. *Israel passes through the covenants while the rest of us come in when the covenants have already been established.*

What I'm trying to do here is outline G-d's plan to save and redeem humankind through Israel from the beginning to the end. This is so we can not only see the timing that has affected us, but also the timing that Israel was brought into, ultimately helping to bring spiritual life to the entire believing world. The call has now been given and established, not just through Abraham, but also through his son Isaac and Isaac's son Jacob. These three make up the patriarchs of our faith, meaning that they are the fathers of our faith.

We Can Relate to Jacob

Most of us can relate to Jacob, can't we? I mean we might not be deceivers like he was, but Jacob was definitely human, and his human characteristics played a major role in his life. In much the same way, we are human and our characteristics play a major role in our lives too, because we are all sinful and in need of redemption.

You probably know the story—Jacob had a dream. In it G-d called him to Himself. And from this time and commitment to G-d, G-d began a redemptive process in Jacob through most of his life and experience. It's amazing how much of the Gospel and our walk with G-d can be clearly seen through the patriarchs. Through Jacob we witness the process of *sanctification* taking place. It isn't until a good deal of time, struggle, and experience in Jacob's life passes that G-d actually promotes him and renames him *Israel*.

It was through a fight with Christ that Jacob finally pressed on, and through his struggle and sanctification the nation of Israel was born (see Gen. 32:22-30). Please take note here that Israel is actually living and walking through each of these dispensations as they are being established, for they went before us to help bring us to the point that G-d could actually give us life and freedom through the Messiah.

Joseph's Struggles

Earlier on, G-d told Abraham that his descendants would go into captivity and it would be several hundred years before they would return to the land. We know the story of Joseph, who was sold into slavery by his jealous brothers, which actually brought the nation of Israel into Egypt. And for a while they were blessed with the finest of lands in Egypt before they were put into slavery. All along, however, while we see the blessings of G-d on Israel we also see the devil's schemes to ensnare and destroy them. Another aspect of the kingdom we all have to deal with in the spiritual realm to this very day are the devil's attempts to destroy Israel so that he will not have to give up his dominion over humanity.

THE DELIVERANCE

It was through Israel's cries in bondage in the Passover story that G-d began to move to reveal the next part of His plan. Gloriously, we see the mighty hand of G-d deliver Israel out of an impossible circumstance. It was with great power, and with signs and wonders that G-d delivered Israel from Egypt, which also majestically portrays the story's spiritual fulfillment of the Gospel itself: how Jesus came with great power, signs, and wonders to deliver us from the bondage of our sin and take us from death into life; how each of us would require a covering on the doorposts of our hearts to save us from the judgment of death against the world because of sin.

Jesus was the Paschal Lamb and His shed blood would be placed on the doorpost of our hearts to cover our sin and save us from spiritual death. It was the elements on the Passover table itself, the bread and the wine, that Jesus took and made eternal through His own body and blood. What a connection from the old to the new!

THE LAW

Israel came before G-d on Mount Sinai, and no sooner are they delivered from Egypt than G-d released His next dispensation, the Mosaic law. And while we know from the apostles that the law is good and holy, we also know it had a divine purpose to expose the heart, reveal sin, and, most significantly, bring it into account. The law also gave the nation of Israel a whole code in which to live by, much ahead of its time when it was given.

This was a crucial part in G-d's plan to redeem us and win us back to faith. It was in fact the law that showed Israel what made them deficient before G-d, and, indeed, they became extremely aware of their need for sacrifice and shed blood in order to find forgiveness and restoration. This should have actually prepared them for the Gospel, which was to bring their final redemption.

The law held up a heavenly mirror to the heart of man, not only exposing what it was that separated us from G-d, but also clearly pointing out the differences in character between us and G-d. It is the moral law that exposes sin, bringing about condemnation not just for Israel but also for the rest of the Gentile world. For without the law we would not know what sin is (see Rom. 7:7-12). However, G-d spared the Gentiles the experience of this dispensation as it was given to His firstborn children, who actually faced the law for us; and look what has happened to them as a result.

FROM THE OLD TO THE NEW

I don't know about you, but I know that with mankind's heart strongly beating in my soul, I could not have been obedient to the law without the power of the Holy Spirit. And, even then, if we are honest with ourselves, it is still always a fight! Nor was Israel able to keep the law because their own humanity could not stand up to it. There was only ever One who kept the law completely, and His name is Christ.

Messiah, in the New Covenant, is at the end of the law; and when we put our faith in Him, we naturally pass from its condemnation through His sacrifice. Scripture tells us that He became a curse for us in order to redeem us from the law's sting, which is death and separation from G-d (see Gal. 3:13-14). For those of us who now believe, we are not under law but under grace (see Rom. 6:14).

The Purpose of the Law

Jesus could not come into the world until the law was given, as sin had to first be brought into account. In addition, through His sacrifice and obedience, Jesus abolished the old system that we could not keep anyway (see Jer. 31:32), freeing us from it, so that the law could be made anew in the New Covenant, a new dispensation, known as the law of Christ (see Rom. 8:2; 1 Cor. 9:20-23; Gal. 6:2). As a result, for those of us surrendering to faith, our hearts would now be circumcised by the power of the Holy Spirit living deeply within each one of us, who, according to the prophet Jeremiah, embodies the very law of G-d (see Jer. 31:33).

Please note here that unlike us in the Church, who have come into the Gospel that brings life because the Gentile world was not called until after the cross and resurrection, Israel was brought into a system that actually brought death, because sin had to first be exposed (the apostle Paul explains this to us in his epistles to the Romans, Galatians, and Ephesians). Therefore, the dispensation of the law was only temporary, until the Isaac of G-d (Christ) was given as a sacrifice for all humankind.

The law of G-d burned truth into the hearts of humankind to expose our natural condition, that, when we believe, convicts each of us of our sinful nature and brings us to Christ into a New Covenant that frees us from its curse. Just as Jesus has said, *"Then you will know the truth, and the truth will set you free"* (John 8:32).

For the most part, Israel could not yet experience the intimacy of the New Covenant until sin was made known in all of our hearts, for it separated us from G-d. The law had now made it official, so that in the right time we could actually be redeemed from it and brought back to G-d, which the L-rd accomplished through His Son.

A good question for all of us to consider is this: Which covenant would we want to be brought into, the one where the law is given to expose sin or the one that gives life and freedom from it? The answer should be obvious to all, but I bring it up in hopes that we can better relate and appreciate what our brother, Israel, has experienced for all of us. Israel was chosen first for this purpose, they have suffered greatly as a result, and they are still yet to come into the Gospel that will give them spiritual life.

EVERY BELIEVER COMES THROUGH THE COVENANTS

As we come to faith through Christ, we actually come through all of the dispensations that G-d established, which have been given to Israel. We have faith in the promises of G-d through Abraham, and our sin is exposed and recognized by the giving of the moral law. When we yield our hearts to Christ and recognize our sin, we find ultimate freedom from it with the great intimacy that Jesus has provided for us through the New Covenant (Gospel). But Israel got caught in-between this process. For the apostle Paul tells us that Israel, who pursued a law of righteousness, did not ultimately do it with faith but with works, which G-d cannot accept (see Rom. 9:31).

Faith is tantamount to every aspect of the kingdom of G-d, from the beginning of belief right up until the very end. In fact, the Bible tells us that everything that is not of faith is sin (see Rom. 14:23). We can clearly see those in Israel's past who operated in faith, those who actually penned the Word of G-d. From Moses and King David to the prophets, wherever faith was applied, even to the system of the law, the grace of G-d abounded and both revelation and relationship were the result. However, for the most part, these great men of G-d were always in a minority amongst the general population in Israel, who eventually went their own way in the pursuit of foreign gods.

THE LAW WAS ONLY PART OF G-D'S PLAN, BUT IT BROUGHT ACCOUNTABILITY

The law, however, was a process in G-d's overall plan, and Moses warned Israel that G-d would deal harshly with us in light of our disobedience. Despite our humanity, we still needed to be accountable to the standard of the law so that there could be no excuse.

Just like the rest of humankind, our sin and selfishness deceived us; and while Israel truly experienced the blessings and prosperity of G-d in the earlier part of their history, it did not take too long for the flesh to rear its ugly head and for sin to take root and control. Similarly, this can be seen today in the modern world where sin abounds and the enemy controls.

The question here for us as believers is this: Would we have done the same thing? And I submit to you, that any race, group, or people would have made the same mistakes and errors that Israel did, owing to the state of the sinful heart of man. In a way, Israel took the rap for us to help us enter the kingdom of G-d. And look how the Church has responded. Please don't get me wrong here, I am not excusing them because they rejected the L-rd and have suffered greatly as a result. But I'm rather trying to show that what they actually went through was no different from the rest of us, because all humanity is the same when it comes to sin.

ISRAEL SEALED FOR A FUTURE TIME

In the latter period of the Hebrew Scriptures, we mainly read of Israel's backslidings. Here, we constantly see the wrath and compassion of G-d's character, His unfailing love for His children, but then His wrath and anger in light of their disobedience to cast Him aside. For G-d longs for their love and obedience, just as any normal father would want of his children.

I truly believe Israel's greatest sin was their idolatry in rejecting their own G-d and turning to the gods of the nations around them. For the G-d of Israel is a jealous G-d, greatly desiring our affection and obedience, showing love to a thousand generations of those who love Him and keep His commandments (see Exod. 20:6). What they failed to see was that their own right to live in the land G-d had given them was dependent on their holiness and obedience to G-d as given through the law. And since the law raised a holy standard, Israel's constant failing and rejection had to bring about consequences and judgment, which G-d was extremely long-suffering to bring to pass.

It seems as if He had finally lost patience with Israel altogether with the dispersion of the ten northern tribes to Assyria, who were never to return again. He then raised up the prophet Isaiah in Judah, where the final two tribes remained (Benjamin and Judah). And He told Isaiah to proclaim a curse of spiritual blindness and deafness over His people in light of their consistent disobedience (see Isa. 6:6-10).

From a humanistic standpoint, this would appear harsh. However, at this point, the entire nation of Israel was backslidden and was fully deserving of judgment, with not even one person operating in any form of righteousness (see Jer. 5). But instead of casting them out immediately, He had Isaiah place a seal upon them. In reflection we can now look upon this as an act of mercy, because it saved Judah from a complete and utter destruction that their sins fully deserved in light of the law. Yet it would ultimately bring Israel into a national wandering and dispersion that Moses forewarned, even after their first return to the land. And I believe this completely blinded them to Jesus's coming.

It was this sealing that Isaiah placed upon them that is still with them today and to which the apostle Paul refers to in his dissertation in Romans 9–11. It is this hardening that has squeezed the spiritual life out of them and which has caused their bones to feel so dry (see Ezek. 37:2). It has completely spiritually blinded and deafened them to the New Covenant until the time of the end, to which they have been sovereignly sealed and set apart for kingdom purposes, and which has been so difficult for us all to understand, especially the Jews.

Despite their rejection and disobedience, however, they are loved on behalf of the patriarchs. And in so many places in His Word, He has promised to restore them, as thankfully we serve an all-compassionate and forgiving G-d who cannot deny Himself or His holy covenants because they were His promises in the first place. This in itself should be enough for us as believers, lending all of our support to the proper fulfillment of His Word.

There had to be consequences for not walking in obedience to the law, just as there are today whenever we break the laws of the land or the rules of our parents. Judgment naturally follows this and action has to be taken. Otherwise, there is no standard for righteous living, which is one of the main reasons our society today is in such turmoil. We allow people to make their own rules, sometimes without consequences, which is never healthy for anyone in the long run. Similarly, the purpose of the law was to distinguish between right and wrong, and action had to be taken if it was broken despite G-d's long-suffering character.

As a result of this, even at the appointed time (approximately some 600 years after Isaiah's proclamation), when the Christ was to be among the Jewish people, they could neither see nor recognize Him for who He truly was. G-d was sending His beloved Son to Israel to lift the veil of sin over humankind. Yet the spiritual leadership could neither hear nor see the truth of the Gospel that would set people free from within because their pride and self-righteousness continued to blind them. And it was only those to whom G-d lifted the veil that could actually see. Jesus touched numerous lives and souls while on the earth, for there were many in need; and a good percentage of Jews followed Christ after His resurrection.

However, the leadership clearly rejected Him and turned the majority of the people against Him. Even His own disciples did not fully understand Him, yet He supernaturally opened their eyes so that they could see and properly establish the New Covenant among us (see Luke 24:45). His Jewish apostles and their followers became the witnesses of the Christ and the G-d of Israel, who together turned the world on its end, the Church being born through them. These Jewish souls helped to lay the foundation for His Gospel to go out to the entire Gentile world so that the baton could be passed to the rest of G-d's spiritual family. And their very names will be written upon heaven's gates along with the names of the 12 tribes of Israel.

THE LAW COULD NOT BE COMPROMISED

What is hopefully clear here in this section is that the holiness of G-d through the law could not be compromised as a result of humankind's humanity, and for this reason the Jewish people were now headed for the Diaspora (dispersion). Just as Moses had foretold in the Torah, they were dispersed and scattered because of their disobedience (see Deut. 28–31).

Though I don't fully understand all of this, there is some kind of divine connection between the suffering of Christ and the suffering of the Jews as His firstborn children. As believers in Jesus it is so easy for us to look at Isaiah 53 and clearly see a line-by-line description of His ministry birthing the New Covenant into the world. However, when some rabbinical Jews look at these Scriptures, they can only see their own suffering as a people; and it is quite evident in our world's history that no other group of people have suffered more than the Jews since their dispersion, or even before that. It was actually through millions of dying Jews, burning in ovens or being poisoned to death in gas chambers in Nazi Germany, that for a very brief period of time the world had compassion on them. Yet through their deaths, their dead, dry bones, the nation of Israel was reborn, almost like a death and resurrection in and of itself (see Ezek. 37:1-3; Jer. 8:2).

Israel, however, got caught into a legalistic system in which religious man (in his own self-righteousness) attempted to usurp G-d's own plan of salvation. Sometimes it is too easy for us to look back when we read the Bible and easily judge them for their stubbornness and disobedience, but most of them never even knew G-d personally and ended up getting ensnared in an extremely legalistic system.

If we think about this for a moment and also look into Church history, we can again see the same spirit working through the Church, causing people to attempt to earn their own salvation. So, indeed, we are all at fault and in need of G-d's salvation.

WE NEED TO HAVE MORE COMPASSION

Should this not cause us to have more compassion and understanding of what Israel actually walked through for us individually as well as for the entire world? Please remember the apostle Paul's teaching in Romans 11, for the Gentile world was indeed offered salvation as a result of G-d's mercy and because of Israel's disobedience. It is only the mercy of G-d that allows all of us to reenter His kingdom, mercy we have received as a result of Israel's journey, being much different from our own. Isaiah prophesied:

> *Comfort, comfort My people, says your G-d. Speak tenderly to Jerusalem, and proclaim to her that her hard service has been completed, that her sin has been paid*

for, that she has received from the L-rd's hand double for all her sins (Isaiah 40:1-2).

ISRAEL TOOK ON THE LAW FOR US ALL

So Israel took on the system of the law for us so that Christ could be given to the entire world. And it is important for us to see the price that has been paid by our Jewish brothers and sisters for all humankind. One must also recognize that their calling has been different to those of us in the Gentile world, who were called into the kingdom after Christ was given.

In Romans 11 the apostle Paul uses the analogy of an olive tree to describe this mystery between the Jews and the Gentiles. Because of their lack of faith and disobedience, Israel was cast out and the Gentile believers were brought in to make Israel envious.

JESUS CHRIST

G-d now completed the system for humankind through Christ to return to G-d, and at this point the Gentiles began to enter into it. This is where the path for the Church and the Gentile believer began. But it was only as a result of G-d's mercy and love through Christ that allowed us to enter in as well as the price Israel paid by facing the law.

THE OLIVE TREE

For the past 2,000 years, the olive tree that was once completely Jewish is now controlled by Gentile believers, the other half of G-d's family. This is because Jesus has passed the baton to reach His other sheep in order to complete the family circle of G-d (see John 10:16).

During the time of the Gentiles (see Rom. 11:25), and since Gentile leadership took control of the Church, G-d has been focused on reaching the rest of His family, and during that time a remnant of Israel has always come in (see Rom. 11:5). However, as He now looks to reconnect His firstborn child, our spiritual brethren, in order to awaken them and restore His kingdom on the earth. *We must begin to adjust our perspective and come into agreement with His end-time plan to establish both camps in our spiritual inheritance, reigning with Christ.* For one cannot exist without the other in G-d's future kingdom, and there is a whole lot of healing, repentance, and forgiveness on both sides that is necessary for this to take place.

THE RECONNECTION

G-d's spiritual family (both Jew and Christian) has not yet experienced unity in the kingdom of G-d in the way He desires. Only Jews populated the vine for a while, then later Gentile believers; and in a time yet to come, which I believe we are now living in, this family of G-d will be finally united.

While we read in the prophets of Israel's backsliding and disobedience, we also read of numerous words and prophecies of future redemption for Israel. When we look at the whole Bible in this regard, it is easier to see this than anything else—that G-d had reserved Israel for a future time.

In hindsight, one can almost see Isaiah's proclamation over them as being spiritually sealed off (see Isa. 6:6-10), where the veil of sin around Israel's heart, which brings blindness in and of itself, was sealed tight to ensure their blindness and deafness to the truth. This was so that the mercy of G-d could be revealed through them to all mankind at a later date, that G-d's covenants would be fulfilled. G-d already knew that in our own humanity we would fail our call and instead stoop to idolatry, which G-d could not condone without consequences.

Isaiah later confirmed this:

Be stunned and amazed, blind yourselves and be sight-less; be drunk, but not from wine, stagger, but not from beer. The L-rd has brought over you a deep sleep: He has sealed your eyes (the prophets), He has covered your heads (the seers) (Isaiah 29:9-10).

One would almost have to be blind themselves to believe that G-d was finished with the Jews, owing to the many promises in Scripture of future redemption and restoration. We know from the apostle Paul that this hardening they received is only temporary, and so in the right time the veil will be lifted and all Israel will come to a knowledge of the truth (see Rom. 11:25-26).

MOSES SAW THE RECONNECTION

Even Moses foretold of this happening with the blessings and the curses sermon in Deuteronomy 30:1-6. Part 1 is being fulfilled before our eyes:

Even if you have been banished to the most distant land under the heavens, from there the L-rd your G-d will gather you and bring you back. He will bring you to the land that belonged to your fathers, and you will take possession of it. He will make you more prosperous and numerous than your fathers (Deuteronomy 30:4-5).

And Part 2 has also begun as many Jews are now coming to faith:

The L-rd your G-d will circumcise your hearts and the hearts of your descendants, so that you may love Him with all your heart and with all your soul, and live (Deuteronomy 30:6).

Interestingly enough, Moses is the first to write of the order of these events. For it is written that Israel is to be brought back to the land first, before the Spirit of G-d is breathed upon them. The words of Ezekiel also confirm the order of these events—where the *breath of G-d* will come upon them to receive the Spirit of G-d *after* they have been brought back to the land (see Ezek. 37).

And the words of the prophet Zechariah also confirm this: *"They will look on Me, the One they had pierced, and they will mourn for Him as one mourns for an only child, and grieve bitterly for Him as one grieves for a firstborn son"* (Zech. 12:10).

THE PROPHECIES MAKE IT CLEAR

Here they will receive the New Covenant in the words of the prophet Jeremiah, where G-d will write the law of G-d upon their hearts and cleanse them from all of their sins, as He has already done with us in the Church who are now living under the New Covenant (see Jer. 31:33). Take a look at Jeremiah to see how definite G-d is about their restoration: He says, *"Only if the heavens above can be measured and the foundations of the earth below be searched out will I reject all the descendants of Israel because of all they have done"* (Jer. 31:37). How certain and definite is this in the Word of G-d, which we must not ignore!

Both the prophet Micah (see 7:18-20) and the prophet Ezekiel (see 36:22-23) clearly point to the reason for Israel's restoration (aside from His unfailing love for His firstborn children): G-d's words and covenants *must* come to pass. Thank G-d that these unconditional covenants to restore Israel are not based on Israel's righteousness to bring them to pass, but rather on the will of G-d to keep His holy Word. For at the appointed time, the complete veil over Israel and the Jewish people will be lifted from their souls. This is in order for them to be spiritually awakened and to find redemption, which has always been G-d's desire for *all* His children, not just for the Jews.

IT IS FOR HIS GLORY

And He will do all of this for His glory. Ezekiel says,

> *Therefore say to the house of Israel, "This is what the sovereign L-rd says: It is not for your sake, O house of Israel, that I am going to do these things, but for the sake of My holy name, which you have profaned among the nations where you have gone. I will show the holiness of My great name, which you have profaned among the nations, the name you have profaned among them. Then the nations will know that I am the L-rd, declares the Sovereign L-rd, when I show Myself holy through you before their eyes* (Ezekiel 36:22-23).

UNCONDITIONAL COVENANTS

To help us further understand this, let's take a closer look at two of the unconditional covenants G-d made with Abraham and King David. Through them we gain a clearer understanding of how significant it is for G-d's words and promises to actually come to pass through the people of Israel, the other half of our spiritual family.

If we cannot count on G-d's Word, where then could we really place our faith? It is His Word and truth that enables each of us as believers and followers of Him to be able to trust Him with our very lives. So why would G-d make promises to Israel and then not fulfill them? He promised them land that they would inherit forever, where they would eventually live, being fully reconciled to G-d with clean hands and pure hearts, loving their G-d with all of their soul and all of their might. And much of this is still to take place.

Would this make G-d out to be a liar, if He did not fulfill His own words and promises to restore Israel? May it never be! For our G-d is a consuming fire with nothing but truth departing from His lips and His holy Word. As a result, to suggest anything different about these covenants regarding Israel would be false. We all need to work hard in the Church to fully expose anything to the contrary before it is too late, that His mercy would be released to us all, including those who do not currently see things this way. It is never too late to change, but it may be in the end.

THE ABRAHAMIC COVENANT

G-d's covenant to Abraham was an *"everlasting covenant"* (Gen. 17:7), which according to *Webster's* actually means "eternal." However, for the sake of theological discussion, I would like to suggest that *forever* actually means until heaven and earth pass away, before G-d makes everything new in fulfilling His promises to us (see Rev. 21:1-5). But even here, interestingly enough, the name of the city in the new heavens and earth is called the "New Jerusalem." Perhaps the verdict is still out on this as actually lasting eternally. But we do know for sure that everlasting is indeed a very long time, if not forever!

We must be clear that this land has been given solely to the Jews for the purposes of establishing G-d's glory upon the earth. With every fiber of our being, as believers and servants of the G-d of Israel, we should want this to be fulfilled, as it is also intricately connected to our own destiny and inheritance in the Church, being vital for us to see. Otherwise, wouldn't we be seen as working against G-d? For the Word of G-d is clear here regarding the land covenant and restoring Israel to it, as well as their spiritual awakening that is yet to come.

THE DAVIDIC COVENANT

The same is also true with the Davidic covenant, another unconditional promise made by G-d that He has total responsibility to bring to pass. Here G-d established David's throne and lineage as eternal, and promises that G-d's own Son will be forever established through David's line (see 2 Sam. 7:11-16). In reality, where would we be as believers today without the fulfillment of these promises through Christ's first coming as the Lamb of G-d? And yet, what happens when He returns as the Lion of the tribe of Judah (see Rev. 5:5)?

G-d promised through King David an everlasting throne with an eternal seat that only Christ Himself can sit upon. But it is only when He returns to the very city He left (Jerusalem) that this will actually take place. So shouldn't we be focused on G-d filling His holy seat? Yet, without Israel's spiritual awakening and our connection to them, which is the missing link up until this time, Christ is not ready to return and take His throne. Nor is His Body ready to move into their spiritual inheritance to rule and reign with Him, which is why this reconnection is so highly significant to all of us at this point in time.

When we look at these Scriptures, we almost have to be foolish to believe anything other than what is written will actually come to pass. G-d has already given us Jesus, who came first as a Lamb, but when He returns He will be like a roaring Lion to take all authority upon the earth. And we will rule and reign with Him, believing Jew and Gentile alike, one spiritual family, all of G-d's children finally united in the kingdom of G-d.

Even in our current time, the land promises to Israel have already been fulfilled, something that the Puritans only believed in their hearts. Millions of Jews from all over the world have already returned to Israel. Isn't that a miracle within itself?

And what about the awakening and return of the Russian Jews from the land of the North, which has also recently taken place, and part of which I was personally involved in? Over 1 million Jews have left these lands to return to Israel or live in the United States. And it was these days that Jeremiah prophesied of thousands of years ago:

"However, the days are coming," declares the L-rd, "when men will no longer say, 'As surely as the L-rd lives, who brought the Israelites up out of the Egypt,' but they will say, 'As surely as the L-rd lives, who brought the Israelites up out of the land of the north and out of all the countries where He had banished them.' For I will restore them to the land I gave their forefathers" (Jeremiah 16:14-15).

ISRAEL: THE GOLDEN KEY

There can be no doubt at this point that G-d is on the move concerning Israel. It is only a question of time for His end-time plans to be fulfilled in the regathering and reawakening of the Jewish people, that His glory may shine to all the nations. So the question that I have as you are reading this book is, Don't you think it's time to get on board with the Father's plans to show Himself to humanity, not only through Israel, but also through the Church? And if not, what is in your own heart or theology that may be stopping you?

For Israel's redemption is absolutely crucial to the Father's end-time plan to show Himself to the world; and without Israel's awakening, Jesus cannot return to take His throne upon the earth. Similarly, without us embracing our own unique role to help rebirth them through prayer and intercession, this cannot take place either as we are currently the missing link in G-d's chain to bring it to pass.

Israel and the Church are forever spiritually connected to G-d and all His covenants *must* be fulfilled—the veil has to be lifted before they are restored into their rightful place to reign with Christ along with the rest of the Church. *The key here for us in the Church, however, is to fully realize the role that we are still yet to fulfill in helping them get rebirthed.* This is why it is so important for us to better understand this mystery, because the glory of G-d completely depends upon it. Could it be that there is indeed a veil over our own hearts that has prevented us from seeing this until now?

Having said all of the above, I want to clarify that I believe His entire plan, including our response to it, is well within the sovereignty and timing of G-d. While we may not have seen this so clearly up to this point as we make the transition in spiritually reconnecting the family of G-d in our hearts, His call and directive will become known to us and we will respond to it accordingly, for Jesus has said, *"My sheep listen to My voice"* (John 10:27).

CRUCIAL CONSEQUENCES

Both our Father and His most precious Son, Jesus, are waiting for us to awaken to His plan, to help Him reconnect His full spiritual family so that His will can be done. We are really talking about Christ's return here and the further establishment of the kingdom of G-d upon the earth with the very seat and throne of David. The apostle Paul wrote, *"For if their rejection is the reconciliation of the world, what will their acceptance be but life from the dead?"* (Rom. 11:15). For when Israel fully awakens, the Father will show His glory through them to all of the nations, Messiah will return, and the dead will be raised in the first resurrection, which are my end-time beliefs (see Rev. 20).

When we embrace G-d's end-time plan, such spiritual power will be loosed upon us that will ultimately bring about the greatest spiritual awakening the world has ever witnessed. So what are we waiting for with our Father's plans to unite His family?

I have been a believer now for almost 30 years, and have spent most of that time in the Church, which has become desperate for revival and spiritual awakening as wickedness has been increasing with such a spiritual grip in the world. Over the past 20 years, we have begun to witness and experience smaller revivals and awakenings. Yet they always seem to be in pockets and they also fizzle out quickly. I believe, that until this Israel piece is fully turned on in us, we are missing the key to the additional power we so desperately need from G-d to awaken our world and its children, because He wants His family to be one with Him.

Although our spiritual reconnection to Israel is not the only thing G-d is doing, His focus on it and our connection to them is probably one of the most important revelations of our time, in terms of how we position it in our priorities. We (the Church) need to awaken to release G-d's mercy back to His firstborn, which is the key to the Father's plan.

As we have seen from the Church's past, however, we have not been able to do this ourselves as our humanity has always gotten in the way. Ultimately, the only way to love Israel in all of their resistance and objections to the Gospel is through G-d's own heart and His completely unselfish love. I call this the *Father's heart*, which is what this book is all about.

Not only will I reveal how to receive His heart and love for His firstborn, but because of this reconnection in G-d's family that we are about to experience, we will be able to place our hands upon the *key* through Christ that will open the door to the unquenchable power the Father wants to give us in reuniting His family as one. As we put His will above our own, by blessing His firstborn children and our own spiritual brethren, we will truly witness the kingdom of G-d upon the earth, for He has promised, *"I will bless those who bless you"* (Gen. 12:3).

As I have already mentioned, when we look at current teachings about Israel and the Church, there seems to be an apparent separation between Israel and G-d, almost like G-d will deal with them separately. However, and I say this with all humility, this is not the heart of the Father longing for His children to become one. He is working His end-time plan to bring us together.

WE ARE MORE CONNECTED THAN WE MAY THINK

To demonstrate the spiritual connection between Israel and the Church, one can often trace movements of the Spirit that are also associated to events in the natural with the reestablishment of Israel. I believe this would be true of the Messianic movement itself (Awakening of Israel), which started in the late 1960s out of the Jesus movement. Was it a coincidence that at the same time Jerusalem was taken back by Israel (1967), that the Spirit of G-d was loosed upon the Jews to begin their awakening? It is especially enlightening in how significant Jerusalem is as the city of the coming King, that there would be a direct correlation toward a movement of G-d's Spirit in establishing the Messianic movement.

This movement, which was first established in thought at the end of the nineteenth century, in an article that appeared in *Our Hope Magazine*,[7] also happened at almost exactly the same time the Zionist movement began amongst the Jewish people wanting to return to Israel.

We can also see this with the reestablishment of Israel in 1948. At almost exactly the same time, the Spirit of G-d moved mightily in the Church and birthed the Billy Graham Evangelistic Association along with the Healing and Latter Day revivals, both of which began to spiritually awaken America and the world, birthing millions of souls into the kingdom.

In addition, probably the greatest awakening of the twentieth century, which also occurred during the infancy of the Zionist movement, was the Azusa Street revival in Los Angeles, California. This revival sparked the great awakening of the Holy Spirit through the Pentecostal movement. This outpouring of G-d's Spirit not only gave birth to untold hundreds of millions of believers, but also became the foundation for much of what is happening today in the Charismatic movement, as well as the ongoing flow of the supernatural gifts of the Holy Spirit that is now happening worldwide throughout the Church.[8]

Amazingly, and I would suggest not by coincidence either, the Azusa Street revival actually started on the same date as Passover that year (April 9, 1906, or *Nissan* 14).[9] Can you believe the timing of this event and its vital spiritual connection to Israel through the Passover Feast and Christ's resurrection, which ultimately gave life to the outpouring of G-d's Spirit among us?

However, we never hear about these types of things, and I was so excited in the Spirit as the L-rd whispered this to me as I was writing this chapter. It was not easy to find a website that showed the past dates of Passover, especially from 1906, but with a lot of prayer and patience I found one. And when I first saw it, my spirit leapt. I feel so strongly about Jew and Gentile believers being intricately connected through G-d's holy calendar and what He is doing concerning the land and its people.

So I think it is fairly safe to say that there is a lot more than meets the eye here in connecting physical Israel to the events tying into the Body of Christ. My hope and prayer is that we would awaken more spiritually to this connection, to the ways in which G-d decides to move and show Himself to His family.

THE EZEKIEL CALL

Our spiritual reconnection to Israel will become the uniting factor in bringing His family into the oneness of G-d, and that now is the appointed time for this to take place. We (the Church) have a prophetic calling and voice to fulfill and release into the earth, that we are to become the Ezekiel of G-d, the intercessors to stand in the gap to breathe His spiritual breath of mercy and life into them. I believe that we are *The Ezekiel Generation*, just as it is written:

> *Then He said to me, "Prophecy to the breath; prophecy, son of man, and say to it, 'This is what the Sovereign L-rd says: Come from the four winds, O breath, and breathe into these slain, that they may live.'" So I prophesied as He commanded me, and breath entered them; they came to life and stood up on their feet—a vast army.*
>
> *Then He said to me: "Son of man, these bones are the whole house of Israel"* (Ezekiel 37:9-11).

Has G-d ever moved upon the earth without an intercessor to bring about His changes? Then why would the end be any different from all of the other times in biblical history? As in the story of my son Joshua's birth, he could not be brought forth until all three forces were in agreement. In this case, we can clearly see the unity of G-d's family—G-d the Father, Jesus, His Son, and the Church all working together to bring this plan to pass. When we think about this from a parental perspective, what a blessing it is to see our family working together with the same goal in mind. And, in this case, what a blessing it is to see our firstborn brother come to life so that all of us may come into our own inheritance as well.

As a Gentile believer, do we want the glory of G-d to be shown to the world? For it is only through the awakening of His firstborn children before He returns that this can take place. Unlike any other Church generation in its history, we have the distinct honor to be personally involved in Israel's reawakening. This is why the mystery of Israel and the Church must be completely unraveled at this time; and this is why much of the confusion in end-time teachings that seem to completely divorce the Church from having any role in this rebirthing needs to be corrected. And I am not referring to our beliefs about the rapture here.

So at this time, we can clearly see it for ourselves, that it will compel us to join G-d's ranks and begin to get the job done so that His kingdom can come down to the earth, so that the Lion of the tribe of Judah can take His seat upon the throne (see Rev. 5:5), and so that we can take up our priestly roles to rule the nations with Him.

HAS THERE BEEN A VEIL OVER OUR HEARTS?

What has prevented us from seeing this before? It is almost like there has been a veil upon our own hearts. For we are indeed exhorted and commanded to love Israel despite their rejection of the Gospel (see Rom. 11:28); but didn't the Church do exactly the opposite over the past 1,900 years?

We will begin to explore this in the next chapter to better understand the separation and our past dealings with Israel in the hope of experiencing healing in G-d's family.

ENDNOTES

1. *Your People Shall By My People* and *God's Promise and the Future of Israel.*

2. For more information about replacement theology and what it is, visit www.replacementtheology.org. This definition was also taken from the above website, accessed on March 28, 2013.

3. For more information about this, you can visit www .gotquestions.org.

4. Derek Prince, "Why Israel?," Study Notes CD 4414.

5. Derek Prince, "Why Israel?," Study Notes CD 4414.

6. See chapter 19 of this book for a fuller discussion of the point I am making here.

7. Arno C. Gaebelein and Ernst F. Stroeter, *Our Hope Magazine*, "The Messianic Jewish Congregational Movement of 1895," www.religion-online.org/showarticle.asp?, accessed April 4, 2013.

8. Azusa Street Revival Documentary, YouTube, Jack Hayford.

9. Passover 1906, www.jewishholidaysonline.com/1906. Passover is also the time Jesus was crucified.

Part Two

UNDERSTANDING THE DISCONNECTION

5

THE CHURCH'S PAST

Aside from G–d's crucial timing, if our reconnection toward Israel and the Jewish people and our role to help rebirth them in the Spirit is so vital in our Father's plans to show His glory to the world, then how come most of us have not yet fully seen the significance of this reconnection up to this point in time?

What I am about to share with you is of a sensitive and extremely delicate nature. I would ask as a result of this that you would try your best to remain open to some of my thoughts in this area, because this may be difficult for you to see at first. However, please know that I bring it into the light for the sole purpose of introducing healing, repentance, and forgiveness in the Body of Christ, especially from our bloodline and ancestral past.

ARE WE SEEING CORRECTLY?

Can we honestly expect most of the Church's theology to be correct regarding Israel and the Jewish people, when our own Church history has been so dark toward them? Can we expect it when a great deal of our ancestry and bloodline has been stained with anti-Semitism, hatred, and persecution of the Jewish people over the past 2,000 years? Could it also be possible that, as a result of this past history toward them, the Church has received its own veil as a measure of judgment? And could it be that at best our theology is blurred toward the end times concerning Israel, especially our own unique role we are still yet to play? Why is it that there is still a great deal of confusion and misunderstanding when it comes to Israel and the Church, and that the mystery the apostle Paul spoke of in Romans 11 is still not clear?

While I write these words, I want us to know that in no way am I pointing the finger here at anyone to lay the blame, but rather bringing our pasts into the light so that we can find reconciliation. Without discussing and fully addressing our past, sometimes it is just not possible to break free, which I believe to be the case here. The enemy of our souls is still using the past against us without us even being aware of it, and it is now of vital significance to the fullness of the kingdom of G-d upon the earth that his grip be exposed.

Neither Jew nor Gentile are innocent here from the past, and a great deal of the persecution within G-d's family was actually started from the Jewish side first. This is quite clear throughout the New Testament, especially within the book of Acts. But it did not stop there, and, as most of us are aware, the tables greatly turned in this regard. In order for us to find complete liberty here, we must be willing to look back and gain a better understanding of how the enemy has sown his seeds against us to keep the family of G-d separated. For that has always been his goal.

WHAT HAS THE DEVIL SOWN?

When we operate in sin and disobedience, whether in the Church or in the world, and do not repent of it, these sins travel down into our bloodline and heritage, affecting our children and grandchildren's lives. This gives root for the devil to take further hold by attaching his spiritual forces and strongholds to it. In fact, isn't this exactly how the enemy works with all sin, by attaching his demonic forces to sinful behavior in order to control and grip souls away from G-d?

As a businessman most of my life, I have traveled all around the world. Quite often, when entering a new place or city, I sometimes feel the spiritual climate that may be controlling those places with some form of oppression. And some kind of sinful behavior is usually always present, because sin fuels the enemy's camp, which is one of the main reasons why obedience is so important in our lives as believers. We need to attempt to remain as free as possible in our walk with G-d.

To get a closer look at what I am writing here, we only have to look at racism to see it more clearly. Generations of people in our more recent history were so clearly convinced that racism wasn't sinful—and look how it affected their thoughts and attitudes as well as their actions. Simply put, sinful behavior further empowers darkness, and the enemy's camp seems to have freedom to associate itself when sin is present. Think for a moment of when we are disobedient to G-d as believers, do we not begin to come out from under an umbrella of His grace, allowing darkness to creep in (see James 1:13-15)?

THROUGH OUR BLOODLINE

Does it not say in the book of Exodus (see 20:5) that the sins of the fathers can travel to the third and fourth generation? Is it not clear, then, that our lives can be affected through the actions of our ancestry? Not just our views and perspectives on the Jewish people, but also many of the habits and behaviors of our parents and our lineage also need to be broken off our lives by the Spirit of G-d.

Many in the world are just simply blind to these facts because they have no real understanding of the spiritual realm that is all around them, often denying its very existence. And to be perfectly honest here, because we cannot see or touch this realm, and can only sense and feel it from time to time, we in the Church are not much more tuned into it either, even though we ought to be.

LUTHER AND GERMANY

For how did a whole German nation turn so viciously against the Jewish people if it had not first been spiritually seduced? The spiritual bloodline of the Church has been tainted by some horrific anti-Semitic acts and teachings that promoted Israel's finality, separation, and condemnation from G-d, especially in light of G-d's call and direction toward Gentile believers that clearly taught that the hardening of Israel was only temporary (see Rom. 11:25-26).

These acts and teachings have continued through most of Church history. While G-d used Martin Luther to bring great revelation to the Body of Christ (he became one of the fathers of the Protestant Reformation), he was most certainly deceived through his bloodline and his ultimate theological conclusions when it came to the Jewish people. He turned violently against the Jews at the end because they rejected him, even suggesting their homes be destroyed, synagogues torched, and their books burned.[1] I would like to suggest that from a satanic point of view, how much overtime did the devil and his demons work on Luther to turn his heart against them, which took place in the latter part of his life when he was actually sick and weakened? For in the beginning of his ministry, he earnestly tried to reach out to the Jewish people.

I respectfully submit to you, then, that satan knew exactly what was at stake here by spiritually attacking Luther. It was so the modern Church would also be infiltrated with an anti-Semitic spirit that was common in the current churches of that time. Thus, anti-Semitism would now continue to travel through the bloodline of the generations, down into the present Protestant movement.

For has not the devil been trying to destroy the Jews since G-d had covenanted with them, even before Christ? Just think of Pharaoh in Egypt, Nehemiah trying to rebuild the walls of Jerusalem, or the Purim story of Haman and Mordecai, where G-d used Esther to come to the rescue and deliver the Jewish people from annihilation. Do you ever wonder why the devil hates the Jews so much? It's because their existence testifies to the G-d of Israel, His holy covenants to sustain them, and, more importantly now, when they get spiritually restored the devil is finished! In truth, Israel's spiritual restoration is the devil's demise, which is why it will become our greatest fight!

THE CHURCH BECOMES ANTI-SEMITIC

For soon after the initial Jewish believers went on to be with the L-rd and the Church began to be controlled by Gentiles, anti-Semitism unfortunately began to take root in the Church with most believing that the Jews had entered into a final judgment. Therefore, if they did not convert to Christianity, there was no hope for them—not understanding that both their call and journey was quite different from the rest of the Church.

This was in spite of the apostle Paul's exhortation to love them despite their resistance to the Gospel (see Rom. 11:28). Even though there were hundreds of Scriptures that spoke so clearly of their spiritual restoration, and even though the Jewish apostles along with all of the Church's original Jewish leadership so readily accepted the Holy Spirit's move amongst the Gentiles, quickly removing any and all obstacles that may have prevented them from coming to the L-rd, they truly opened their arms and fully embraced their Gentile brethren as equals in Christ.

It is not my intention to delve into these details about the Church's position toward the Jews, as there are already some good books that have been written on this subject.[2] You could also read chapter 8 from my first book, *The New Covenant Prophecy,* which goes into greater detail into the Church's past in this area. But I want to say that by the time Rome controlled the Church in the fourth century, it had already become extremely anti-Semitic.

Unfortunately, this was also promoted by many of the teachings of the early Church fathers, who may have been deeply loved by the Church but sadly misunderstood G-d's plan for Israel. They even looked to completely separate Christianity from any of its Jewish roots; so much so that when a Jew looks at Christianity today, they are rarely drawn to jealousy despite the apostle Paul's exhortations to all believers (see Rom. 11:11). The Church has become separate from its heritage, even though we have been grafted into a Jewish vine. In a lot of our theology, however, it is almost as if that vine is completely Gentile, with hardly any room for Jewish believers to be restored.

From Dan Juster's book, *Jewish Roots,* which has just recently been updated, we read that by the early second century, Church fathers such as Justin Martyr strongly encouraged full separation from any Jewish heritage whatsoever, teaching that Christ had eliminated them. These practices and other anti-Semitic positions continued to gain strength as each generation passed; so much so that by the fourth century, Bishop Ambrose actually suggested that the burning of their synagogues was not a sin because of their rejection of Christ. They overlooked the founding apostles as well as the hundreds of thousands of Jews who actually followed Yeshua into the New Covenant, establishing and building the Church.

The greatest damage done in this area was through John Chrysostom,[3] an important Church leader of his time in the fourth century, who was greatly loved by the Church but was obviously off regarding his theology toward Israel. He seemed to be threatened by Christians who were visiting synagogues in Antioch to gain a better understanding of their roots and heritage. He reacted by giving eight different sermons full of hatred and anti-Semitism, strongly teaching any and all disconnection from our Jewish past.

Sadly, in light of his favor and influence in the Church, these teachings laid a strong foundation for the Church's future position toward the Jews so that by the time the Church had really gained strength throughout the East and the West, nearly all of it was anti-Semitic. This caused the Jewish people immeasurable suffering throughout the centuries that we could hardly imagine as great pressure was constantly applied to them to convert or face the consequences.

So the Jews were forced into the faith, which only deepened the divide between the two groups. And those who would not convert suffered great persecution and even death; the ones who did were forbidden to continue any association with their own roots.

Can you even imagine this? I truly find this hard to believe as a Jewish believer, that the very people who received mercy as a result of Israel's disobedience were now chastising their older brothers in the kingdom of G-d because of their rejection, even when the apostle Paul tried to prepare us for it in advance. Perhaps he wrote of this because of what he saw coming.

What a tragic mistake it is to wrongly interpret some of the apostles' writings against the Jewish resistance as vilifying an entire race. For while these godly Jewish men, who built the Church, may have encountered resistance from their own Jewish brethren that opposed them, they would have considered themselves cut off so that their brothers could find faith in Christ: *"For I could wish that*

I myself were cursed and cut off from Christ for the sake of my brothers, those of my own race, the people of Israel," (Rom. 9:3-4) the apostle Paul said.

How wrong could we have been, and what did the Church fathers open the door to, when we turned against the Jewish people so that satan was able to seduce the Church in this area, using the other half of G-d's spiritual family to begin to wipe the Jews out? What chance would there be, except for the grace of G-d, of any Jews in the future really having the opportunity to return to G-d through Christ, when all of Christianity along with its Christian symbols were used to persecute and kill the Jews? I hate to say it, as I never like to give the devil credit for anything, but what a masterful, despicable plan the enemy had to be able to achieve this! Yet in our own humanity, our ancestry fell for it!

IT's IN THE BLOODLINE

I know this is hard for us to consider, especially now that most of us in this modern day do not act this way toward anyone. However, we must do our best to face the past so that if there is any negative influences that have affected us, especially through the bloodline, G-d may be able to free us from them.

The last 1,500 years were actually worse, where at one time the Jews were completely vilified and killing them seemed to be acceptable. From the Crusades to the Spanish Inquisition, the Russian Pogroms and then to Nazi Germany, the Gentile world sought to completely eliminate the Jews from the face of the earth. And most of this was done in the name of our L-rd.

Is it difficult for us to imagine today, as a result, why any Jewish person could even go near a church. For we have to gain a better understanding of our own history toward the Jewish people and why they are so resistant to Christianity today. For it is no longer only the fact that they might of rejected Christ that keeps Jewish people away from faith, but rather because of all of the horrific acts that have been done to them in the name of Christ. For truly, as Dr. Michael Brown says, the Church has blood on its hands from our past.

My Own Bloodline Resistance

Even in my own return to faith as a Jew, it was extremely difficult for me to overcome all of the inherent barriers against Christ from my own heritage and bloodline because of how my people have been persecuted in the name of Christ. I also felt that if I accepted Christ, I would be betraying my people. Oh, what has our ancestry done to our firstborn brother? What did they do to Joseph, who was cast into slavery by his own brothers?

For it was only through the love and grace of G-d that I was able to overcome this myself and fully embrace the little church the Spirit of G-d led me into, despite the fact that I knew a lot of the Church around me was still affected by anti-Semitism. For G-d quickly taught me that He was not the One to blame for this; and that wherever man has placed his hands, it is rarely pure and clean, even including the Church.

Do we honestly believe in our heart of hearts that the founding apostles or Jesus Himself could have condoned the Church's action toward the Jews? Or what of Christ Himself, that in the midst of His torment on the cross, cried out for their forgiveness (see Luke 23:34)?

I know these are strong words, but please know that they are not said with any condemnation. Rather, I say them to bring us to a reality of how the Church has misunderstood Israel's calling throughout history and their past toward them. I say it so that we can come into cleansing, healing, and repentance so the bloodline that is still affecting us from the past can be cleansed, that G-d's family can become united, and that our Father's will can be done through both of us to show His glory to the nations.

WE MUST PROPERLY FACE THE CHURCH'S PAST FOR OURSELVES

In order for this to happen, we need to be willing to face the past along with its mistakes if we want to get it right in the end. This is just like Israel will do when they finally look upon the One they have pierced and realize what a tragic mistake they have made (see Zech. 12:10). For certain, the Church's past has been full of wickedness to the very people who gave us Christ. And many of our ancestors condemned them for killing Him.

The Jews did not kill Christ any more than the Romans did, even though they were both used in that fateful day. G-d designed it so that all humanity, both Jew and Gentile alike, were involved in the Lamb's sacrifice. The Father gave Him up as a love offering for all of our sins. In Jesus's own words to Pilate, the Roman governor, He said, *"You would have no power over Me if it were not given to you from above"* (John 19:11). "Christ killers!" is an anti-Semitic lie that we still hear to this very day in some places, and that has been handed down through the centuries.

For Jesus was always painfully aware of the death and sacrifice that He would end up making for all of us, which He did of His own free will to take on all of our sins. In the words of Isaiah the prophet, which I have paraphrased,

> *It was the L-rd's will to crush Him and cause Him to suffer, and though the L-rd makes His life a guilt offering.... After the suffering of His soul, He will see the light of life and be satisfied...because He poured out His life unto death and was numbered with the transgressors.*

For He bore the sins of many and made intercession for the transgressors (Isaiah 53:10-12 personal paraphrase).

A REMNANT OF BELIEVERS

Not everyone in the Church, however, was anti-Semitic. Interestingly enough, there has always seemed to be a remnant of believers who fully understood G-d's promises toward Israel, just like there has always been a remnant of Jewish believers in the New Covenant, up until the time that the veil will be officially lifted from their hearts (see Rom. 11:5).

Some of these different Church groups, such as the Puritans from England in the sixteenth and seventeenth centuries, firmly believed that the Jews were still G-d's chosen people in light of the Word of G-d. They believed Israel would not only be restored to the land but also spiritually reconnected when G-d would lift the veil from over their hearts. Some also believe that through their many prayers for Israel and the Jewish people, the Puritans may have helped to birth the Zionist movement in the Spirit, which was to come centuries later (end of the nineteenth century) through the Jewish people crying out for a return to the land. The Puritan's beliefs also had a strong influence in the establishment of the United States through its founding fathers. Many of the first settlers of North America were from a Puritan background as well.

There have also been many Christians who have actually helped the Jewish people, even risking their own lives to do so. A great number of them are honored and remembered at Israel's Yad Vashem Museum in Jerusalem, which remembers the Holocaust. However, most of the Church and the majority of Gentiles were not so kind or loving toward the Jews, to say the least. As a result of these actions from our past, our bloodline has been stained toward Israel and the

Jewish people; and few of us have been unaffected by it if we are truly honest with ourselves.

GENERATIONAL ANTI-SEMITISM

Generational anti-Semitism is the main reason our theology has been blurred and confused toward Israel and the Church, which can cause us to become more anti-Semitic. But even those of us who may now profess to love Israel and greatly desire and support their regathering can still be affected by this generational curse. This is why it is so deceptive, as our bloodline can unknowingly influence us while the enemy has been using it against us. This is because our ancestry and blood have been stained against the Jews. And it will continue to affect us if it has not been broken off and renounced, both corporately and individually. The main reason why I'm raising these issues in the first place is for us to get free from anything that might hold us back.

YOU DON'T HAVE TO BE ANTI-SEMITIC TO BE AFFECTED BY GENERATIONAL ANTI-SEMITISM

If you have operated in anti-Semitism, any hatred or negative slurs, or any acts or comments toward Jewish people, then you obviously need to repent of it. But in this section I am not addressing blatant anti-Semitism, but rather something more inconspicuous—*generational anti-Semitism*, which is not necessarily blatant or obvious at all. In fact, it is oftentimes extremely subtle.

Most who have good intentions toward the Jewish people and Israel would rarely even know or feel its effects, yet be affected by it as a result of their lineage. To be perfectly clear here, one does not have to be anti-Semitic to be affected by generational anti-Semitism and the actions from our ancestry. This is extremely important for us to understand. But because it still exists through our bloodline, the enemy has a right to influence us in this area in the spiritual realm.

This so easily explains why we may be disconnected to the calling we have in the Church to help rebirth Israel in the Spirit, because we have been unable to see it or its significance in our lives. I believe that the sins of our fathers have blinded us from seeing the fullness of G-d's plan through both groups up until this time. But now is the hour for G-d to reveal it to prepare us for His final act in uniting His spiritual family. Now is the time for G-d to make it known, as we are entering a time of transition between Jew and Gentile, except this time to usher in the L-rd's return.

IN THE MIND, BUT NOT IN THE HEART

For those of us who are already pro-Israel, this can also result in us having an intellectual knowledge about Israel and their regathering while still lacking a real love and connection for them in our hearts and spirits. And this ultimately affects our discernment in this area. Thus, we cannot see what our Father wants us to know and fully understand about the reconnection and His end-time plan to show Himself through both groups because of what has gone on through our bloodline. Because of this, most of us have hardly any knowledge at all and are disconnected from perhaps one of greatest callings in the Church, which is to release the mercy of G-d back to Israel (see Rom. 11:30-32).

As an intercessor for Israel and the Jewish people for most of my walk with the L-rd, I started to recognize this in prayer meetings specifically aimed at Israel. I felt that certain good-willed, good-intentioned believers, who were actually praying for Israel, seemed to be discerning incorrectly from the Holy Spirit about these matters. These were matters He had already made clear to my spirit, especially through my son Joshua's birth.

G-D STARTED TO SHOW ME

I did not first jump at these issues either, and instead became prayerful about them, even questioning my own theology. However, it didn't stop there as it seemed I had entered a phase when I started to experience this a lot, almost as if the Holy Spirit was definitely trying to show me something. And this continued for several months until one particular prayer meeting when one of my close friends in the church I was attending at the time suddenly recognized that his understanding and discernment was off regarding Israel.

So we sat and talked for a few minutes. In our conversation, I asked him if he felt any negative feelings toward the Jewish people, and shared that others might have affected him in his family. It could have come either from his immediate family or his ancestry, being passed down by how they felt or what they may have said negatively against the Jewish people.

This dear brother, who has a deep love for Jesus, was immediately convicted of anti-Semitism from his past, and right there on the spot, confessed it to the L-rd. At once he became free, was filled with a new love for Israel and the Jewish people, and quickly described to me how clean and pure he felt in his heart.

This continued as I spiritually grew up in my church experience. I would recognize certain Gentile believers, especially pastors and leaders as having a theologically intellectual commitment toward Israel because of their understanding of the Word of G-d, that indeed G-d would once again spiritually reconnect Israel as we came down to the end of time. Because of this, they understood that we had to be committed to Israel. Yet their hearts and spirits still seemed to somehow be distant or disconnected to the Jewish people as well as to the fullness of G-d's plan, almost like they were missing the greatest piece of the puzzle.

THEY SHOULD BE LIKE US

Why is it that, with most of us, whenever a Jewish person comes to faith in the Church, we fully expect Jewish believers to conform to all of the Gentile customs? We don't really recognize their spiritual call as Jews to restore their Jewish identity and to help make way for G-d's covenants to be fulfilled through Israel's spiritual awakening. Could there be some misunderstanding here? After all, whose vine is it?

While we are all called to the oneness in Spirit of the New Covenant in Christ and are now co-heirs with Him, it is apparent that we have not yet fully understood that Israel's call is different from the rest of G-d's spiritual family, as well as not yet understanding our own unique role to help rebirth them. Therefore, fully exposing the generational anti-Semitism issue brings all of this into the light, as it has veiled us from properly seeing the roles we are both supposed to play out in order for G-d's kingdom to come. The moment we think of Jewish believers practicing their customs and traditions, we become fearful of them returning to the law.

However, the New Covenant that Jesus gave us truly brings these customs into a new light, just as the Jewish apostles discovered. As long as there is no dependence on the law for salvation, do the Jews not have a right to intertwine the old into the new, especially to reach their own?

THEY NEED TO BE WHO G-D
MADE THEM TO BE

In light of the times in which we are living, in order for G-d's end-time plan to take place, we must reevaluate how we both see and recognize Israel as well as the calling on Jewish believers, and stop comparing them to other nations. While they are definitely a people, they are not like other nations, but instead are a covenant people whose very existence and restoration depends solely on the promises of our G-d to reestablish them into His priesthood by upholding His holy Word (see Isa. 61:6-9).

It is for this reason that we must bless them into their inheritance so that we may also receive our own. It is so we may both reign together as a spiritual family throughout the world, for this is the plan of G-d in our time, to truly make us one (see Rev. 5:9-10)! It is to encourage them into the fullness of their identity and traditions and cause the Messianic body to strengthen and flourish among themselves. It is to shine a brilliant light back into the rest of the Jewish community to help awaken them (see Matt. 5:14-16), whether that comes from within church groups or through the Messianic body (which is also part of the greater Church). In reality, the New Covenant in Christ is the only true and proper extension of Judaism and it needs to be appropriately reflected in order to make Israel envious.

GENERATIONAL ANTI-SEMITISM HAS AFFECTED US ALL

I respectfully submit and truly believe that nearly all of us in the Church from a Gentile background have been affected by generational anti-Semitism. This is because of the Church's past action against the Jews that the enemy has been able to sneak in and use it against us. Now is the time for us to address it; now is the time for it to be exposed; and now is the time for us to get free so that we may all come into our rightful destinies, both Jew and Gentile believers alike.

WE HAVE BEEN CALLED

Despite Israel's current rejection of the Gospel (see Rom. 11:28), there can be no question that we were called and even commanded to love them. The apostle Paul again writes to the Romans: *"I am talking to you Gentiles. Inasmuch as I am an apostle to the Gentiles, I make much of my ministry in the hope that I may somehow arouse my own people to envy and save some of them"* (Rom. 11:13-14). This was not a wish or desire of the apostle Paul, or the L-rd Jesus exhorting us through the Holy Spirit, but rather an edict and positioning G-d was establishing for us to have toward the Jews, G-d's firstborn children. Yet in light of our past history, up until this modern time the Church has failed the L-rd in this place. Why? Because without the grace and love of G-d in our own humanity, it has been impossible for us to love the Jewish people who have continually rejected Christ and us as a result.

Instead of loving them as they are, which takes a supernatural love, the Church was deceived, went to the other extreme, and became the instruments of their wrath, thoroughly deepening the chasm that exists between Jews and Gentiles. And this is something that only G-d's healing touch can now transform. Just like Israel failed to become a light to the world (because in its own humanity it could not stand up to the law), up to this point the majority of us in the Church have failed to bring the light of G-d back to Israel because of our own humanity, despite our calling to draw them to jealousy (see Rom. 11:11). There is an interesting parallel here, as both occurrences reveal man's humanity and our inability to operate in our own strength. We must rather operate fully in the Spirit of G-d. We must rather operate fully in the Spirit of G-d, which will bring us back to His mercy, which is actually His intention and plan (see Rom. 11:32).

EXPOSE THE ENEMY AND ALLOW G-D TO HEAL

This may be challenging for us to comprehend, but the Church has experienced its own veil in light of its disobedience here as a measure of judgment concerning Israel, so that it has been unable to properly see G-d's plans in these days. This should not totally surprise us, as it is only by G-d's grace and revelation that we can fully see His Word in the first place. Until our bloodline is properly cleansed, the blurring and confusion will remain (see Matt. 7:1-2), which we must also be willing to face if we want to get free from its prejudice.

As difficult as it may be for us to face, we have received a measure of Israel's blindness coming back upon us as a result of our actions toward them (see Matt. 7:1). Therefore, we are not the only ones who are veiled when it comes to Israel, the Church, and the last days. It is as if a mirror of Israel's blindness has come upon us. And this is why our theology concerning both groups is also in need of adjustment and correction.

RUTHS AND CORNELIUSES

What is also interesting, though, is that while there is only a remnant of Jewish believers currently in the Church, even the remnant appears to be mirrored spiritually among Gentile believers who already have the Israel revelation. This was something Jesus showed our intercessory prayer group at Messiah's House several years ago.

In many churches there always seems to be a handful of believers who truly get the whole Israel piece and hunger and thirst for anything to do with Israel being regathered. Interestingly, when you talk to many of these believers—who I like to refer to as Ruths and Corneliuses because G-d has already spiritually reconnected them— they will tell you that it was as if a veil was lifted from their hearts concerning Israel, so that they could begin to see this fresh perspective from G-d's own heart.

APPEAL TO PASTORS AND LEADERS

As difficult as this may appear, however, most of the leadership in the Church is still spiritually disconnected, especially in light of what they are taught in seminary regarding eschatology (end-time theology). If you are a pastor reading this book, my heart goes out to you, and I really want to encourage you to be extra prayerful about what I am saying here. Ask G-d if what I am saying is true or not, because I believe a great deal of what you may have learned in seminary regarding Israel and the Church is in definite need of adjustment. And I say this with all humility and respect for our theological institutions.

As we now move closer to this end-time period, it is slowly beginning to change, and we truly need to pray for our leadership to get this revelation. And this is especially true if we are going to get on the same page as our L-rd concerning His end-time plans to return to the earth.

THE VEIL OVER THE CHURCH

This veil over the Church has affected us in a number of ways, for much of the Church still believes it has actually replaced Israel. Replacement theology was established by a number of the early Church fathers, being passed down from one generation to the next, which is why the Church has been so entrenched in these teachings. They taught that the Church had superseded Israel in light of their rejection of Christ; and despite the mercy that has been bestowed on the Church through Christ, we have failed to see G-d's mercy back to Israel as well as His heart as a Father, to keep His multiple promises to restore them through His holy covenants.

While Israel definitely entered a major period of judgment in their dispersion and greatly suffered the consequences of their own sin and disobedience toward G-d, it was never supposed to end there. On the contrary, for within G-d's plan, their rejection meant riches for the world so His Word could go out to the nations to help make Israel jealous. However, the great mystery about Israel is that they have to be restored in order for the kingdom to come, as G-d is forever connected to them as His firstborn children, just as He is to the rest of His children.

Needless to say, this was a tragic mistake for the Church. And in furthering our separation from the Jews, we also sadly lost a great deal of the connection to our roots and heritage. However, there are also warnings contained in G-d's Word for those who would mistreat any of His children (see Deut. 32:43).

Didn't the apostle Paul also caution us about this, about not being arrogant concerning our position compared to theirs?

> *Do not be arrogant, but be afraid. For if G-d did not spare the natural branches, He will not spare you either. Consider therefore the kindness and sternness of G-d: sternness to those who fell, but kindness to you, provided that you continue in His kindness. Otherwise, you also will be cut off* (Romans 11:20-22).

These are strong words used by the Holy Spirit in how to position ourselves toward Israel; and they should not be taken lightly.

ROMANTIC BELIEVERS

There are others of us in the Church who believe that Israel still has a place in G-d's plan and will be restored before the end, yet see no role for the Church to play in this reconnection, except perhaps helping them return to the land. Still others of us, who may have seen the light of G-d's Word toward Israel, now reach out with love and compassion, but are almost romantic with our approach, even financially supporting Jewish groups in the land of Israel, who may actually be persecuting our very own Messianic brethren.

Finally, as G-d's awakening has begun in this area between Israel and the Church, can we please consider allowing G-d to bring forth healing, cleansing, and deliverance from our past? This is so the Father's heart for Israel can be placed in our spirits in order that His plan can be fulfilled in these days we find ourselves living in.

GOOD QUESTIONS

You may ask me, "Who are you that G-d would reveal this to you? And how do you know this for sure? Why would G-d allow my heart to be affected through my family tree like this? Why would G-d allow our theology to be confused in light of the Church's behavior toward the Jewish people?" And these are all valid questions, which is why we need to consider the message of this book carefully.

As a Jewish believer coming into the Church, this does not necessarily affect me like my Gentile brethren. I am also not as affected by some of the unfortunate divisions that exist between our Catholic and Protestant brethren, which are also heavy in the bloodline, and as a result are in great need of their own repentance and healing. Could it be possible that the division in the Church, which is dramatic, may also stem from the division that exists between the Church and the Jewish people, the first separation?

JEWISH PEOPLE CAN BE AFFECTED

Believe it or not, however, this anti-Semitic spirit can also affect Jewish people, but this is obviously a small percentage. This spiritual stronghold can be stronger in some places than in others, depending on what kind of anti-Semitic activity has occurred in the past. But certain Jewish people can be affected by it, causing them to not really like their own people.

This can also be true of Jewish believers that come into the Church, wanting nothing to do with their Jewish heritage and roots. These

Jewish brethren should pray and ask G-d about this, as every Jewish believer has a call in the Church to be a light back to their own people, to help draw them to jealousy. This call is not exclusive to the Gentiles; but as a Jew in the Church, I should not have to be instructed to reach out to my own, it should be completely natural for me, just as it was for the apostles. Unless, of course, there is something preventing me from flowing in this calling, then I would need to look into my heart and ask G-d to change me and give me a love for my people.

Coming from the Jewish side, I had to overcome my own bloodline issues that are more common to Jewish people. This was actually resistance to Christ through all of the horrible persecution of my people. It wasn't unusual for me as a child growing up in England to be confronted by anti-Semitic remarks at my school, often getting into fights defending myself against the slurs. When I became a believer, I had several barriers to deal with in this area in my own walk with G-d, entering the Church that as a whole was still quite full of anti-Semitism.

However, there were also many believers that I was beginning to meet that loved the Jewish people and also embraced me as a spiritual brother; and G-d quickly showed me that He was not the One to blame. After a while, I knew by the Word of G-d that any Gentile believer in Jesus was now part of my family as I was part of theirs, and that I was called to love them just as I was called to love my own people. I did this despite some of my own people rejecting me for embracing Christ and my Gentile believing family.

We Jewish believers are an interesting lot—not wanted by some in the Church and not wanted by our own either. It is not always an easy place to live and exist in. However, in light of my background and my walk with G-d in the Church, He has used my life and experience to bring this message to you at this time.

ONE FAMILY

As remnant Jewish believers now coming into the Church, instead of fueling the divide, we are called to help heal the gap that exists between G-d's family, and so rely on His all-sufficient grace. I have also received a great deal of love from believers in the Church, and I am personally indebted to many who have helped me walk and mature in the Spirit of G-d. Not only has G-d given me a great deal of love for my own people, but He has also given me a great deal of love for the Church. I am acutely aware that both groups are in great need of the mercy of G-d, and that G-d loves each person in His family equally.

Second, for a very short period of time in my walk with G-d, I actually became angry toward the Jewish religious leaders of Yeshua's day because they caused us to reject Him and therefore withheld Messiah from us. However, it was this attitude in me that G-d actually used to change my heart back toward my own people and give me a supernatural love for them.

Not only is the Church in great need of healing and deliverance from any form of anti-Semitism, but the enemy has also cloaked this generational spirit and we must work now to expose it.

A DEEPER LOOK

Let's now take a deeper look at this issue to gain a better understanding of it. It is a crucial part of the unlocking of our hearts in the Church that must spiritually take place within us, if we are going to get on the same page as our Father in regard to His end-time plan to reveal Himself to the world. Please understand that as a Jew I went through this process from the other side, to break away from the bloodline of my relatives that would prevent me from reuniting with my Gentile believing family. In truth, we are all in need of healing and cleansing from our stormy past.

By now I had attained this understanding because of my own experiences in the Spirit of G-d as a Jewish believer and intercessor for Israel. Of course, when I first started to get this revelation and these senses from G-d, I naturally questioned them. But the Holy Spirit led me through a number of real-life circumstances that continued to reinforce what I was beginning to see. All the evidence I ever needed came about through believers themselves. Then I began to share these thoughts and insights about generational anti-Semitism and people started to get supernaturally healed and delivered from it. Whenever I would teach on Israel and the Church, I would always include a section on the Father's heart and subsequently lead people in confession, renunciation, and repentance on anything anti-Semitic through their bloodlines and ancestry.

Usually, almost immediately after repentance, an overwhelming presence of G-d's Spirit would come into the room and weeping would naturally follow with healing, cleansing, and deliverance. Then the Holy Spirit would release a full measure of His love for His firstborn children as we prayed and petitioned Him. This is ultimately what we must have in order to come into agreement with G-d for His firstborn to be redeemed and is what this book is all about. For it is impossible for us to love them in our own strength and humanity as we have seen through the Church's actions over the last 1,900 years.

WE HAVE ALL BEEN AFFECTED

Last spring, while I was writing *The New Covenant Prophecy*, I was visiting with Pastor Don Finto in Nashville, Tennessee, who is one of the leaders in the Church spearheading this spiritual awakening toward Israel and the Jewish people. He runs Caleb Company with Tod McDowell, a ministry that is focused on training leaders in the five-fold ministry (see Eph. 4:11), with a top priority to reconnect the Church with Israel and their Jewish roots.

It was here, however, that something unique happened in the Spirit, more fully confirming this message to me. I had no plans to share or teach, but rather to reconnect with my old friend and soak in all of their spirituality and love for their Jewish brethren. Don immediately felt led to introduce me to Thomas Boehm, also a Jewish believer who sits on the board of the Caleb Company ministry.

Over a spirited lunch that day, I shared my heart and thoughts with Thomas and Don about the Church's position in regard to Israel and how generational anti-Semitism was affecting it. However, without knowing, Tod McDowell had planned a leadership meeting the next day for the entire team at their ministry facility on the outskirts of Nashville. Tod had asked Thomas to share on Jewish roots. When we got there the following morning, nearly all of the group's ministry team were present, and there were about 20 people in the room.

It goes without saying that all of these ministry leaders already had a deep love for Israel and the Jewish people. It was their main ministry focus, not only to help retrain Church leaders on receiving the Israel piece, but also to realign themselves with the Jewish roots of our faith. Most of them were already experienced intercessors for Israel.

As Thomas started to speak to the group, the Holy Spirit suddenly stopped him. He then told everyone that he felt I was to share the burden on my heart for the Church reconnecting to Israel. I had obviously not prepared anything because I had not planned to speak. Over the next several minutes, the Holy Spirit truly led me to capsulate the thoughts and insights He had revealed to me to this wonderful group of people. Much of what I shared that day, you have just read about in this book, except I shared it from my own perspective and personal experience. When I finished, Tod asked me to lead the group in prayer in response to what I just shared.

As was my habit by now, I would usually always lead people straight into confession and repentance, breaking off their ancestral bloodline through generational anti-Semitism. *Was it really necessary to lead these people through this kind of prayer and confession?* I thought to myself. After all, everyone in the room not only had a love and passion for Israel and the Jewish people, but they were also very busy in their own individual lives sharing the reconnection message with everyone they knew. So who was I to bring this message to them?

However, thanks be to G-d, because with Tod's encouragement I still felt His leading to proceed. As I did, we could not believe what happened next. After we prayed, confessed, and renounced any spiritual ties from our bloodlines toward the Church's past actions, and even that of our own families, the presence of G-d fell in that room—such as I had not experienced for many years. Not only was everyone in the room weeping, but they were also wailing with the heart of G-d for His lost son, Israel. We could feel His pain and separation as a Father for His firstborn son as well as His love for them at the same time—it was an amazing moment of intercession in the Spirit of G-d.

I had the sense from the Holy Spirit, that if these beloved people—who had already given over their lives to the service of G-d to help reconnect G-d's spiritual family in the Church—actually needed to go through this renouncement, then every one of us in the Church would actually need it too. This was another prompt for writing this book.

Tod McDowell's Thoughts on What Took Place

Tod wrote me about his experience that day as well, which I would like to quote here at length.

As Grant shared our need to break off any generational anti-Semitism through the bloodline that may have unknowingly been passed down from our ancestors, I thought that it would be good to affirm him and his teaching. But I was stepping out in faith as I didn't think that our group had any need for this—especially me. I had already confessed and repented of my own "ignorant replacement theology" that discounted the relevance of the current nation of Israel and the Jewish people according to G-d's biblical covenants and promises. I also have taught around the world, sharing G-d's heart and purpose for Israel to be connected to the Gentile Church and the nations.

I believed that what Grant shared was true, and that it wouldn't hurt to pray as he encouraged, but I had no idea of the potency of this transaction. As I began to pray with our staff and leadership team concerning my ancestral anti-Semitic roots, the Holy Spirit flashed before me my eastern European roots that I had not thought about, and suddenly a pain rose up in my heart. I felt the broken heart of G-d erupting in my soul concerning the hatred, bias, and "treating lightly" of the Jewish people in my ancestral line. I didn't know this from my family stories, but now the Holy Spirit was revealing it to me because I was opening up to it.

It became so intense that I began to weep and wail with the weight and burden in my spirit. As this began, I was shocked that I had such deep places in my heart of anti-Semitic curses passed down from my family line. I have never consciously felt this before, but in that moment I experienced an internal cleansing and freedom from this defiling and dark curse that I now know the enemy has not only used against me and my family but also the Church. Through my tears, I repented and renounced this family history, and, as I did, waves of healing love showered over me as I felt the forgiveness and restoration from the Father.

In addition, I was not the only one. As I looked around, all of the brethren in the room seemed to be affected in the same manner. The presence of G-d in the room was intense as He washed us all from the enemy's hold through our bloodlines.

Looking back on this, I believe that this was a major stepping-stone on my journey into understanding and embracing G-d's heart and purposes for Israel on a personal level. I would encourage you to ask the Holy Spirit to reveal this to you about your own family background and perhaps you will experience this surprising and freeing reality as I did.

Dealing with generational anti-Semitism is much like dealing with many other issues or sins that may be in our hearts and that need to be confessed or repented of. Though in this case we were not directly responsible for it, the process of healing is still much the same. What is tricky here is that when there is sin from our past that is passed down through our bloodlines or ancestry, much of it can go undetected. However, that does not eliminate it from being there nor does it free us from any deception or spiritual hold that the enemy can have over us that still needs to be broken in light of our ancestry.

Please understand that I am not raising this issue to lay blame. On the contrary, without us facing our past through the Church and our ancestry, the enemy has divided us and is still using this against us—more than we will ever know or fully understand. And in order for us to get free, we must bring it into the light. We are not to blame for the actions of our forefathers. However, if they are still affecting us like they can in other areas of our lives, and the enemy is still using it, shouldn't we want to deal with it and be free?

If we don't, it is like putting the cart before the horse. Everything we do in this area without renouncement will still keep us separated, which is not our Father's will at this time. In addition, the enemy would still be free to move because our hearts are not fully cleansed from the sins of our past, and we could more easily be deceived.

END-TIME TEACHINGS

This is also why a lot of our theology is either confused or misguided when it comes to Israel and the Church, and in need of adjustment. For where the heart is not fully clean, the enemy has an opening to bring in confusion and deception. He has obviously been very tricky here, which we should not be so surprised with, as this is what the enemy does. He looks to keep dominion and control, but now is the time for him to be exposed by bringing incredible change into the Church, or at least to those in the Body of Christ who will receive the reconnection.

PROPHETIC SCRIPTURES

I have heard, read, and seen so many teachings on the end times, conclusively addressing every tiny little detail in the book of Revelation that leaves nothing left to interpretation. Yet, when you read the book of Revelation, almost every word is written in riddles and metaphors. And I know that after Jesus comes to establish His kingdom, we will be able to look back on these Scriptures and teachings and say, "Ah, that's how it was meant to happen and that's what was meant by those words." At that time, everything will so easily fall into place and make sense. However, up until then, it is simply not possible for us to see fully, but rather somewhat dimly, like in a mirror (see 1 Cor. 13:12). Perhaps we were not meant to see fully, and there are other reasons for this than the L-rd just hiding the Word and truth from demonic forces.

These are what I call the *prophetic Scriptures*. And while we all may have different understandings of them, nothing should be carved in stone or written in doctrine. To be perfectly honest, we simply do not know and should instead try to fully appreciate our different opinions in the Body of Christ and enjoy each other's points of view and perspectives without judging one another. The Orthodox Jews are actually much better at doing this than we are in the Church, as the Talmud presents so many different opinions, many times without a definite conclusion. We need to do a much better job at loving and accepting each other in the Church, even if we have to agree to disagree.

G-D ALWAYS USES AN INTERCESSOR

However, one thing is clear in nearly all of these teachings about the end times that have come out of a Gentile perspective: there seems to be no reconnection between G-d's family in the last days before Jesus returns; that the salvation of Israel and the Jewish people will just happen supernaturally between them and G-d. Needless to say, I believe this to be false. For when has G-d ever done anything major in our spiritual history without using an intercessor to help bring it about?

Could G-d have saved the world without Noah? Was Israel established without any agreement from its patriarchs—Abraham, Isaac, and Jacob? Would Israel have been saved from famine and starvation without Joseph? Did G-d supernaturally bring Israel out of Egypt without Him first raising up Moses? Did the Red Sea part without Moses raising his staff? Did the walls of Jericho fall without Joshua marching and shouting? Were the walls of Jerusalem rebuilt without Nehemiah? Could the Father have saved the world without Jesus? And where is Jesus right now; is He not sitting at the Father's right hand interceding for us (see Rom. 8:34)?

I could go on and on with many other examples, including all of the prophets, just as the writer of Hebrews did in chapter 11, when he penned the history of all those who had gone before him, who stood in the gap, and took a position for G-d's Word and plan to come into fruition.

G-D'S MERCY PLAN

G-d has indeed already told us in His Word how the Jews will be spiritually restored through His mercy plan (see Rom. 11:30-31). Won't it be G-d's mercy that will ultimately forgive and restore Israel and the Jewish people in the last days? G-d's mercy and forgiveness are there for us to finally get it right toward Israel and love them the same way our Father does. G-d has called us to be the vessels of mercy and forgiveness He wants to use to pour out His love upon them. So why would everything be so separate in the last days? And why wouldn't the enemy do everything he can to keep it that way if he knew what was at stake?

We are talking about the return of our L-rd and the establishment of His throne upon the seat of David, that both Jewish and Gentile believers would take on their priestly roles to rule and reign upon the earth with the Almighty. Let us also not forget that we are also talking about the end of the devil's reign upon the earth, where he will be bound for a 1,000 years. So don't think for one moment that he is going to give up without a major fight!

This is why we in the current generation have a different calling from our ancestors, because G-d is calling us to stand in the gap and help reunite His family in this new era and time of transition between His kingdom children. There is much that needs to be exposed and brought into the light in order for this to happen. Are you beginning to get it now?

We know from G-d's Word that the time will come when He will supernaturally lift the veil from Israel's spirits and suddenly those who have been blinded will finally see. To a certain extent, this has already begun as many Jewish people are supernaturally awakening to the L-rd. However, this cannot happen on its own, not without us nor without our intercession and agreement to support the Father's plan. For up to this point we have been the missing link because most of us have been unable to see.

OUR EYES NEED OPENING

This message can only come through the Holy Spirit's revelation to our hearts. In reality, we in the Church need our most precious L-rd to open our minds regarding this awakening of Israel. We need the Spirit's help so we can properly see the Scriptures in light of our unique call in reconnecting with our firstborn brothers and sisters, helping to restore them spiritually (see Luke 24:45). This is so that G-d's mercy would be released into the earth. As the Spirit opens our eyes, we'll be able to see how G-d will reestablish Israel back into His kingdom, which in turn will establish both groups into our inheritance and priestly roles.

G-d cannot loose His mighty hand and outstretched arm to bring them forth if the Church is not fully working with Him. For Jesus to bring this about, we will provide the fuel of prayer in the heavenly realm. Not only so, but also think about what a woman actually goes through to bring forth new life: the pain, the struggle, and finally the push. All is required of her in order that the child be born, and this is what it will take from us so that Israel will come forth and Jesus can return.

THE HEART MUST BE CLEANSED

But before any of this can actually take place, our hearts need to be changed. We need to be cleansed, purified, and to be rid of anything that would want to separate us from our spiritual family, especially from *the spirit of generational anti-Semitism,* as G-d plans to reveal Himself to the world. It is probably one of the most deceptive spirits of them all as it has been so cloaked throughout the years.

Which will it be for us as we are reading this book? Will we allow our past to continue to affect us regarding the fullness of our hearts toward our Jewish brethren and remain as we are, to find and hide behind some theological reason to throw this word off so as to not have to respond to it? Or will we allow our loving Father to touch our spirits and change our hearts so that He may be glorified through both Jew and Gentile in these last days?

HAS THE CHURCH BEEN LIKE THE PROPHET JONAH?

When we think about it, hasn't the Church been a bit like the prophet Jonah, who was called to Nineveh? Have we not been called by G-d to supernaturally show His love back to Israel and make them jealous? Through our past, haven't we completely gone in the opposite direction? Isn't it time for us to correct this now and to permit G-d to release His love and mercy back to Israel?

For the blindness and confusion can be removed in an instant, because we serve an all-loving, all-forgiving, uncondemning G-d. It is Him whom greatly desires His mercy to be shown to all mankind through this unbelievable mystery called Israel and the Church, which is ultimately our Father's plan through both of us.

For it is only in the Father's love and strength that we will be able to fully shine this light back to the Jews, because until that spiritual veil is lifted from them, they don't want it and have absolutely no interest in receiving it. But they must be restored for all things to take place. For in the words of Topol, from the story of *The Fiddler on the Roof*: "L-rd, could please You chose someone else?" However, just like my son Joshua, who did not want to be born but was born, and who represents Israel through his journey to life, so will Israel be born. For as it is written, so shall it be!

Because of all of this, it will become a work for us. But it is with gladness and joy that we should willingly take it on. For it will be a glorious work that will ultimately loose such heavenly power upon the earth that it will be forever changed. *Israel is the golden key that we must now use to unlock the answers to these times as well as our spiritual reconnection toward them.*

ENDNOTES

1.   The quote below is taken from excerpts of Martin Luther's booklet, *The Jews and Their Lies*, 1543, quoted on http://www.jewishvirtuallibrary.org/jsource/anti-semitism/Luther_on_Jews.html, accessed April 1, 2013.

> What shall we Christians do with this rejected and condemned people, the Jews? Since they live among us, we dare not tolerate their conduct, now that we are aware of their lying and reviling and blaspheming. If we do, we become sharers in their lies, cursing and blasphemy. Thus we cannot extinguish the unquenchable fire of divine wrath, of which the prophets speak, nor can we convert the Jews. With prayer and the fear of G-d we must practice a sharp mercy to see whether we might save at least a few from the glowing flames. We dare not avenge ourselves. Vengeance a thousand times worse than we could wish them already has them by the throat. I shall give you my sincere advice:

> First to set fire to their synagogues or schools and to bury and cover with dirt whatever will not burn, so that no man will ever again see a stone or cinder of them. This is to be done in honor of our L-rd and of Christendom, so that G-d might see that we are Christians, and do not condone or knowingly tolerate such public lying, cursing, and blaspheming of his Son and of his Christians. For whatever we tolerated in the past unknowingly—and I myself was unaware of it—will be pardoned by G-d. But if we, now that we are informed, were to protect and shield such a house for the Jews, existing right before our very nose, in which they lie about, blaspheme, curse, vilify, and defame Christ and us (as was heard above), it would be the same as if we were doing all this and even worse ourselves, as we very well know.

> Second, I advise that their houses also be razed and destroyed....

Third, I advise that all their prayer books and Talmudic writings, in which such idolatry, lies, cursing and blasphemy are taught, be taken from them....

Fourth, I advise that their rabbis be forbidden to teach henceforth on pain of loss of life and limb....

Fifth, I advise that safe-conduct on the highways be abolished completely for the Jews. For they have no business in the countryside, since they are not lords, officials, tradesmen, or the like. Let they stay at home....

Sixth, I advise that usury be prohibited to them, and that all cash and treasure of silver and gold be taken from them and put aside for safekeeping. The reason for such a measure is that, as said above, they have no other means of earning a livelihood than usury, and by it they have stolen and robbed from us all they possess. Such money should now be used in no other way than the following: Whenever a Jew is sincerely converted, he should be handed one hundred, two hundred, or three hundred florins, as personal circumstances may suggest. With this he could set himself up in some occupation for the support of his poor wife and children, and the maintenance of the old or feeble. For such evil gains are cursed if they are not put to use with G-d's blessing in a good and worthy cause.

Seventh, I commend putting a flail, an ax, a hoe, a spade, a distaff, or a spindle into the hands of young, strong Jews and Jewesses and letting them earn their bread in the sweat of their brow, as was imposed on the children of Adam....

2. Such good books would be *Jewish Roots* by Dan Juster, *Our Hands are Stained with Blood* by Dr. Michael Brown, and *Your People Shall Be My People* by Don Finto. I highly recommend each one of them.

3. Dan Juster, *Jewish Roots: The History of Anti-Semitism* (Shippensburg, PA: Destiny Image, 1995), 141.

6

THE FATHER'S HEART

THE STORY OF TWO SONS

Nowhere is this relationship between G-d's family, as Jew and Gentile believers, more clearly seen in Scripture than in the story of the prodigal son (see Luke 15:11-32). For a moment, let us reflect upon it, with G-d being the father and the two sons being the Jew and the Christian, respectively. This will help us see the changes we need to make in these times we find ourselves living in.

Sometimes, when looking at this story, it is hard for us in the Church to see ourselves as the older brother because Israel is the one who came first. However, except for the apostles and many of the first Jewish believers who helped establish the Church in the first century, the rest of the Jewish people have still to come into the New Covenant. This is one of the reasons Jesus said, *"So the last will be first, and the first will be last"* (Matt. 20:16).

We must be clear here to hold onto G-d's Word, as salvation only comes through faith in Jesus Christ (see Rom. 3:22). That means Israel is still to experience redemption through the Messiah alone. As a result, what was once completely Jewish before the New

Covenant was given has been handed over to the Gentile believers who now run and operate our Father's house exclusive of our firstborn brother, who is still yet to be redeemed.[1] So when we read the story of the prodigal son, we can understand how the faithful brother feels. He thought he was being obedient, doing everything he was supposed to do, and part of him was probably happy because he knew he would end up in control of it all—it was his inheritance. After all, he had worked years for it.

Now faced with his brother's return, however, he does not respond like his father, who is full of compassion and mercy, but rather with anger, hostility, and jealousy: *How dare he even think about returning here!* he thinks to himself. His brother, who went his own way and squandered everything he had and then realized the error of his ways, being truly humbled by life, returned home in the hope he could become one of his father's servants.

On the other hand, the father's response is completely different from that of the elder brother. After all, he was a loving father who stood in the gap for his lost son. He was faithful to love him despite his rejection. He was grieved and heartbroken that his son walked away from him in the first place, and he never stopped feeling the pain of this separation—he wept and he mourned. But he never lost hope, waiting patiently for his son to return as he knew it was only a matter of time.

Time as we know it seems endless, but the father said, "I will never give up, I will never surrender until my lost son is properly restored." Then all of a sudden, an incredible thing happened, the fullness of joy swept over the father's heart, and the love of G-d consumed his soul like a river flowing at springtime. Suddenly, from his rocking chair on his front porch, he saw his lost son at a distance down the path leading up to the front of the house.[2] He immediately knew and understood what happened, except now his heart was filled with compassion as tears of joy ran down his face. *"My son! My son! My son!"* he exclaimed.

Full of overwhelming excitement, he ran down the path to greet his son. When they met, he threw his arms around him and hugged him like a bear, kissing him all over his face. His son humbled himself and sought his father's forgiveness, even asking to become like one of his servants. Yet none of that seemed to matter now, because today, this son who was lost, his son who was dead, had been found and is alive again. His son, whom he never stopped waiting for, whom he never stopped praying for, returned. Immediately and without question the father restored him to his rightful place as an heir along with the obedient son.

The father said to his servants:

Quick! Bring the best robe and put it on him. Put a ring on his finger and sandals on his feet. Bring the fattened calf and kill it. Let's have a feast and celebrate. For this son of mine was dead and is alive again; he was lost and is found (Luke 115:22-24).

The father is so overjoyed that he just cannot contain himself.

SPOKEN PROPHETICALLY TO GENTILE BELIEVERS

The Father says to the Gentile believers:

For I have promised to restore Israel, I have given My word, I have covenanted with him in the same way I have covenanted with you. And all I have already belongs to you. I am willing to forgive him the same way I am willing to forgive you. For just as he was unfaithful to Me by rejecting Me, so you have been unfaithful to Me by rejecting them.

The son's loving father is filled with compassion, his heart filled with mercy and grace. The father lovingly embraced him and immediately restored him to his place in his family; something the older brother couldn't even fathom or understand.

Yet we know our Father in heaven is full of mercy and grace, and His Gospel is full of the same. He is able to wash away all of our sins, even as He has already done, so we could enter into the kingdom in the first place, all as a result of His great love for us. Didn't the veil of sin also blind us before His grace supernaturally lifted it from our souls?

So who should we be like in the Church? We should be like our Father in heaven. But in reality we are often not, instead being like the elder brother in this story. It has been impossible for the Church to love the Jews in our own humanity without the supernatural love of G-d, yet they are elected as a result of the patriarchs (see Rom. 11:28), which has been a dichotomy for the Church.

But because our Father loves Israel and has chosen them, He is able to look on them with compassion. Even in their disobedience and resistance, and even in their blindness and deafness, He still loves them because they are His very own. His Word must be accomplished through them because of His own integrity as a holy and righteous G-d. Look how they have suffered as a result of this. And remember, by the time he came home, the prodigal son had truly learned his lesson.

It is only in the Father's love that we could even come close to moving in this. However, this is exactly what it will take to get this job done, and nothing else short of it will work. So what are we to do? And how should we act to move in this direction if we believe it to be G-d's Word and call for us?

SEARCH OUR HEART

We need to be honest with our own hearts and with the Holy Spirit, as well as become honest with the prior actions of our families in past generations that may have affected us without our knowing of it. Have we felt like the brother in the prodigal story feels toward Israel and the Jews? Have we lacked G-d's mercy toward them? And have we been anti-Semitic toward them? Have we been indifferent, cold, or jealous? Does the thought of their restoration make us angry or even insecure?

We may be a lover and supporter of Israel, but as we've been reading this book, we know that our heart has been touched and even convicted of our ancestral line toward them, or even our current family member's opinions. We may understand Israel in our mind because of the Word of G-d, but we know our heart is still not right and needs to be cleansed because of the past.

We also need to come to terms with how the Church has sinned against our Jewish brethren in the past. And, if we are willing, we need to make our hearts right with the Almighty who calls Himself by their namesake, the G-d of Israel. And, ultimately, Israel needs to come to terms with its past as well. As already mentioned, cleansing is needed all around (both Jew and Gentile), but it must start with us first!

The moment that we confess, the moment that we renounce, the moment that we repent, G-d is more than able to wash us clean and purify us so that we can receive His heart—the Father's heart for His lost son. This is so that His unconditional love can pour through us, that He would open our spirits as well as our minds to move into the fullness of His direction and plans in these last days. It is so we can fulfill the unique role He has given to us as His other sheep in His spiritual family (see John 10:16), except now it is reversed. And this is all in order that Israel may fulfill its own unique role in the earth to glorify G-d in fulfilling His Word so that the kingdom can come.

For the Word of G-d is clear through the apostle John: *"If we confess our sins, He is faithful and just and will forgive us our sins and purify us from all unrighteousness"* (1 John 1:9).

RESTORATIVE PRAYER

If we are willing, all of us in the Church, especially pastors and leaders, need to pray through these confession, renouncement, and repentance prayers in order that the Holy Spirit may fully cleanse our hearts from anything negative toward our firstborn brothers and sisters. This, of course, is not just from our own lives but also from our bloodlines and ancestry.

Not everything that is written may actually apply to each of us personally. However, for the sake of the Church at large and all of us in it, let us read through this prayer with an open heart. As you do, pay particular attention to any sensitivities the Holy Spirit might touch within you, asking Him to shed more light on them for additional confession, renouncement, and repentance.

In addition, please do not rush through this. Create the right environment between you and G-d, in stillness and quietness, to say this prayer so you can address this issue properly. You may also want to pray through this prayer with others, or even in church if the pastor or elders are leading.

In some parts you may feel conviction, and in others you may feel nothing at all. However, please complete the prayer fully allowing the presence of the Holy Spirit to work through you as you pray. As you start to pray, you may also feel your emotions welling up inside of you. If this is the case, I would encourage you to just let it flow. This is the presence of G-d cleansing and purifying your heart. Not all of us react in this manner, and that is completely okay.

The key for us here is to fully confess, renounce, and repent of anything that has come against our Jewish brethren, whether through us or through our family line, so that the enemy's influence can be fully broken off us, freeing our spirits to receive the Father's heart for our lost brother. In addition, we need to be careful of distractions, for neither the devil nor his demonic forces are happy about these prayers.

PRAYER OF CONFESSION

Dear heavenly Father, I come to You in the precious name of Jesus Christ, the Jewish Messiah.

L-rd, I ask You to forgive me personally of any anti-Semitism against Jewish people: whether through words spoken, thoughts, or words received through any of my family members, any of my friends, or any other person who may have spoken negative words against the Jewish people that may have affected my heart. L-rd, I confess all of these words and thoughts to You, and I ask You to forgive me for all of them.

L-rd, I confess any jealousy or envy in my heart toward them, and that You would forgive me for it.

L-rd, I confess any anger that I may have in my heart toward the Jewish people, and I ask You to forgive me for it.

L-rd, I confess any indifference in my heart toward the Jewish people, for not caring about them the way You do, and I ask You to forgive me for it.

L-rd, I confess any insecurity in my heart toward the Jewish people, thinking that I may be any less than them. And I thank You that You have made me equal with them as Your heirs in the kingdom of G-d.

L-rd, I ask You to forgive me for buying into any of the lies that I've been exposed to in my lifetime about the Jewish people and the nation of Israel.

L-rd, I confess any ignorance in my heart about Israel and the Church in light of the apostle Paul's teachings in Romans 11, for not understanding their significance in the kingdom of G-d and in Your overall plans, and I ask You to forgive me. L-rd, please show me and teach me Your ways for Israel and the Church in these last days.

L-rd, I confess that in my humanity I have not been able to love the Jewish people the way You love them, and I ask You to change my heart.

L-rd, I confess the sins of my fathers and mothers toward the Jewish people, and anything in my bloodline from my family tree through the generations who may have operated in anti-Semitism against the Jewish people. And I ask You to forgive them for any acts against them, and as a qualified heir, I repent on their behalf.

L-rd, I confess the sins of the Church against the Jewish people. Any anti-Semitism, any hatred, any jealousy and envy, any covetousness, any anger, any indifference, any lies, any persecution, any torture, any murder, and any false teachings—I ask You to forgive the Church for operating in deception against them and not being able to love them in our own humanity.

L-rd, I ask You to help me forgive my Jewish brothers and sisters for their past and current rejection of Jesus as well as their indifference to the Gospel. I entrust them totally to You in the lifting of the spiritual veil that is upon them. I invite You to use me in any way to help bring Your love toward them, in the hope that they may see You through me and my life in You.

L-rd, I confess the sin of believing or embracing replacement theology, which says that the Church has replaced Israel, and I ask You to forgive me for it.

L-rd, while I know Your Word tells us that both Jew and Gentile are one in the Spirit, I now fully accept and embrace the unique roles that You have for Israel and the Church during these times. I pledge my allegiance to You and Your plans for us both, so that You will ultimately be glorified throughout the earth. And I say, "Come, L-rd Jesus, and have Your way amongst us."

L-rd, I ask You to forgive the Church and all of its leaders, teachers, and pastors that may have helped to promote any anti-Semitic doctrine, words, or teachings that have brought division and persecution on the Jewish people.

L-rd, we ask You to forgive the Jewish people for rejecting Yeshua, their Messiah; and we ask that You will lift the veil from their eyes and the deafness from their ears, as You have done for us, so that we can all love You together as Your spiritual family; and that we would be one so that the world would know that You, Father, have sent Jesus to us all.

L-rd, we confess the sin of separation as Gentile believers from our Jewish roots and heritage, and we ask You to forgive us for it. L-rd, please reconnect us by the power of Your Holy Spirit.

PRAYER OF RENOUNCEMENT

Dear heavenly Father, I come to You in the precious name of Jesus Christ, the Jewish Messiah. L-rd, I formerly renounce all of these sins that I have prayed: all anti-Semitism in my own heart and any anti-Semitism from any other influence, through family members, friends, or anyone in my bloodline and ancestral past.

L-rd, in the most powerful cleansing name of Jesus Christ, I come into agreement with You and break any form of generational anti-Semitism that has either affected or influenced me or anyone else in my family; and I take authority over it in Jesus's name, rendering it powerless over me and my family.

L-rd, I also formally renounce and break any form of replacement theology that I have believed, been influenced or affected by; and in the power of the name of Jesus Christ, the name above all names, I take authority over it and render it powerless over me and my family.

I also renounce and break any attachment to replacement theology from any of my prior family, through my bloodline and ancestry. And in the power of the name of Jesus Christ, I take authority over it and render it powerless over my family and me, releasing it all to Jesus to break its hold.

Prayer of Repentance

Dear heavenly Father, I come to You in the precious name of Jesus Christ, the Jewish Messiah.

L-rd, I truly ask You to help me to repent of all of these things that I have just prayed about. I ask You to teach me Your ways and to give me Your heart for Your family, both Jew and Gentile alike, that I would be in agreement with You and that You may be fully glorified through both Israel and the Church during these days.

L-rd, I pledge my allegiance to You and offer You my full support, that Your will would be done upon the earth. In Jesus's precious name I pray, amen.

PRAYER FOR PASTORS AND LEADERS

Pastors and leaders have a greater responsibility to pray and renounce any anti-Semitic thoughts or teachings in light of the influence they have over G-d's flock. They especially have a responsibility to disavow any connection to replacement theology that may have been learned in Bible school or university, or through books, CDs, or DVD teachings.

If you are a leader in any of the denominations in the Body of Christ—Roman Catholic, Greek Orthodox, Anglican, Protestant, Episcopalian, Presbyterian, Pentecostal, Charismatic, Baptist, Lutheran, Methodist, Church of Christ, Faith Churches, or any other denominational or nondenominational church group—and you are in agreement with these teachings, please pray the following:

Dear heavenly Father, I come to You in the precious name of Jesus Christ, the Jewish Messiah, as one of Your shepherds and leaders.

L-rd, I ask You to forgive me of any connection and association to the teachings of replacement theology, or any other teachings about Israel that are or may be in contradiction to Your Word, either through what I was taught in Bible college or university, or various churches or church groups that I may have been associated with.

L-rd, I formally renounce them and ask that You will fill my mind and heart with the truth of Your Word concerning Israel, the Jewish people, and their restoration in the last days. I ask that You would reveal to me any role that the Church will need to play and fulfill to help You achieve Your plans here in the world so that You would be glorified in all of the earth.

L-rd, I pledge my allegiance as one of Your shepherds to uphold this reconnection in Your spiritual family and give it my full support. In Jesus's most holy name I pray, amen.

RECEIVING THE FATHER'S HEART

As already discussed, it is simply not possible to fully love the Jewish people in our own strength in light of their continued rejection of Jesus. Without a doubt, G-d's supernatural love is needed to flow through us for this to happen.

I call this the Father's heart in light of the prodigal story discussed above. And for us to receive this heart is one of the main reasons for me writing this book. His heart for His spiritual family will truly change us and give us what we need to help Him achieve His plans through us in order to redeem Israel and restore His kingdom in the last days.

This calling of the end-time generations of the Church have a unique and distinct role to play to assist G-d to spiritually rebirth Israel, which is why we must no longer be ignorant about this mystery. We have a major part to play in it, which, up to this point, we have not seen too clearly.

We are now free to receive the Father's heart—His unconditional love through the power of the Holy Spirit for His lost son. Upon receiving the fullness of His love and mercy, we can begin to fully embrace Israel and the Jewish people in light of the covenants that our Father has made with them. This is not only to restore them, but also to redeem them into the kingdom of G-d and reestablish them back into His spiritual family so that we would reign with them through Christ when He returns to the earth.

WOULD YOU PRAY THIS PRAYER WITH ME?

Dear heavenly Father, I come to You in the precious name of Jesus Christ, the Jewish Messiah.

L-rd, I ask You to fill me with the fullness of Your heart for Your lost son, the Jewish people, who are also my spiritual brothers and sisters, though most of them are still yet to receive Your redemption for their lives.

L-rd, I fully embrace them as Your children and my brothers and sisters, as well as the covenants You have made with them, not only to redeem them, but also to show Your holiness and righteousness through them.

L-rd, please give me Your heart, Your passion, and Your unconditional love for them. Please keep them upon my heart to always remember to pray for them, that Your will would be done not only through them but also through us.

L-rd, as You prayed in John 17 that we would be one, I pray now for the uniting of Your spiritual family and that You would truly bring us together upon the earth. In Jesus's most holy name I pray, amen.

MY PRAYER

Now L-rd, please fill Your loving child with the fullness of Your heart for Israel and the Jewish people, in the precious name of Jesus, amen.

Congratulations, you have just received the Father's heart for the Jewish people. Some of you may feel like weeping, and, if so, I would encourage you in this. However, if you do not feel this touch, it is also okay. But expect to see things a little bit differently from now on; not only in regard to your understanding of the Word of G-d as it relates to Israel and the Church, but also in the way you may feel or act toward the Jewish people.

ENDNOTES

1. I did not make reference to the remnant of Jewish believers in the Church here because it is still such a small percentage of believers and is also not relevant to the point I am making.

2. *In that Day* by Rabbi David Levine has some interesting thoughts on this parable.

7

THE EZEKIEL GENERATION

UNDERSTANDING ROLES

Now that we have dealt with generational anti-Semitism, and the Holy Spirit has washed away anything unclean from our past and filled us with the Father's love toward our Jewish family, we are now ready to take a fresh look at the role G-d wants us to play in the end times. We are also going to look at His plans to show Himself through the Church and Israel in these days in which we are living.

OUR GENERATION AND THE ONES THAT TARRY

In this light, I believe that our generation and the ones that may tarry before the Messiah returns have a greater responsibility to play than in other generations that have preceded us. This is why the message of this book and the Father's heart is so relevant for us at this time. The fact is that we were born at this point in history and placed into one of the most exciting spiritual times that has ever existed. Can you imagine being the very generation that is taken up to meet our L-rd, ruling and reigning with Him upon the earth

155

(see Rev. 5:9-10; Isa. 61:4; 62:1-12)? Because of this, G-d is looking for His Church (Jewish and Gentile believers) to begin to involve themselves more than ever before with His end-time plans to establish His kingdom.

G-d's heart is that Jew and Gentile would become one, His spiritual family dwelling together in unity. In addition, if we in the Church are in fact the vessels of mercy that He has chosen to help win Israel back to faith (see Rom. 11:30-31), then we must have full confidence in our rights so that we are fully secure to come into the Father's heart to help win back the rest of our spiritual family. We know that there is nothing to lose and everything to gain through their spiritual awakening, which will ultimately bring about our L-rd's return, where we reign together with Christ (see Rev. 3:21-22).

The only difference between us now is where we will actually serve, as I have already pointed out in earlier chapters. For it now pleases the Father to use the Church in this capacity that His supernatural love and mercy would flow through us to help awaken Israel. However, we must also fully recognize that rebirthing Israel is like unlocking the golden key—the key of David that once again reopens Israel's door to their spiritual restoration.

WHAT AN HONOR

As we read on, we will begin to see what an honor G-d has actually bestowed upon the Church in His end-time plan, for He has already given us the key of David. But we must learn to place it in the right door along with the power He has already given to us, which is still to be loosed upon us as we make this connection (see Matt. 16:19).

Sometimes I think about this whole story like a *L-rd of the Rings* movie, with the different spiritual forces on both sides opposing each other. And, believe me, this is the part of the movie script where the battle is ferocious. Israel's significance as a group of people, therefore, and their spiritual awakening is not only vital but also crucial to the advancement of the kingdom of G-d. The battle will definitely intensify as we get closer to the end; to this I have no doubts.

ISRAEL'S ROLE

We must get away from the concept that Israel and the Jewish people are just like any other nation or group in the earth, though they fall into this category. While Israel may not be any more special to G-d than the rest of us—because we are all special to Him—they are still the apple of His eye and are distinct because of His promises to them. We must be able to bless the distinctions that G-d Himself has created between us, *"first for the Jew, then for the Gentile"* (Rom. 1:16).

If we have not already seen them in this light, we must begin to distinguish them as a *covenant people without overexalting them.* As G-d's firstborn children, they are directly tied into G-d's prophetic words and promises to reveal His glory in the last days for Jesus to return to the earth (see Ezek. 36). For Jesus shall not return until His firstborn children declare, *"Blessed is He who comes in the name of the L-rd"* (Matt. 23:39). But we must also understand that in light of their current spiritual condition, not everything they do is righteous, and so we must learn to discern accordingly so we know how to pray. Israel's specific role in G-d's end-time plan is actually to receive His redemption and salvation, which will prepare them for their future role as priests when Jesus returns.

THE CHURCH'S ROLE

In contrast to this, we must also recognize the distinctive role that G-d is calling the Church into, that we have the great honor to help the G-d of heaven rebirth His other children into the kingdom of G-d. The question we need to ask ourselves in the Church is, Do we want our Father in heaven and His blessed Son, Jesus, to be glorified in all the earth? For if the answer to that question is yes, which it should be, then we need to start thinking about the changes we need to make in our spiritual ilks and theology, as well as some of our activities, to help bring this about.

Taking the golden key and turning it into that heavenly door will not only unlock all the power that we need to reach a lost and dying world, but it will also unleash the greatest spiritual awakening that we have ever witnessed (see Joel 2:28-32; Rom. 11:15). Our role here, however, is to come into agreement with the G-d of Abraham to rebirth Israel and to help restore the Church's apostolic roots, which is also instrumental in helping the L-rd get the job finished and crucial for His kingdom to come and be established upon the earth. So we cry out, "Come, L-rd Jesus!"

THE KINGDOM IS JEWISH

How Should the Commonwealth Associate Itself?

First, belief in Jesus is not a Gentile concept, even though He is currently portrayed in this manner by most of the Church. I hope you understand me here: it is as if Christianity is a separate religion, although it is truly the only real extension of Judaism. And our own reconnection to the roots of our faith will help us dramatically during these days as the L-rd begins to unite His Body for His return. But what will the Church look like at this time? For when He returns, He will come as a Jew, as the Lion of the tribe of Judah (see Rev. 5:5).

We need to give this some serious thought, because what we are currently presenting in the majority of the Church is still so separate from our Jewish roots and heritage that the New Covenant (which actually authorizes Gentile believers to join into Israel's covenants) now appears utterly Gentile when in reality it is Jewish. Are we not children of Abraham? Do we not become a part of the commonwealth of Israel? Are we not grafted into their vine even though they are temporarily cut off (see Rom 11:17)?

For such a time as this, with our calling and role in the Church to help Israel reconnect with their Messiah, we must seriously begin to rethink how we present the Gospel to our Jewish family, which will dramatically change the way they perceive us. This is especially true when we fully sanction their own unique calling to live as Jews from within the Church.

Let's not forget that the Church was founded by the G-d of Israel, a Jewish carpenter with His Jewish apostles, who is coming back to sit on a Jewish throne, to reign in a Jewish city, and on whose heavenly gates will be written the names of the 12 Jewish tribes of Israel and the 12 Jewish apostles. For during the time of the Gentiles (see Rom. 11:25), the focus has obviously been on the rest of G-d's children throughout the nations. But as Israel now awakens to the presence of G-d, we need to rethink our reconnection to them, not just in the Spirit but also in the natural, so that both groups will fulfill their destinies.

I am not proposing for one moment here that Gentile believers become Jewish: please do not misunderstand me as both Jews and Gentile believers have different roles. However, as we look to reconnect in the Spirit, we must fully embrace their rights to live in their calling as Jews. We must also reflect the Jewishness of the Gospel in a manner in which we communicate it back to them so they can ultimately fulfill their destinies, enabling us to also fulfill ours. This happens because we are intricately connected in the Spirit of G-d, and neither of us can advance without each other, which is G-d's design.

In addition, as we look to connect more to our Jewish roots, which definitely has a better chance of making them envious, I think we will be surprised by some of the rich heritage Israel has that we may also now share in as followers of Christ.

JEWS ENTER THE SAME WAY AS EVERYONE ELSE

Second, like the apostle Paul, who would have considered himself cursed and cut off for the sake of his own people (see Rom. 9:3-4), we must come to understand that Jewish people come to faith in the New Covenant just like everyone else: without accepting Yeshua, they cannot cross over into new life.

There is no other way for my people to come into the kingdom, except through Messiah, who *"is the end of law so that there might be righteousness for everyone who believes"* (Rom. 10:4). In the apostle Paul's words, *"I am not ashamed of the gospel, because it is the power of G-d for the salvation of everyone who believes: first for the Jew, then for the Gentile"* (Rom. 1:16). For there are some brethren in the Body of Christ who are teaching that Jews are under a separate covenant and therefore do not need to be saved the way Gentiles do. But this is simply not the case and not true to the Word of G-d or the New Covenant, which was also given to Israel before it went out to the rest of the world (see Jer. 31:31-34).

We must bring correction to these teachings. As with all good wishes and intent toward the Jewish people, they are not only promoting confusion to the Word of G-d, but also a continued separation toward the unity that Christ Himself is calling us to in these days, as we look to reexamine our theology and His will for us in His end-time plan.

BLESS THE DIFFERENT ROLES

Third, in acknowledging the differences between our roles, we must begin to loose our blessings upon Jewish believers, fully supporting their rights to live as covenant children as they return to their G-d. We must not only enjoy their reconnection as Jews but also desire to see them fully awakened to their callings. This was very much my own experience, which you can read about in *The New Covenant Prophecy*, that tells the story of my own Jewish testimony. Indeed, let us keep in mind that the vine we now live in is still Jewish, and they are still Jews as they return to faith and begin to move into the New Covenant.

G-d not only wants us to bless them in this but also to help strengthen them in the Spirit, along with the ministries in the Church that are already focused on blessing this reconnection. Just like Aaron and Hur, the priests of G-d who held up Moses's hands so that the Amalekites could be defeated (see Exod. 17:8-16), G-d is calling us to lift up Israel's hands and strengthen them as they enter into the New Covenant.

Many of us in the Church, who walk with the Spirit, can actually help to strengthen the Messianic body in the deeper things of the faith. As I have noted as a Jewish believer, I have learned from my Gentile believing brothers and sisters how to move and operate in the things of the Spirit. For I can tell you as a Messianic believer that the Jewish believing body is in great need of help and maturity in these areas, although many might not admit it.

It is also true to say that even as the Church needs to reconnect to the believing Jewish body, a good deal of the Messianic movement also needs to reconnect with the Church. They are often guilty of the same separation as we in the Church and are in need of their own healing and repentance, which must also take place in connecting with their Gentile brethren. In addition, because the Messianic body has not been properly understood up to this point, many of the congregations tend to be smaller groups and often struggle financially as they are caught in-between two main religious groups (Jews and Christians) who don't really understand them. This is all due to a great lack of understanding on both parts—Jews who still believe that belief in Christ is forbidden, and Christians who believe that when Jews believe in Christ, they should conform to the Gentile Church, which has no outlet for any Jewish expression.

Embracing the Father's heart will change all of this for both groups (Jewish and Gentile believers) and begin to straighten it out. If we want G-d to change Israel, then we must first allow Him to change us in the Church, especially in the days we find ourselves living in.

LOOK AT THE TIMES

If we are truly moving into the final days before Jesus returns, then everything I am writing is of vital importance. My hope and prayer is that we will all be prayerful about its content. None of us can tell for sure if we are the last generation on earth before Jesus returns. But I also think it is fair to say that we are definitely close to these times, which is all the more reason why we need to prepare ourselves.

Jesus tried to prepare us through various warnings, earthly signs, and shakings. He said there would be earthquakes, famines, and pestilences, as well as rumors of wars (see Luke 21:5-37). The year 2011 alone witnessed more natural disasters than in any previous year on record according to the Obama Administration and ABC News;[1] not to mention that the Washington Monument was severely damaged in the August earthquake. We must be blind if we can't see that something is definitely happening in the earth today, signifying it is the end times.

Aside from the most devastating natural disasters, we have also been affected by several pestilences with thousands of dead fish and birds showing up all over the globe.[2] This has really caught my attention in light of Jesus's prophecies about pestilences in the last days. These, Jesus said, *"are the beginning of birth pains...but the end will not come right away* (Mark 13:8; Luke 21:9). It seems as if now we have entered this prophetic age that He foretold. Even as I was working on the final edit of this book in the spring of 2012, right before Passover, swarms of locusts by the billions hit different parts of the world in Egypt, Israel, and Madagascar.

It's simply not possible for us to always understand events and catastrophes, but this does not mean that we should not be willing to look. Times and dates are important and highly significant to G-d, and sometimes they can be clearer than at other times. We must also act carefully in how we discuss them, because through every catastrophe innocent people are involved, so we must show compassion and mercy more than anything else. However, these things will take place and shakings will come because of the imperfect, sinful world we currently live in.

Let's also take a look at a couple of other events that I believe to be relevant to this new prophetic era. These have already begun and have already occurred, interestingly enough, on two of the Jewish feasts.

SHOFAR BLOWS: THE THREE "7S"

On the eve of Rosh Hashanah in 2008, for example, which is the Jewish holiday that celebrates the Harvest, the New Year, and the Feast of Trumpets, where the shofar is blown, the stock market fell 777 points and plunged the world economy into the worst recession since the 1929 crash. I wrote to the Messiah's House ministry at that time, and have encapsulated much of it below.

> The next morning on my prayer walk with the L-rd, I sought His will and insight. While I do not profess to know everything about the time and craziness we currently find ourselves living in, I can share the significance

of what He said to me. It has been burning on my heart since that moment I noticed the numbers on the TV, and I now feel compelled to share it with you.

Knowing a little bit about numerical significance in the Bible, I know that the number 7 represents completion, and as a result many theologians refer to the number 7 as G-d's perfect number. I was immediately impressed that this may be a sign. As I continued to walk, the Holy Spirit led me to Revelation 5:6, and again I was shaken by what I read concerning the three 7s. It was as if the L-rd was making a proclamation to the Jewish people by giving them this sign on the eve of the Festival of Trumpets:

> *Then I saw a Lamb, looking as if it had been slain, standing in the center of the throne, encircled by the four living creatures and the elders. He had seven horns and seven eyes, which are the seven spirits of G-d sent out into all of the earth.*

In this text, John was describing what the Spirit of G-d was showing him about the end days. He retells the vision he saw that Yeshua, who was the three "7s," was the only One worthy to open the scroll that begin the final stages of history before His return.

Again, I want to be clear here: I am not saying that this is the beginning of that time, although it could be. But I know that what has come clearly to me is that the L-rd was sounding His trumpets on the holiday of Rosh Hashanah, and that we needed to hearken to His voice. The three 7s in Revelation speak of the Messiah, and it is G-d's message to raise Him up to the world to draw all men unto Himself, both Jew and Gentile alike, like the bronze snake that Moses raised up in the desert for the Israelites to find healing and life (see Num. 21:8). G-d has given His Son, Yeshua, to all people in the world, to the Jew first and then the Gentile, that they may have eternal life.

This proclamation marked a time in our history where G-d would once again refocus on His firstborn, on His covenants and promises to Israel. We are living in the beginning of the era when the veil that is over the hearts and souls of the Jewish people, preventing them from hearing and seeing the Gospel from a spiritual perspective, will now be lifted (see Isa. 6:8-10).

As the apostle Paul had written to the Romans, no longer will there just be a remnant of Jewish believers as has been over the past 2,000 years, but as the time of the Gentiles now comes into its fullness, Israel must be reawakened and spiritually return to the G-d of Israel (see Ezek. 37). At this time, many more will come to know Jesus personally and intimately, like He intended our relationship with Him to be in the first place.

There are two messages here for those who will listen to their call: the first is to the Jewish people and the second to the Church. Both have to do with awakening and repentance, and both are a sign of love from a living, loving G-d who deeply loves all of His children. G-d loves this country we live in, and not only has He richly blessed us but His mercy and grace are still upon us.

In addition, America has staunchly stood next to the nation of Israel throughout her history. In Genesis G-d covenanted with Abraham and stated that those who would bless His people would be blessed (see Gen. 12:1-3). However, the G-d of Israel is not a humanist, He is a consuming fire; and many in our country have sadly forgotten or are completely ignorant to the fact that He is a holy and righteous G-d, and *nothing* sinful can come into His presence. G-d has set up the universe so that when sin reaches a certain point, judgment naturally comes down upon it (see Gen. 15:16). This is evident to me with the 2008 financial crisis, which is a result of the sin of greed in Wall Street and Washington. However, this crash is still a warning compared to what is to come upon us without true repentance.

There is more here than meets the eye, and knowing G-d like some of us do, we know that He uses all circumstances for the good of those who love Him (see Rom. 8:28). I believe this is a second trumpet; perhaps 9/11 was the first one to wake us up, the spiritual impact of which has since diminished. But what better way for G-d to get our attention than with our pocket books.

After that crisis, I was convicted of how much I depend on my earthly wealth more than my faith in G-d. I confessed this to the L-rd and asked Him to change me and make me ready for the time we are about to enter, whatever that may be. Again, let me be clear here: I am not saying G-d brought that upon us, but rather through our own actions and our sins as a nation, He has used it to get our attention. Today, more than ever before, we are way too consumed with the material realm, and as a result we have borrowed ourselves into oblivion, attempting to reach all of our wants and desires, both as a nation and as individual people.

It is my desire for the Jews to awaken from their spiritual sleep and to earnestly search out the truth about G-d's firstborn and His calling upon their lives, for our spiritual awakening as a people and a nation is soon to come. And this is so we will look to G-d and make our hearts right before Him, as proclaimed by the prophets of old and the apostles.

G-d is also blowing the trumpet to His Church regarding His physical children, the Jews, as they are also a part of His kingdom and complete the family portrait. As Israel gave birth to us, we must in turn give birth to them (see Rom. 11), praying and interceding for Israel to be awakened, that the glory of our Father in heaven would be made known to the world though them (see Ezek. 36).

The prophet Ezekiel told us that G-d would show His glory through Israel in the last days. And this is the trumpet that is beginning to blow, the shofar is sounding aloud to Israel and the Jewish people, and He will use the world and its circumstances to get our attention to awaken us to His call to accept the Lamb of G-d into our lives.

The angel of death in the Passover story is a prophetic picture of this final act. And it is important for us to understand the age we are beginning to live in because G-d really wants to get our attention before it's too late.

I also felt that materialism was getting out of hand in light of all the prosperity that the Western world has been experiencing. So during this time, I started to seek G-d about changing my own heart and getting my priorities straight. There was hardly a person in America that did not feel the effects of the financial crisis in 2008. And for the first couple of months, at least, it was like the world froze up and everyone stopped spending. I think we were so shocked by it and the actual vulnerability of our own system that we became numbed to it.

THE HANUKKAH FIRE

I also felt that the fire in Israel on the first day of Hanukkah in 2010 was also a prophetic sign, even though it may have started as an accident. The newspapers and headlines reported that Mount Carmel was ablaze with the greatest fire in Israel's history. If you know your Bible, you may know the significance of Mount Carmel, as it was on this very mountain that the prophet Elijah challenged and humiliated the prophets of Baal, calling fire down from heaven to burn up his offering, which they could not produce themselves (see 1 Kings 18).

There is an interesting parallel here between this incredible story and the fires of Hanukkah that preceded all of the natural disasters in 2011. For the gods of Baal are very similar to the gods of our age, the things that people attach themselves to and hold dear, more than G-d Himself. Yet, behind Baal is a very deceptive devil who is looking to steal and kill souls, and, without knowing it, the world is following him.

In this fire upon Mount Carmel, I believe G-d was making a statement that the gods of this world would ultimately be shaken and exposed. For G-d will not be mocked, and there comes a time where our actions and sinful choices in the world can cause heavenly reactions because sin reaches a point of judgment (see Gen. 15:17). For through Hanukkah, which remembered the miracle of light and deliverance for Israel, in which Yeshua substantiated Himself as the light of the world to deliver all mankind (see John 9–11), G-d was presenting the world with a sign.

It was almost as if those fires on Mount Carmel during Hanukkah were like a torch that preceded all of the natural disasters of the following year. For the G-d of Israel has not forgotten the Jewish calendar nor His position to the Jew and the Gentile, and neither should we. There are great prophetic insights that can be gained from the Jewish holidays and the significance of their fulfillment in the New Covenant. However, we should not be surprised when major things happen in our world in and around the Jewish feasts, because He created these events, and they not only belong to Him but they also bring glory to the G-dhead.

We have seen an even greater increase in natural shakings upon the earth. And these signs are only the beginning of a prophetic period where the world truly begins to see the results of its own sins and disobedience before a holy and righteous G-d—who many think is either not there or does nothing.

SIN WILL BE JUDGED

G-d has designed our world so that He does not always intervene, because He has given us free will and choice. Somehow, this story of sin and righteousness must be played out before He returns to the earth to establish His kingdom. But we are now witnessing this as the sins of the world are on the increase. Make no mistake about it: it will eventually come because sin must face its judgment before the L-rd shows Himself to the world.

While G-d has given us free will and choice, which has actually caused so many of humankind's problems in the world, none of us will ultimately escape the final judgment unless we choose life over death. And this is a reality the world does not want to face—otherwise its sins would be exposed. What an interesting parallel here between sin, righteousness, and the free will that G-d has given us to choose between life and death.

Just with these two signs alone, not to mention the shakings in the earth, it seems as if we have entered the prophetic age and therefore need to take a more serious look at where we may be in light of Jesus's return and what needs to take place in order for that to happen.

DO NOT BUILD YOUR HOUSE ON SAND

More recently, Hurricane Sandy has hit the Northeast with devastating effects, and some of our most innocent dear children were savagely murdered at Sandy Hook Elementary School in Connecticut. Abnormal things are happening to us and it is as if someone or something is trying to get our attention. Jesus warned us not to build our house on sand (see Matt. 7:26-27), yet isn't this exactly what we are doing? It will have its consequences.

Another Messianic brother, Rabbi Jonathan Kahn, whom G-d is raising up as a prophetic voice at this time in our country, has written a must-read book, *The Harbinger*. It clearly points to many of the prophetic warnings that are coming to America during these days because of our indifference to G-d and His Word. The attacks come, and for a brief moment we are shaken, but it does not last long. We are still not getting the message to repent and turn to G-d before it is too late. Instead, we just turn back to our old ways, which ultimately have their effects.

It definitely seems like we are entering some challenging times, and who of us will not be tested by it? It is not G-d's heart to punish us, for He is slow to anger and wrath. But it is His heart for us to turn from our evil ways and repent before it is too late. All of these occurrences are warnings, and without us turning back to G-d we are only heaping greater judgment on ourselves as a nation before a holy and righteous G-d.

WE NEED TO GET IT RIGHT

This is all the more reason for us now in the Church to get it right and allow G-d to transition us into this time of the uniting of His family so we are able to glorify His kingdom upon the earth.

Could it be, like the apostles themselves, that we in the Church need our own Jerusalem counsel (see Acts 15)? Except this time, instead of the Jews meeting to embrace the Gentiles, the Gentiles could meet to reembrace the Jews back into their own vine. But how can we possibly help bring them back into their own vine, to draw them to envy as we are commanded to do through the apostle Paul (see Rom. 11:14), when we have made the vine so Gentile, so separate, and so foreign for them as Jews to even consider it? Are we willing to make some changes and adjustments like the apostles did to accept the Gentiles?

WE NEED TO MAKE THEM ENVIOUS

In receiving the Father's heart and His call to a oneness between us as His spiritual family, we must be willing now to look at all of the areas and issues that have separated us. Can we please consider reconnecting to our roots and heritage in a way that will make them jealous of our own relationship with their G-d? For, as I am trying to point out to us in the Church, it is Gentile believers who were specifically given the mission to win Israel back to faith.

However, in wanting to bring the balance here between Jewish and Gentile believers, did the apostle Paul need anyone else's direction to want to draw his own people to faith? As a Jew, wasn't this just natural for him? G-d knew that it would not be for the rest of us; hence, the additional Gentile edicts became necessary for all believers to stir Israel to faith in Yeshua.

Just look at the pure numbers: 7 billion Gentiles, approximately 18 million Jews (if you include the children of the fathers—the Jewish religion only acknowledges children born from their mothers to be Jewish). How long would it really take to reach the Jewish population if Christians in Jewish areas really committed themselves to the Father's heart, to prayer and intercession, and to lifestyle evangelism? Like I always suggest to our group at Messiah's House, just start with one Jewish person and commit them and their family to prayer.

Please do not get me wrong here. I am not suggesting for one moment that we go back and become like Jews from the Old Covenant, but rather that we reflect the intimacy of our New Covenant relationship through their covenants and promises we are now sharing in. For this can make a huge difference in how we approach our Jewish friends and neighbors when sharing our faith with them. For example, when speaking to a Jewish person, we could say, "I love and serve your G-d, and I am so indebted to your people for giving Him to us," or "Thank you for helping lay the foundations to our faith. Thank you for giving us Yeshua!"

THE HOLY SPIRIT WILL BE OUR GUIDE

It is not my purpose in this book to tell us how we should specifically act, because the Holy Spirit is our guide and we always need to be careful of legalism. But I do want to offer some insights and guidelines to what we might want to think about now in light of the changes we need to make in order to win Israel back to the faith. It is my desire to stress that we must be dependent on Him for this.

Let us be so prayerful about it that we are fully led by the Holy Spirit with any adjustments that we may need to make to present the New Covenant in light of its roots. This will have a far greater impact on our Jewish friends and neighbors (if we have them) than anything else, and it will also bring us into obedience to our call to show them their G-d.

PRAY INTO THE MERCY PLAN

The greatest role for us all to play in these times is to pray and intercede for Israel's rebirth and for the L-rd's return. For it is through the circle of G-d's mercy that we may be able to shine His light back to our firstborn brothers and sisters:

> *Just as you who were at one time disobedient to G-d have now received mercy as a result of their disobedience, so they too have now become disobedient in order that they too may now receive mercy as a result of G-d's mercy to you. For G-d has bound all men over to disobedience so that He may have mercy on them all* (Romans 11:30-32).

And again,

> *How, then, can they call on the one they have not believed in? And how can they believe in the one whom they have not heard? And how can they hear without someone preaching to them? And how can they preach unless they are sent? As it is written, "How beautiful are the feet of those who bring good news!"* (Roman 10:14-15)

In other words, whom will they hear the good news from, if not through believers?

FAITH INTO THE MERCY PLAN

I am not just connecting this teaching to witnessing and evangelism, which I think the apostle Paul was referring to in the above passage. But I'm rather connecting it to a position of faith in the Spirit, that at this time Israel and the Jewish people must now spiritually come forth in light of G-d's words and covenants to them. This attitude of faith is what G-d is looking to birth in us that will affect and change everything else we do, including our evangelism back toward them. For it is with the Father's heart and mercy that we can pray and intercede for their spiritual awakening, with His spiritual eyes that we must see them through His word, already awakened and reestablished back into the kingdom, and nothing else will do. We are all called to share this prayer burden with the L-rd.

And while it is true to say that some of us are called to greater works amongst the Jewish communities around us because we live in more heavily populated Jewish areas, many of us who may be reading this book may have never even met a Jewish person before. This would not release us from the burden of prayer, intercession, or our spiritual connection to them that is the actual catalyst in bringing them forth in order to unite G-d's family, which will help to usher in His return for both groups (Jewish and Gentile believers). You may not be aware of this, but there are already churches in different parts of the world that may have never even seen a Jewish person and yet they are gathering for regular fasting and prayer to help spiritually rebirth Israel.[3]

Nor should we think of new programs and ideas alone with all of our good intentions to want to reach out to them. Everything must come from His heart and by the power of His Spirit if we are going to succeed; it must be done in His strength and not our own. We have already seen from the past what happens when we try to love from our own humanity and strength. We should not forget that until the veil is removed, most Jewish people will resist anything to do with Yeshua. This is why the Holy Spirit has so carefully tried to position us, fully understanding their resistance but never changing our position toward them in the Spirit.

The apostle Paul wrote, *"As far as the gospel is concerned, they are enemies on your account; but as far as election is concerned, they are loved on account of the patriarchs, for G-d's gifts and His call are irrevocable"* (Rom. 11:28-29). For if they rejected Martin Luther, they will reject us too until their appointed time, which will be brought about through love and effective, fervent prayer, and all this through G-d's tender mercies and timing.

PRAYER AND INTERCESSION ARE THE GREATEST ROLES

Calling to mind Joshua's birth story, it was through the struggle, the pain, and the intercession that the Church moved in that allowed both the Son and the Father to bring Israel forth. Without a doubt, prayer and intercession are the greatest roles we can play in this end-time plan. And everything must come from this place before anything else will happen.

In the words of the great intercessor, Rees Howells, "It reminds us that no great event in history, even though prophesied beforehand in the Scriptures, comes to pass unless G-d finds His human channels of faith and obedience."[4] In fact, if we go back to the Scriptures that speak of Israel's spiritual awakening, who is it that G-d actually uses to release His heavenly breath toward Israel to awaken them?

THE EZEKIEL GENERATION: THE ROLE OF THE CHURCH

Let's take a look at Ezekiel 37 once again. There are two specific prophecies in this chapter—the first deals with the land being restored as we have already witnessed and discussed; and the second deals with Israel's spiritual awakening, which is still obviously yet to happen (see Ezek. 37:9-11). Is G-d the One to breathe the breath of G-d back into the dry bones of Israel? Or is it Ezekiel, whom He commands to prophesy?

Then He said to me, "Prophesy to the breath; prophesy, son of man, and say to it, 'This is what the Sovereign L-rd says: Come from the four winds, O breath, and breathe into these slain, that they may live.'" So I prophesied as He commanded me, and breath entered them; they came to life and stood up on their feet—a vast army.

Then He said to me: "Son of man, these bones are the whole house of Israel" (Ezekiel 37:9-11).

Here, in his prophetic role, Ezekiel is told by G-d to call on the four winds of the earth and breathe the breath of life into Israel and the Jewish people, just like we are now called in the Church to stand in the gap for Israel and breathe the breath of G-d into them. For at this time we in the Church are the prophetic fulfillment of this prophecy in taking up Ezekiel's role to release the mercy of G-d back into our firstborn brethren in the family of G-d, which is why this message is so important for us to grasp.

We and the generations of believers who tarry before the L-rd returns are indeed called into the Ezekiel generation; and He is looking for His Church to stand in the gap, to pray, to intercede, and to bring Israel forth. We are called to proclaim the breath of the New Covenant, to release it into His firstborn children. So let us gather together in unity and speak with one voice in the Spirit of G-d, "Israel, come forth!"

LED BY HIS SPIRIT

There will be times for us to reach out, especially those of us who live around Jewish people, and let the evangelism and witness come from a leading of His Spirit that is bathed in His love, wisdom, and patience. But, most importantly, our witness should be bathed in intercessory prayer, which is the foundation of everything we do.

As we can never take this battle on as our own, but rather must first be filled with His power and strength, for this battle is truly divine.

At this time in history, may we become ever so conscious of this intercessory role, that as the Ezekiel of G-d we may come into agreement with the G-dhead to pray and push, to fight and to stand, to see Israel come to life in the Spirit. May we be used of His Spirit in such a manner that will help give birth to the establishment of the kingdom of G-d upon the earth. Would you like to receive the Ezekiel anointing?

PRAYER TO RECEIVE THE EZEKIEL ANOINTING[5]

Dear heavenly Father, I come to You in the precious name of Jesus Christ, the Jewish Messiah. And I ask You to release to me the Ezekiel anointing, to stand in the gap and help rebirth Israel and the Jewish people in the Spirit and into the family of G-d.

L-rd, I call upon the four winds to loose Your breath into them, that they may spiritually come alive according to all of Your covenants, prophecies, and words that You have given us in Your Scriptures that promise their spiritual restoration after they have returned to the land. L-rd, loose Your power upon the Church as well as Your anointing and guidance to pray and intercede for the Jewish people to come forth. And release Your wisdom and insight in the Spirit to know how to pray and move during this time.

L-rd, give me Your love and release Your mercy into the depths of my heart, that I may stand with You in agreement with Your end-time plan not only to regather your firstborn children but also to unite us as one spiritual family in Your kingdom.

I ask that You would help me to pray for the Jewish people, to pray for the Church, to pray for those under Islam, as well as those in the world, and, most importantly, to pray for Your will to be done through Your Body in these last days, so that You will be glorified before all the nations of the earth. In Jesus's most precious name I pray, amen.

MY PRAYER FOR YOU

L-rd, with the burden You have given to me for Your people Israel, and for the Church to reconnect to Israel, I come into agreement with Your Holy Spirit and I release the Ezekiel anointing to all of my brothers and sisters in Christ who are praying this prayer. In Jesus's special name I pray, amen.

PRAYER FOR BELIEVERS WHO LIVE AROUND JEWISH PEOPLE (SEE 1 COR. 9:20-23)

L-rd, please give me the wisdom and the patience to shine Your light back to the Jewish people around me in a way that may cause them to feel reconnected with You, to reach out to them through the guidance of Your Holy Spirit.

Help me, L-rd, to fulfill my call as a Jewish or Gentile believer, to draw my Jewish friends and neighbors into a jealousy that would cause them to want You. Teach me to be able to present You in a manner that will accomplish this, that I could become one of Your vessels to help win Your Jewish children back to the faith. In Jesus's precious name I pray, amen.

ENDNOTES

1. This was from a report on ABC News, October 28, 2011, by Amy Bingham.

2. These events are easily accessed on the Internet. You can search for "dead birds and fish" or "plague of locusts" and read about these events.

3. You can find more information about this here: http://www .charismamag.com/site-archives/1441-0511-magazine-articles/ features/13395-rise-of-the-praying-church, accessed May 13, 2013.

4. Norman Grubb, *Rees Howells: Intercessor* (Lutterworth Press, 1952), 263.

5. Pastors and leaders, please think about leading your body corporately in this prayer.

8

UNDERSTANDING THE VEILS

When we think of the word *veil* in Scripture, several things come to mind: the veil over Moses (see Exod. 34:29-35), the veil between the Holy Place and the Holy of Holies (see Exod. 26:31-35), the veil over the disciples' eyes in understanding the Scriptures (see Luke 24:45), or even the veil that has been removed from us when we first believe (see 2 Cor. 4:1-6).

However, in the modern Church, perhaps the greatest memory that comes to mind with the word *veil* is actually the veil over the Jewish people. But what do we really know and understand about this veil, and of the other veils that G-d is going to remove in the end times? Let's try to gain a better understanding of the veils, and we'll start with Israel first.

Please get ready, because what you are about to read may be quite surprising to you. My hope is that it will also be illuminating as it was to me when G-d first began to reveal it to me.

THE VEIL OF SIN

We know from Scripture that Israel experienced a hardening: *"G-d gave them a spirit of stupor, eyes so that they could not see and ears so that they could not hear, to this very day"* (Rom. 11:8). The veil that was placed upon them, however, did not happen in light of their response to Christ as some of us might think. The blindness and deafness was placed upon them hundreds of years before Jesus's coming—when G-d used the prophet Isaiah to close their eyes and ears as a result of their constant idolatry and backsliding (see Isa. 6:9-10).

Was this a veil that was placed upon them, or was it a sealing to what was already in their hearts? When we look back at it, does it not look like the Jewish people were signed and sealed for another time? And hasn't the rest of the world been able to come into the kingdom as a result of their struggle and disobedience to G-d (see Rom. 11:30)?

When most people refer to the veil over the Jews, they usually refer to something quite separate and unique to Israel. This is what I used to think as well regarding the veil until G-d began to shed more light on the subject as we were seeking Him about a deeper understanding of the veil in our intercessory prayer group for Messiah's House several years ago. Even though there is still a difference here with Israel, there is only one veil that exists on the heart of mankind, and that is the veil of sin.

Let me address this issue first, and then we will hopefully be able to see more clearly how the Jewish people have been affected by it. Israel was called first, especially to the law, so let's take a look at this in order to see where the veil was first introduced and, more importantly, first recognized. But to gain a proper understanding of the veil and its origins, we need to understand how the law functions.

THE LAW EXPOSED THE HEART

In my mind, the giving of the law on Mount Sinai (see Exod. 19–20) is one of the most powerful accounts of Scripture in the entire

Bible, where G-d not only showed up on the mountaintop in fire and smoke, but actually spoke the law of G-d with His own voice to the people of Israel. It was both an awesome and fearsome moment.

Let's pay particular attention to Exodus 20:18-19. For it is here that for the first time we see the heart of man respond to the giving of the law. At that very moment, something quite unusual and dynamic took place as G-d revealed the Ten Commandments to the hearts of the Israelites.

> *When the people saw the thunder and lightning and heard the trumpet and saw the mountain in smoke, they trembled with fear. They stayed at a distance and said to Moses, "Speak to us yourself and we will listen. But do not have G-d speak to us or we will die"* (Exodus 20:18-19).

This was the first time the law was introduced to all of humankind. And what did the law do, which we learn from the apostle Paul in the New Covenant? It exposed our sinful heart and brought it into account (see Rom. 3:19; 7:7-13).

People could not come close to G-d as a result of their own sin. Instead, the Israelites insisted that Moses do it for them; that he be the intercessor G-d raised up for Israel. You have to read between the lines to see this, but in light of our New Testament understanding of Scripture and the main purpose for the law that the apostle Paul has taught us, I believe this is indeed what is happening on the inside of man's heart during this crucial moment in time.

The veil of sin inherited through Adam and Eve had just been exposed and brought into account through the giving of the law. As a result, they pointed their arms forward and stepped back with their feet as they could not deal with G-d's presence. This was not only a result of the fear of the moment, but also because of their own sinful nature. It immediately separated them from a holy and righteous G-d, whom sin could not touch. It is sin's consequences that produce spiritual blindness and deafness in the heart and soul. Is not sin like a veil around the heart that separates us from a holy and loving G-d, actually blinding and deafening us to the truth?

At that very point in time, the veil of sin, not just in the hearts of the Israelites but also in all of mankind's, would be exposed and brought into account through the giving of G-d's holy law, which did not actually bring life but death (see Rom. 7:10). And this happened even though G-d's timing was different for the Gentiles to come into His holy covenants. While it is true to say that G-d chose Israel apart from the world to experience the law and its consequences, the rest of humanity experiences its effects. This has been greatly misunderstood in the Church as a result of the Church's disconnection from Israel.

THE LAW BRINGS ALL SIN INTO ACCOUNT AND LEADS US TO CHRIST

For while the New Covenant brings us into a new system that is free from the law (see Eph. 2:15), the law itself has not been done away with. It is this that has been greatly misunderstood by the Church, and any mention of it creates all sorts of rumblings because it still needs clarification.

The law is still in place in order to bring us to Christ, who is at the end of it and freed us from its curse—spiritual death and separation from G-d (see Gal. 2–3). In fact, have we not died to the law through Christ's sacrifice and been crucified with Him to cross over into life (see Rom. 7:4; Gal. 2:19-20)? However, we must understand that without the law sin would not be officially recognized. Even though the Gentile world will not be judged by the system of the law (see Rom. 2:12-16), this does not negate the fact that the law brought about sin's judgment. There is a definite distinction here that we need to recognize and be aware of.

The best possible way for me to explain this is to back my way into it to show you what happens to any soul that does not receive Christ. Lest we're mistaken, Christ could not have come if the law was not given to Israel first, because, as the apostle Paul explains to us, sin had to be fully exposed and brought into account (see Gal. 3:19; Rom. 4:14). And where there is no law, there is no transgression (see Rom. 4–7).

For is it not true to say that if anyone does not accept Christ, they remain under the curse of the law, which is sin and death? But how would we know that if the law had not been given to us first, because this is how most of the Church believes and operates while leading sinners to repentance, freeing them from death's curse? What is it that calls sin into account other than the law of G-d that ultimately brings its wrath?

For when we accept Christ, we pass from spiritual death to spiritual life (see Eph. 2:14-22). We then become free from the old system of the law, which brought about sin's condemnation, because Christ's sacrifice has brought us into a New Covenant where His Holy Spirit circumcises our hearts with the law of G-d (see Jer. 31:33-34).

CHRIST IS OUR *KIPPUR*

Through Jesus's sacrifice and resurrection, He has freed us from the curse of sin and death and brought us into a new way of the Spirit through grace (see Eph. 1:7). So the old order has passed away in order to bring His Word and truth into a new system that the Bible refers to as the New Covenant, which is nothing other than the Gospel. The veil that separated all humanity from G-d, the veil of sin that the law exposed and brought into judgment, was destroyed by Christ's sacrifice and resurrection. Therefore, when we accept His atonement, we pass from death into life; but the law remains in place for sinners to come into repentance.

THE VEIL IN THE TEMPLE

G-d has given us a picture of this, with the veil that was set up between the Holy Place and the Holy of Holies in the temple of G-d, separating us from the presence of G-d. For when Jesus died on the cross, the veil in the temple was torn into two (see Luke 23:45) as the barrier that actually separated us from life and death was opened to us in the New Covenant. This was because Jesus destroyed it with His own life, His *kippur*, or atonement.

Through His sacrifice and His shed blood, which paid the penalty for sin, He opened the door to the Holy of Holies where we could pass from death through the law into life in His Son, being able to know G-d intimately for ourselves (see Jer. 31:34). It was here that the presence of G-d hovered over the Ark, to which we have now gained access through Jesus's life and the giving of the Holy Spirit.

This new passageway was not just for the Jews but also for the rest of humanity to enter into spiritual life where we could be free of sin's curse. The law then, as the apostle Paul tells us, is a schoolmaster to bring us to Christ (see Gal. 3:24 KJV). But it is only when we believe in Him that we cross over into life; otherwise, we still remain under the curse of the law as well as its judgments. This is one of the main reasons why Jesus explains to us, *"Until heaven and earth disappear, not the smallest letter, nor the least stroke of a pen, will by any means disappear from the Law until everything is accomplished"* (Matt. 5:18). These words cannot be nullified; otherwise, we risk the chance of taking G-d's Word out of context. For there has to be a decent explanation here that brings all of G-d's teachings about the purpose of the law into account.

WHAT'S THE FIRST THING MOST OF US DO WHEN WE FIRST BELIEVE?

Indeed, what is the first thing that any new believer does when they accept Christ as their Savior? What happened to you when you first believed? Did we not confess our sins to a holy and righteous G-d and tell Him of anything unclean in our hearts that may have separated us from His love and peace?

After we confessed our sins and turned from our old ways, did it not seem as if a veil had been lifted from us, and suddenly we could see what we were once blinded to before? Then, all of a sudden, the things of the kingdom and the Word of G-d now seemed so perfectly clear, whereas before it was as if we were blinded to them. Speak to most believers and they will tell you that after accepting Christ, they see and hear completely differently than the way they did before.

For me, personally, I can clearly remember that day. It was as if a veil had been lifted from my soul. I think most who have come to Christ out of the world have experienced that veil being lifted, because, when we believe, the veil of sin is lifted and removed. This is so the Spirit of G-d may indwell our spirits and awaken us from the spiritual death we have been under because of sin. And this also happens when we put our faith and trust in Jesus and make that spiritual crossing from death to life. As the famous Christian hymn goes:

> *Amazing Grace, how sweet the sound,*
> *That saved a wretch like me.*
> *I once was lost but now am found,*
> *Was blind, but now I see.*[1]

IT IS THE SAME VEIL FOR US ALL

As we may have just discovered, the veil of sin over our hearts is the same for all us. The only difference is that G-d addressed it to the Jew first and then later to the Gentile through Christ. G-d brought Israel through the law and brought Gentile believers in at the end of it. However, all humanity has been affected through the giving of the law as it brought sin into account; and all humanity must go through Christ in order to be saved out of it. So all those who do not accept Christ, His atonement and His sacrifice, remain under sin's curse (spiritual separation from G-d) and their hearts remain veiled to the truth. It was the truth that the law actually exposed and, as a result, brought sin's consequence into account.

The apostle Paul confirms this when he writes:

> There will be trouble and distress for every human being who does evil: first for the Jew, then for the Gentile; but glory, honor and peace for everyone who does good: first for the Jew, then for the Gentile. For G-d does not show favoritism (Romans 2:9-11).

In another Scripture he explains why we do not nullify the law with the faith of the New Covenant, but rather uphold the law because it actually brings us to Christ (see Rom. 3:31). There has been tremendous confusion and misunderstanding about this in the Body of Christ throughout the centuries, even until today. We are in definite need of greater clarification on this most significant subject.

FROM ADAM TO CHRIST

Try to look at it this way for a moment: it was sin that separated Adam and Eve from G-d. So G-d would have to devise a system that would show us exactly what it was that caused us to be separated from Him in the first place. In giving Israel the law, G-d was able to bring sin's punishment into account, which was judgment and death, in order that at the end of law He could send His Son to redeem us from it and give us life.

He achieved this with the giving of His one and only Son in the New Covenant, who was completely obedient to the law. Jesus said of Himself, *"For G-d did not send His Son into the world to condemn the world, but to save the world through Him"* (John 3:17). However, the confusion with the law comes in with our understanding of its purposes, while the apostle Paul so masterfully explains its main function to us throughout his epistles.

LOST THE CONNECTION

A great deal of this has been lost in our understanding because of our separation from our heritage and roots. This was just so natural for the apostles in their thinking because of their own Jewish heritage and their understanding of the Old Covenant. But many in the Church today believe that the law has no consequences because Christ has done away with it. And while this may be true for believers, it is certainly not the case for those who have not yet passed over into life. It is actually the law that will bring their sin into account before the judgment. So in reality, it has affected us all.

THE MORAL LAW

It is sometimes difficult in the New Testament to gain a clear understanding of what Jesus and the apostle Paul were referring to when they spoke of the law. Many times we think they are referring to what is known as the *moral law*—the Ten Commandments—and at other times it may seem like they are referring to the 613 commandments that comprise the entire Mosaic law.

Amusingly, I think of myself when reading these texts of Scripture, beaming back to these very moments in time, if only I could just ask them the question, "Yeshua, Shaul, do you mean the Ten Commandments or the entire Mosaic law?" However, we have exactly what we need from G-d's Word, and it is always good to dig deeper to gain a better understanding of what they were talking about. We must always be prayerful about His Word, as revelation comes from His Spirit, not just through our minds.

When G-d spoke the law on Mount Sinai with His own voice, He only spoke the Ten Commandments, although the other laws were given by G-d through Moses and are recorded throughout the remainder of Exodus as well as other parts of the Torah. But it does not appear as if they were included in His dissertation of the Ten Commandments. In addition, only the Ten Commandments were to be written on tablets of stone and stored in the Ark of the Covenant, not the other laws that were recorded later.

There seems to be a difference here between these two aspects of the law. And while we are all obviously free from the old Mosaic system when we accept Christ, are not the Ten Commandments now circumcised into our hearts and spirits in the New Covenant? If we break one of them, do we not immediately have the conviction of the Spirit of G-d working in our spirits to bring us to confession and repentance? Just because Jesus summarized the Ten Commandments into two new commands does not necessarily nullify the original text, but rather further substantiates it.

TRUTH IS TRUTH

In addition, does truth spoken by G-d ever change? And if truth has been spoken and taught by G-d, would it not indeed transfer from the old to the new? Just to be clear here: I am not referring to any of the Mosaic laws that related to the sacrificial system, or even the dietary and civil laws that made good sense back then. I am only referring to the other truths spoken of in the Torah or the rest of the Hebrew Scriptures.

G-d did not just wipe the slate clean and start over. No, the old system was done away with as it achieved its main purposes.

However, G-d's truths were brought into a new way and a new system, what the apostle Paul calls the law of Christ (see 1 Cor. 9:21), so that with the power of the Holy Spirit we could finally have an opportunity to be victorious in it.

Even Jesus references the most important aspects of the law, which were *"justice, mercy and faithfulness"* (Matt. 23:23). They are obviously a major part of the New Covenant, which we hopefully practice every day in our lives as we walk out our faith as believers and followers of G-d. Why is it in the Church that if the New Testament laws,[2] of which there are many, do not reaffirm the old, that we just naturally discount the old truths? What about some of the references to sexual relations and uncleanness that may not be written of specifically in the New Testament? Are not many of the Old Testament truths now working in us through the power of the Holy Spirit in the New Covenant? An example of this is where Jeremiah explains to us that G-d will put His law into our hearts and minds so that we will obey it (see Jer. 31:33).

THE OLD IN THE NEW

Please do not get me wrong here, for I am not suggesting for one moment that Gentile believers go back to an old system and look to reapply it. Rather, we need to understand how the old system actually works in the New Covenant, and how it has actually freed us and brought us into spiritual life. After all, where did all of the apostles get their authentication from in most of their thoughts and their presentations of the New Covenant, if it wasn't from the Hebrew Scriptures?

And what exactly does the apostle Paul mean when he says, *"And so He condemned sin in sinful man, in order that the righteous requirements of the law might be fully met in us, who do not live according to the sinful nature but according to the Spirit"* (Rom. 8:3-4)?

In addition, it behooves us in the Church to better understand exactly how the law is still currently working in our world despite our own acknowledgement of it, because the whole world will ultimately be judged as a result of sin unless we have passed over into the life that Jesus has provided us. Just as Isaiah prophesied many years ago: *"We all, like sheep, have gone astray, each of us has turned to his own way; and the L-rd has laid on Him the iniquity of us all"* (Isa. 53:6).

THE VEIL OVER ISRAEL

If all humanity is veiled to G-d because of sin before they accept Christ, then what is this veil that people speak of over the Jewish people? It is important to understand this because there is a difference that we must explore and comprehend.

I like to answer that question with this response: G-d chose Israel to face the law; however, in our humanity He knew that we would turn away from Him even before He gave it to us. Our sinful hearts, it would cause us to turn to our own ways, including following the gods of the people around us. This is quite apparent in the Old Testament passages where Moses speaks of the blessings and the curses (see Deut. 28–32). Despite the choice we were given to follow G-d, He knew sin would lead us away.

G-D HAD TO EXPOSE THE HEART

As part of the dispensations to lead humanity back to faith, G-d had to expose the place in our hearts that caused us to be separate from Him in the first place. And His firstborn son, Israel, was chosen for this purpose. However, who of us in the world, from whatever nation or country or peoples, could have stayed obedient to G-d, overcoming our sinful natures and facing the law without the presence of the Holy Spirit? Did not the law render us powerless to overcome because of our own sinful natures (see Rom. 8:3)? None of us are free from sin except for G-d's one and only Son who had to be completely obedient to the law in order to redeem us from it.

HAS ISRAEL SUFFERED FOR US?

Has not our older brother, therefore, actually endured the law for us, and, as a result, greatly suffered the consequences? Since the law brought a clear understanding between right and wrong, there also had to be consequences for not keeping it. As I have mentioned in earlier chapters, there is something uniquely correlated between the suffering of His firstborn and the suffering of Christ that is hard to put into words. Look for one moment, though, to see just how the land of Israel was actually restored. Was it not through the death, destruction, and loss of 6 million Jews? Was it not the dry bones of the Holocaust that G-d used to redeem the nation (see Ezek. 37)?

Just like the rest of mankind, Israel was given free will to obey the law and keep focused on their G-d. But our sinful nature stripped us of any real power to keep our faithfulness to Him. In addition, it wasn't just our sins that caused G-d to depart from us, because the law made provisions through the sacrificial system; it was sin's hardening that caused Israel to turn away from G-d, constantly denying Him and wanting instead to be like the nations around them, following idols. They wanted to control their own lives and their own destinies instead of trusting G-d and putting Him first, which, consequently, is what He actually requires from all of us, both then and now.

Was this heart condition unique to Israel, or does not the whole world suffer from the same thing? Or was it just that they were a stiff-necked people? But doesn't sin make all of us sniff-necked? As I have already mentioned, because the standard was raised and the law given to Israel, they had to be held accountable to it. Therefore, their actions did not excuse them, just like our sins today do not excuse us either, as we will all face the judgment. This is why we are so in need of His blood that has freed us from the law and sin's curse.

THE VEIL WAS SEALED OVER THE JEWISH PEOPLE

As a result of this, instead of destroying us completely, which our rebellion warranted, G-d hardened us and put a seal upon the hearts of the Jewish people (see Isa. 6:6-10). This would then reserve them for a future time such as the one we are now living in, which explains how the veil is different over Israel compared to the rest of the world.

This also explains the dryness of the bones described in Ezekiel, especially amongst secular Jews who seem so distant and cut off from their G-d. The veil has been so tightly wrapped around their souls that it has squeezed dry any form of spiritual life. Because of this, they have little desire for the things of G-d and instead cling tightly to the things of the world—often excelling in them in light of their giftings to lead (see Rom. 11:29).

Religious Jews have a different ilk, for wherever the Word of G-d is promoted there is always life. In this case, however, it is bound with such legalism that it squeezes dry all the liberty G-d has given them through Christ, instead focusing them on their own works to find godliness.

In truth, both groups are in great need of spiritual life. Because they have been dead for so long, it will take a tsunami of prayer and intercession to awaken them. Remember the fig tree that Jesus cursed; Yeshua Himself put an end to any spiritual life that could come from them (see Matt. 21:18-19). On top of all this, most have little or no desire at all to be awakened, just as we witnessed through my son Joshua's birth experience. *We must begin to understand the battle that is before us, for Israel does not want to come forth even though they must come forth.*

This blindness was also evident when Yeshua was to be given to them as they did not spiritually see or hear Him. Only those whose lives G-d had prepared for this time would be reborn and brought first into the New Covenant, whom G-d used to establish the Church. Please remember Jesus's own words as He cried over Jerusalem's rejection of Him:

> *O Jerusalem, Jerusalem, you who kill the prophets and stone those sent to you, how often have I longed to gather your children together, as a hen gathers her chicks under her wings, but you were not willing* (Matthew 23:37).

Even with the apostles, before the Holy Spirit was given, we see Jesus opening their minds so that they could properly understand the Scriptures (see Luke 24:45). If this is not some kind of a veil lifting, what else could it be?

G-D RESERVED ISRAEL TO SHOW HIS MERCY

In light of Israel's journey, the veil of sin was not to be lifted from Israel until the end; and so G-d has reserved them to show His mercy and glory to the world in this time and hour by ultimately keeping His covenants and promises to them despite their disobedience and resistance. For this was the plan of G-d from the very beginning, because He knew they would not stand up to the law: to release His mercy, which the Church has received as a result of Israel's disobedience, then give that mercy back to Israel through the Church (see Rom. 11:30-32). What a plan, that He may show His mercy upon us all (see Rom. 11:29-32)!

The first were to be last, and the last were to be first. For has not G-d used their rejection to reconcile the whole world to Himself (see Rom. 11:15), and have we now not received G-d's mercy as a result of their disobedience (see Rom. 11:30)? Israel has paid dearly so that the world could be redeemed through Christ. This certainly puts their role in a different light, perhaps one that we have never quite seen before. So shouldn't this give us a whole lot more appreciation and compassion for what they have actually experienced for us as a people?

ISRAEL WAS GIVEN FOR US ALL

In His mercy for us all, G-d has used Israel to bring sin into account with no real strength of their own to face it, because before life could be given through Christ, sin had to first be exposed and brought into account. Aside from giving Israel all of the covenants and promises along with the patriarchs, as well as the human ancestry of Christ (see Rom. 9:4-5), their human inadequacy to the law laid the path for all of us to find redemption. Who of us could have done any different in light of our humanity and sinful nature?

We can now conclude, as the apostle Paul has done in his one and only dissertation to the Gentile Church about their positioning toward the Jewish people as well as to the rest of us, that it is all about G-d's mercy. One thing is for sure: G-d wants us in the Church to be the vessels of His mercy—especially to Israel, His firstborn children whom He loves just as much as He loves us—because they are the golden key to unlock the door to the resurrection power of G-d, through the love of Christ, and that will see the end times fulfilled amongst us (see Rom. 11:15).

So if the veil needs to come up from the Jews, which we know is just a question of G-d's timing and plan, then we must also be willing to address any other issues that may stand in the way of this or that may be hindering it from happening. As we have hopefully already discovered in this book, when G-d brought us into confession and repentance in regard to our own hearts from our ancestral line toward the Jews, and when we received His heart for His firstborn, did not a veil get lifted from our hearts? Will not our understanding change as G-d breathes on us in this regard? As this happens, we will suddenly see the fullness of G-d's plan to redeem Israel through us, and the significance of our reconnection to them as our family in the Spirit.

THE BATON OF G-D

It is only when we in the Church (the assigned vessels of G-d's mercy) pick up the baton of G-d as His Ezekiel generation by listening to the Father's voice, that the breath of G-d will be loosed into Israel, finally lifting the veil that has been over them. This will then free them to come under the conviction of the Holy Spirit (see Ezek. 36:25-28; Zech. 12:10), just as it did to us when we first believed. Israel will once again call upon our G-d, never again to turn away from Him (see Ezek. 36), so that Yeshua can return to the earth to take His seat upon David's throne, that we would both come into our priestly roles to reign with Him forever.

THE VEIL OVER THE CHURCH

The Bible says that judgment first begins in the house of the L-rd (see 1 Pet. 4:17). And if the veil over the Church has been such a hindrance, shouldn't it be our first target to tear down in order to awaken the sleeping giant into the Father's plan and to show His glory to the world? Isn't the devil most afraid of Jesus's return, and won't he continue to do everything in his power to prevent the control of the world from being taken from him?

The restoration of the Jewish people, spiritually restored and holy in the land, is exactly what G-d is looking forward to so that the Lion of the tribe of Judah can now return to the earth and take His seat. And this is exactly what the devil is trying to prevent.

If Israel is called into such an amazing role, then what about the rest of us in the Church? G-d has given us the honor to help see His spiritual family restored so that both groups can finally come into our inheritance so the family circle is completed. For we already have what was given to them; now they need to receive it. What a plan, that His mercy would be shown to us all!

CLEAN HOUSE AND THEN GET THE WORD OUT

We first have to clean up our own act and get our hearts right before this can happen; we have to receive the Father's heart for Israel and reconnect to our spiritual family. Should the Church, therefore, not be one of our main targets in our prayers and intercession to help bring this about? And if we believe this message to be the word of the L-rd, then we should trumpet it throughout the Church so that others can be made aware of it and come into the same repentance.

MAJOR INTERCESSORY BATTLES AHEAD

There are massive spiritual strongholds in the heavenly realm the devil has put in place that will take major battles in prayer and intercession to be broken. And I'm not just speaking only over us in the Church and Israel, as we have discussed, but also over those caught under Islam, who have their own distinct veil, along with the rest of the people of the world who are veiled to G-d because of sin. G-d showed me a long time ago that we cannot have a true heart for Israel unless we are praying for everyone else, especially the Muslims.

G-d wants us to target those billions of souls caught under the veil of Islam. The only way we are going to set them free is by looking to prayer and intercession and to the power of the Holy Spirit, which are our only hope to get the job done. Everything we do for the kingdom of G-d is good, but if it is not bathed and saturated in prayer and intercession beforehand, it will lack the power it requires to be successful; and this is especially true with all of these veils upon us that need to be broken in the heavenly realms in order for the kingdom to advance. Jesus said, *"From the days of John the Baptist until now, the kingdom of heaven has been forcefully advancing, and forceful men lay hold of it"* (Matt. 11:12).

Without a major shift in the Church to prayer and intercession (first to the Jew and then to the Gentile), we will remain powerless. Listen to the apostle Paul here:

> *For though we live in the world, we do not wage war as the world does. The weapons we fight with are not the weapons of the world. On the contrary, they have divine power to demolish strongholds. We demolish arguments and every pretension that sets itself up against the knowledge of G-d, and we take captive every thought to make it obedient to Christ. And we will be ready to punish every act of disobedience, once your obedience is complete* (2 Corinthians 10:3-6).

As we know from Scripture, Jesus will not come until His Word has gone into every nation, and these lands and peoples *must* hear the Good News. Despite Islam's hold, the Gospel is going forth, for His holy Word cannot be stopped. But G-d still needs our prayers to shake the heavenlies so His Word can go forth in greater power.

The grip of Islam must first be effectively dealt with in prayer and intercession before we can see these barriers come down—from the roots of jealously and power, which has enabled this veil and seeded the oldest divide between Abraham's physical children, to become the greatest threat to our modern world. Prayer must penetrate the strongholds of Islam so that G-d's Word can go forth and bring salvation to the millions upon millions of souls that are caught under this deception.

I can assure you that there are many in the Muslim world cursing us and praying for the West's downfall in the hope that they can take it over. The Church has its work cut out for it. So what are we waiting for? It is time to awaken from our sleep into greater prayer and intercession, moving mountains. We also need to gain a greater understanding of the authority we actually have in the Body of Christ, especially through prayer, as it is here that the demons will truly shudder! Let us pray for godly teachers who have been given this kind of revelation from the Father and who will release it to the Body, because we are going to need it in this day and hour.

A WORD OF CAUTION TO US

This awakening of G-d for the reconnection of the Church back toward Israel has already begun and is gaining momentum by the day. It is still much like a stream and will enlarge as it grows. I believe in these coming years, we in the Church will be asked the main questions that this book raises and brings into the light, for we will need to make a most definite choice in this regard. I say this with all humility and love, for in these days if we do not side with the people of Israel, will we be seen to be working against our own G-d? Woe to the enemies of the Jews when the Lion of the tribe of Judah returns!

Please read Jesus's teaching in Matthew 25:31-46, and how He relates the story of the sheep and the goats not only to His return, which I believe He is focusing on in this discourse (see Matt. 25:31-33), but also to our treatment of Jesus's brothers (see Matt. 25:40). Does this text just refer to G-d's brothers in the sense of those of us in the New Covenant who may be struggling and how we treat them, which has been the Church's main understanding of this Scripture? Or does it also suggest Jesus's relationship to His physical brethren, the Jews? This puts a different light on these Scriptures and one that we should seriously contemplate for the end times.

WE MUST NOT BE ARROGANT

If you have not yet received the message of this book into your heart, please carefully consider it as it has immense consequences for our present generation. We must be careful. If there is any arrogance in us, which the apostle Paul warned us about (see Rom. 11:20-24), we must allow Jesus to take it from us and cleanse our hearts so that we may still become the vessels of mercy He longs for us to be. It is not too late and there is never any condemnation in Christ for past behavior; He always wants us to get it right now so we can change our future actions.

Before a dam busts, there is a gradual process that takes place, which is where we presently are with Israel's awakening and reconnection—it is just passing its embryonic stage. The Body of Christ is truly beginning to awaken to G-d's message and timing in this regard, which is one of the main reasons we need to focus much of our prayer and intercession on the rest of the Church. The veil over us must be lifted before we can gain the power needed from G-d to address the other veils that must also be lifted before Christ returns.

As Jesus breathed on the disciples and they immediately began to understand the Scriptures, so we also need G-d to breathe upon us so we can see His end-time plan (see Luke 24:13-35).

WE WILL BE AWAKENED

I sometimes get frustrated with the slowness of this awakening, especially in light of the shortness of time that may be left before end-time events actually begin. But having been an entrepreneur most of my life, and having started several different companies, people are always slower to the vision in the beginning than the one used to initiate it. However, there always comes a time when its success, and in this case, truth, turns the tables, and all of a sudden everyone seems like they are coming onboard. This has been a lot of my experience with many of the brands I have built over the course of my career, and it is the same here with this movement of G-d that must awaken the Church into its role. For G-d will have His way through and amongst His Body, and it will all be in His perfect timing, which is often not the same as ours.

Similarly, like with a wedding, there is so often great panic and pandemonium right before it is about to take place. But right at the last minute, everything seems to calm and the service ends up being beautiful as the bride walks down the aisle in all of her beauty and glory. This is certainly true of us in the Body of Christ, as there is a lot of confusion for many of the reasons I have already pointed out. But thank G-d that He is sovereign and He will have His way among His sheep who truly know His voice.

This is all the more reason why those of us who have already received the Father's heart should trumpet this cause wherever we go. It will most probably be one of the greatest issues that we will face in the Church in our modern day before He returns. Will you help your church place its hands on that golden key to ignite the power of G-d through Christ that we so desperately need to win our generation to His majesty?

IF WE TAKE CARE OF ISRAEL, HE WILL TAKE CARE OF THE REST

Once the Church has effectively dealt with its past in regard to Israel, like the prophet Jonah who also repented (see Jon. 3:3), it will have all that it needs to properly deal with its mission fields. This will not only be to the Jews, which it must approach first in its positioning, but also to the rest of the world. In addition, greater power and authority in prayer and intercession is waiting to be loosed upon us so that we can more effectively address the demonic forces in the heavenly places that keep the veils so tightly knit around us all.

MUST BE IN HIS STRENGTH AND NOT OUR OWN

For we can never think to deal with these places in our own strength or power, but must first approach them in prayer before we do anything. We must also learn to become more targeted, being led more effectively by the Holy Spirit, who has all the power we need to get the job done.

I cannot stress the significance of prayer and intercession enough as G-d is calling us to a battle that we have no power or strength of our own to fight. Yet, with our dependency upon Him, the Holy Spirit will lead us to victory; all He needs from us is our willingness to obey. It wasn't just Jonah's message that brought the Ninevites into repentance, but the Spirit of G-d brought conviction to their hearts so they could properly respond to it.

MILLIONS UPON MILLIONS OF CHRISTIANS PRAYING

Reflecting again on the analogy of Joshua's birth experience: it was the agreement between the Father, the Son, and the Church that released the power of G-d to bring Israel forth. Up until now we have been the missing link. Can you imagine millions upon millions of Christians praying for Israel's awakening? The effects would be astounding.

This is the movement the Spirit of G-d is bringing us into. And as we come together with this focus in mind, it will also loose the power of G-d upon the rest of us, ultimately lifting the veils over the balance of mankind's souls—those who respond to its call. This is so that all those who are to come into the kingdom in the end-time harvest will hear His voice, repent, and obey, for they will also have been freed up spiritually to do so, which His prayer and intercession through us will help bring about.

Joel prophesied of the end times:

> *And afterward, I will pour out My Spirit on all people.*
> *Your sons and daughters will prophesy, your old men will*
> *dream dreams, your young men will see visions. Even on*
> *My servants, both men and women, I will pour out My*
> *Spirit in those days. I will show wonders in the heavens*
> *and on the earth, blood and fire and billows of smoke.*
> *The sun will be turned to darkness and the moon to*
> *blood before the coming of the great and dreadful day*
> *of the L-rd. And everyone who calls on the name of the*
> *L-rd will be saved; for on Mount Zion and in Jerusalem*
> *there will be deliverance, as the L-rd has said, among the*
> *survivors whom the L-rd calls* (Joel 2:28-32).

The choice is ours!

Endnotes

1. "Amazing Grace" by John Newton (1725-1807).
2. There are 1,050 commands in the New Testament according to www.Purtian-books.com.

Part Three

UNDERSTANDING THE RECONNECTION

9

RECONNECTING

There is no question in my mind that the greatest thing we can do for the reconnection of G-d's family is to pray and intercede. I also believe that there are some major differences between prayer and intercession that can dramatically help us in this regard, which we will thoroughly explore in the next chapter. Before I do that, however, I would like to address some of my thoughts about our reconnection and what it might actually mean to us in the end times.

WHAT DOES RECONNECTION LOOK LIKE?

In raising the issue of reconnection between the Jew and Gentile in this book, I am sure that a good number of you may have already asked the question, "Well, what does he mean by reconnecting?"

While I may have addressed the disconnection between the two groups and the great need for us to reconnect, I have not yet fully focused on our response to it, except for getting our hearts right first, which we have hopefully already prayed about and received. If you haven't yet, I would strongly encourage you to do so as you will not be able to properly address this reconnection unless it is done in the Spirit first, making sure your bloodline has been properly cleansed.

WHAT IT IS NOT

To be clear about the reconnection, let me first state most definitely what it is not in order for us to be able to enter into a more comfortable zone with these thoughts and ideas. I am not suggesting or proposing any type of Judaizing[1] that a number of the apostles were challenged with in the first century; I hope I have made myself quite clear in this regard. I am not proposing that there would be any direction for Gentiles to go back to the law, which Christ Himself has freed us from. But I must say, through my experience at the mere mention of Jewish topics from within the Church, one can often be accused of moving into Judaizing,[2] which is obviously not correct either.

This reaction shows a lack of understanding to these matters. The apostle Paul has instructed us that we are not to be ignorant to this mystery, and there is a lot for us to learn at this time (see Rom. 11:25). So I want to make it perfectly clear that not only is this not in my heart, but it is definitely not G-d's will either.

G-D CREATED US JUST AS WE ARE

G-d created the diversity amongst us through the nations. Not only is our G-d the most creative force in the entire universe, but He is also exceptionally talented in His creative outlook and design. Just look at the beauty of creation, or that of humankind, for example— there are currently over 7 billion of us on the planet and yet not one of us is exactly the same. Not only that, but within this uniqueness, He has also brought each of us into different nationalities and groups of people, each of which He loves.

G-d does not want any of us to be any different from what He has created us to be, except for us to be reconnected to our heritage, which the Church moved away from and which we must now look to restore. If He created us to be Jews, we should be Jews; if He created us to be Gentiles, with all of the hundreds of different nationalities and cultures that have developed among us, then we should be as we are. He takes great pleasure in all of us—in our foods, our cultures, and even our different languages.

On the other hand, sometimes when a Gentile believer's light goes on for Israel, they can get a little carried away in wanting to become like Jews. This is evident today in some Messianic congregations where some Gentiles look more Jewish than their Jewish brethren (with all of the garb), which I think is also out of balance. G-d wants us to be at peace with who we are and what He has created us to be, and this reconnection comes from within, through the heart and the Spirit, not though the clothes we wear.

THE GREAT FEAST

Have you ever thought or wondered for a moment what kind of food will be served at the great banquet, the wedding supper of the Lamb (see Isa. 25:6; Luke 13:29; Rev. 19:9)? It could be entirely possible that when we sit at that table, before each of us are our most favorite foods and delicacies. I am not saying this for sure, for only the L-rd knows these details. But I say it to point out how much He loves our uniqueness as well as the distinctions and diversities among us. And I would not put it past our L-rd for being so sensitive to our different wants and needs.

ACCEPTING JEWISH AND GENTILE ROLES

This would also be true of the differences He created between the Jews and the Gentiles, as well as His distinct purposes to reveal

Himself to mankind through both groups. The main point here is that we should be at peace with who we are and should not look to be anything that we are not. Jews should not have to become like Gentiles and Gentiles should not have to become like Jews when coming to Christ. This was stressed by the apostles in establishing the rules for their acceptance and ingathering Gentile believers in the formation of the Church (see Acts 15).

Within the distinctiveness He greatly desires us to dwell together in unity and to fully embrace one another in the Spirit of G-d, which the New Testament is clear about. I can see this quite plainly, assuming we allow His love to increase our tolerance for one another, to accept the various differences among us and the unique roles He has called both groups to from within that spiritual unity. Having said all of the above, as we reconnect in the Spirit I also believe that Christians will have a greater freedom to enjoy the richness of their Jewish heritage, especially through the feasts, which are G-d ordained holidays for us all.

HEALING OTHER DIVISIONS

This renewed unity could also apply to the various divisions in the Body of Christ, between Catholics and Protestants as well as various other different denominations all believing they are right, allowing the enemy to foster barriers and even hatred among us that strips us of our divine power to further promote His love to a lost and dying world. How foolish can we be, that we allow our pride to fuel the enemy's divide? During these days, G-d is going to use all the circumstances around us to bring His Body together, and, if we are totally honest, we can find a lot more that we actually agree upon than not.

Could it also be that as we allow the Spirit of G-d to fully heal the divisions that exist between Jew and Gentile, that He will also heal the divisions in the Body of Christ? Does it not say that this must happen to the Jew first and *then* the Gentile? As we put His principles into action, we will see it affect and heal other divides as well. It is an interesting concept, isn't it?

CAN WE BLESS ISRAEL'S CALL FROM WITHIN THE BODY?

The key here, however, for both groups (Israel and the Church) is to be able to bless each other into our own unique callings while fully understanding that Israel has not yet received the fullness of its spiritual awakening. This would also include how we relate to Jewish believers from within the Body, because up to this point we have not yet fully understood their call and role, expecting them to be just like the rest of us in the Church when they are most definitely not.

For Jewish believers have been called to reflect their Jewish identities from within the faith in order that His light would shine back to His firstborn to help provoke and awaken them to faith. And we must give them our full support to help create a place of comfort for the many other Jewish souls who are still to come in. We must also learn to honor each other as we come into the fullness of our roles. For how else will we coexist in the millennium without fully blessing each other?

As I've already said, we must look to spiritually reconnect first, for there is no doubt that the New Covenant brings us into one spiritual family where we all become joint-heirs to the future kingdom of G-d. So we must learn how to operate together as one Body and bless our distinctive calls.

MESSIANIC BELIEVERS NEED TO CHANGE

The Church is not the only group keeping us apart, for many of the Messianic groups (Jewish believing congregations) that exist today have also become separate. So repentance is required on both sides.

This may have arisen in the beginning of the Messianic movement as a result of the Church's position toward them, not really accepting their roles to live and function as Jews with their newfound faith in Yeshua. But now many don't want to have anything to do with the Church either, which is equally not healthy for our Father's family, whose heart is that we would be one in the Spirit of G-d.

In our Messiah's House ministry, we promote the oneness of both Jewish and Gentile believers operating together in the Spirit. At some of our get-togethers, usually around the Jewish holidays, I have so often felt the Father's joy in the Spirit when we come together as one family, honoring and respecting the differences between us. The presence of G-d among us has a uniqueness to it that comes from His pleasure of us dwelling together in unity as He expresses His love for us both.

RECONNECTING THE NEW TO THE OLD

The reconnection is not so much about taking the old into the new as I have stated above, but rather reconnecting the new with the old. This is not for us to associate with the Mosaic covenant, but rather to all of the promises, covenants, and heritages given to Israel as a whole, as well as to its apostolic foundations, which the Gentile Church looked to sever as it moved away from its Jewish roots. For is not Christianity really Jewish, and is not the New Covenant the only real and proper extension of Judaism? Are we not brought into all of the covenants and promises of Israel, and grafted into their vine? Again, the apostle Paul says, *"Theirs is the adoption as a sons; theirs the divine glory, the covenants, the temple worship and the promises. Theirs are the patriarchs, and from them is traced the human ancestry of Christ, who is G-d over all, forever praised"* (Rom. 9:4-5). It was also from them that salvation has come (see John 4:22).

When we become a believer in Jesus, do we not really inherit what was given to Israel first? How Jewish can our faith really be? So why would it be difficult for us to present their own message back to them in a way in which they can fully relate? The reason it has been difficult is because of the great separation from our roots, heritage, and apostolic foundations. Christianity is now presented as a Gentile faith, which is quite separate and distinct from its Jewish origins.

As a result, the Church is not able to properly function in its calling to win the Jews back to faith (see Rom. 11:30-31). However, as believers fully embrace their Jewish roots and the reconnection toward Israel in the Spirit with the Father's heart we will receive all we need from the G-d to properly operate in a new reconnected mode. This, in and of itself, will more easily draw the Jewish people to envy because they will begin to question what is being presented to them if it is shown to them in a Jewish light that is attached to its origins.

As Gentile believers, are we not already fully operating in the New Covenant that was given to Israel, which up to this point their ancestry has rejected? If we present it to them as if it was theirs in the first place, however, it can make a major difference in how they perceive it. This is not the be all and end all because their blindness is a spiritual one; but it is definitely a move in the right direction.

Of course, those church groups living in and around Jewish neighborhoods may need to make more adjustments than those where no Jewish people are actually living. However, as we come down to the end, we are all called to reconnect to our roots. This will not only loose the power of G-d upon us all, but it will also better prepare us for a Messianic kingdom when Jesus returns.

Reconnection is foremost in the Spirit of G-d, that we would be fully reconciled to Israel in our hearts. Not only embracing Jewish believers as our very own brethren, but also taking on the balance of Israel as family yet to be restored. Also, reeconnecting the Gentile branch in the vine to its Jewish origins will help to prepare the Church for its ministry to Israel and for the L-rd's return.

THE JERUSALEM COUNCIL IN REVERSE

As I have already stated, perhaps the Church is in its own need of a new Jerusalem council that now properly focuses on the Jewish ingathering, and exactly what adjustments it intends to make so that the Holy Spirit has complete liberty to bring them in and reestablish them. Just look how the tables have turned!

Isn't this an interesting concept? For not only does our witness need to be reconnected so that we can also fulfill our calling in drawing them to jealously, but the manner in which we present our faith should also reflect its reconnection to our roots as, in my mind, it was never G-d's intention for us to depart from it in the first place. To the Gentile Church, He has been faithful to His covenants but never accepting of the manner in which His firstborn has been treated. And as a Father, He will continue to weep for lost sons and daughters until they are restored. Wouldn't you lament for your children if they were lost?

RECONNECTION IS FIRST IN THE HEART

Reconnection takes place first in the heart and the spirit before anything else, that we would be fully reconciled to Israel as family; I truly want to emphasize this. In this day and at this time, G-d is calling us to restore and reconnect the Gentile branch to its Jewish vine, fully blessing the Jewish branches, while also taking on the balance of Israel by faith as future family yet to be restored into the olive tree. Reconnecting the Gentile branch in the vine to its Jewish origins will help to prepare the Church for its ministry to Israel and for the L-rd's return. This will not change who we are as G-d's children from the nations, but it will restore us to our Jewish heritage and roots, which will only loose greater power and blessings of heaven upon us. As Gentile believers, it is about how we position and anchor our faith in Christ to what our Father has associated Himself with through the covenants and heritage of Israel. For the kingdom of G-d is a family, and it is time for us to be operating as such—with a deep love and connection for each family member.

When we receive the Father's heart, we are not only automatically reconnected to G-d's plans for His end-time family, but we are also reconnected to our firstborn brothers and sisters. Scripture states, *"A cord of three strands is not quickly broken"* (Eccles. 4:12). G-d, Israel, and the Church—His love will forever change us and continue to bind us as we begin to move together into our destinies to reign with Christ. How exciting is that!

Christianity was not a new religion but rather a new extension of an old one. When we live and operate from that place, the witness of our faith will naturally change, and, without even knowing it, our lives will more effectively touch the Jewish souls around us.

LET THE SPIRIT LEAD THE RECONNECTION

I want to be really careful in exactly what I say regarding this reconnection as there is no definite list, even though we are called to certain fundamental changes in the Church as Jew and Gentile come together in the Spirit of G-d. Those of us who live in more heavily Jewish populated areas will obviously need to do more. As a result of this, we must be led by the Spirit of G-d in this direction, especially in the days that are ahead of us.

Once we have made our hearts right before G-d, He will show us how to properly respond to our calling for these days, both as Jewish and Gentile believers, in our prayer and evangelism as well as in our theological and eschatological positions. I do not want to write a definite outline in this regard, but rather help make some suggestions for us to consider and pray about as we seek the L-rd on this most crucial subject.

Whatever changes or adjustments we decide to make, either as a Church, a Messianic congregation, or as individuals, let the direction for it be clearly from above. I hope we can now see placing our hands upon that golden key as the Father places His hands upon His Church to unlock it.

IT WILL NATURALLY BECOME A PRIORITY

We will now begin to see what a priority it really is, and how these changes will have a dramatic effect on us as well as those around us. For placing the Israel piece into the puzzle through Christ ignites the power of G-d into His end-time plan and truly allows His fullness to flow through our spirits—then it be will for us like it was for the disciples when He opened their minds so they understood the Scriptures in this regard (see Luke 24:45).

As we seek to reestablish the kingdom's position—to the Jew first and then the Gentile—in how we prioritize ourselves, then look out! Again, this is not making them any more important than the rest of us, but rather reaffirming what G-d has already established with them, coming back into agreement with it. This makes a huge difference in the spiritual realm, where all of the power of G-d exists and is waiting to be loosed.

Don't ask me why He has waited for this time to make these changes among us, except to say that as we draw closer to His return, He must make us fully ready for all that is ahead of us. So why not now? This is also true of some of the other changes G-d is looking to make in His Church at this time, concerning leadership and how the Body is equipped for ministry.

CHURCH GOVERNMENT

While the Israel piece should be fundamental in our new reconnected mode, what about Church government? Is the Church not built upon the foundation of the apostles and prophets? Did the L-rd not establish a five-fold ministry to prepare and build us up for works of service (see Eph. 4:11-13)? So why is the current Church so focused on pastoral or priestly leadership that tends to keep most of us too comfortable in our pews, when it is the Body who is supposed to be doing the work? What I loved about my first pastor is that he always looked to work himself out of a job by trying to equip us to do the work of the ministry in whatever capacity we were called. Change is on the horizon for sure, and may the winds of the Holy Spirit have their full way among us to reposition us where we need to be during these days.

One of the best reads on this topic in light of Israel's calling is by my dear old friend and mentor in the faith, Art Katz.[3] He was definitely one of pioneers of this great movement of G-d with a huge prophetic vision to see this time and to help prepare us for it. He wrote a book about this subject, called *Apostolic Foundations*. You may also want to download some of his teachings on Israel and the Church, which are some of the most brilliant discourses I have ever heard on the subject.

PRAY! PRAY! PRAY!

As I mentioned at the beginning of this chapter, the greatest thing we can do is pray for these changes to take place in the Church. If you do not already have a prayer group that is focused on Israel and the end times, please consider starting one and establishing a leader in your group or church whom G-d has burdened for such a role. Interestingly enough, while there has always been a remnant of Jewish believers coming to faith over the centuries from the Jewish people, there is usually always a remnant of believers in most churches who already have a deeper burden for Israel.

RUTHS AND CORNELIUSES

As I have already suggested, it is almost as if the remnant of Israel is mirrored in the Church, small pockets of Jewish believers and small pockets of Gentile believers who already have the Father's heart toward Israel. I call these believers "Ruths" and "Corneliuses" in whom G-d has released a deeper desire to be reconnected with Israel.

Ruth was a Moabitess, but she was filled with a greater desire to connect with Israel and G-d's people. She said to her mother-in-law, *"Your people will be my people and your G-d my G-d"* (Ruth 1:16). Similarly, Cornelius was one of the first Gentile male converts who had a great respect for the Jews as well (see Acts 10).

If you are a pastor or leader in a church, quickly recognize the Ruths and Corneliuses among you, giving them a place in your body that will enable the Spirit of G-d to flourish among you. Whether in prayer, teaching, or both, encourage them to better connect to others outside your church who are doing the same thing. There is probably a good deal that you can learn from them as they are already carrying this torch in G-d's Body to reconnect with Israel. However, they may also need more teaching in this area, depending on their level of understanding.

DON'T THINK IT WILL BE EASY

You should also know that any key that can unlock such great power will also have great opposition. Because of this, much wisdom is required in how we should approach our body or other believers in our group with the Israel key. Satan does not want this message getting out. I would actually highly recommend submitting this whole issue to prayer first and release the timing of it to the Holy Spirit, who has the ability to pull the strings of all people's hearts.

The Israel key is like the Word of G-d itself, which is a sharpened double-edged sword (see Heb. 4:12). As hard as we may pray, some will still not receive it, owing to the strongholds and the deceptions of the past that they just will not let go of for one reason or another. Look at the reaction of the elder brother from the prodigal son story once again—for if we do not change our ways here, we will remain separate, which is not the will of G-d.

It is here as a church leader or layperson that we will have to make a decision where we stand in this regard in the hope that all those we share with will eventually come around to our Father's plan to show His glory to the world. But we must not be controlled by fear either. Some in the Body are more intellectual than others; and before the heart can be reached, additional teaching may also be required, which should always be balanced in the Word of G-d.

THE CONEHEADS

A prayer vision we received in our Messiah's House intercessory meeting back in 2006 may help reflect a greater understanding of the spiritual climate that we will be facing with the Father's heart message. I have called this vision "Coneheads." Below are the notes that were taken from that meeting:

Veil-Lifting Meeting: October 27, 2006, 9–11 p.m.

The L-rd led us into stillness when He began to impart a vision through Grant. This vision did not come easily, coming in parts as we continued to give it back to the L-rd for understanding.

I started to see a tornado-like shape, without the point and not as definite, but felt as if it was the Spirit. The wind blew into a congregation full of people sitting in a church-like meeting. The wind blew from the left, and, as it did, I noticed a lot of the people's hair was sucked up into the wind and they became bald. Not everyone lost their hair, but a lot did. This was the first picture.

We discussed the Scriptures in the Word that refer to hair in Corinthians (see 1 Cor. 11:15). A woman's hair is to her glory, and concluded that those who lost their hair were shamed. We also discussed how Adam and Eve felt naked after they sinned in the garden. As we continued to seek the L-rd, there were gaps of time and then the L-rd gave the next picture.

This time the wind blew in front of the congregation, right toward the leadership. There were several leaders, but one lost his hair, and then the wind blew into the choir and only a few people in the choir lost their hair through the sucking wind. Then I saw the piano player lose her hair—it was literally sucked up by the wind, which I no longer saw, but must have been above her.

We went back to the L-rd again, seeking understanding. I then read from Matthew 25:30 about the talent that the servant buried, and the L-rd was angry with him as he had done nothing with it. That which he had would be given to someone else, owing to his unfaithfulness.

We continued to ask the L-rd for further understanding, and the L-rd showed us the next picture. Now the back wall of the congregation had opened and there before me was a long, winding path. The understanding here was that this was the path of the L-rd and G-d's will.

The journey on the path sped up very quickly and continued to get faster.

Then I saw a large Star of David above the path, and then a cross move into the Star of David. It continued until it locked straight into the Star of David, and then great light and power came from the joining and locking of both symbols. Then finally, the words LAST DAYS kept flashing over the path several times.

I also felt that the cross and Star of David coming together was the merging of the Jew and the Gentile into one new spirit. This was the plan of G-d, and the question we asked each other was, "Were the people able to repent and follow G-d's plan?" I then went back into the vision and wanted the L-rd to put back people's hair, but He clearly said, "No!"

The final understanding was that this had to do with G-d's plan in the last days: that Israel was very much intertwined into His plan (see Ezek. 36); and the cross represented the Church, which must come into this plan and which will ultimately bring the revival that the Church hungers for. This is His plan, He is sovereign; and just like we must submit and follow Him for salvation, so we must submit to His authority and plan to reveal Himself to the world through Israel.

After discussing the L-rd's response here, we discussed how this could be the last days when He would separate the wheat from the tares (see Matt. 13:24-30 KJV). However, I must point out that this was a vision of the those in the Church, not in the world, so we need a deeper understanding here; please give it to us, L-rd.

Conclusion: continue to seek Him for more insight and revelation on this vision as there are many parts to it, and we must have full understanding to know how to pray. Please G-d, give this to us and help us see that which we have not yet seen, that we might know Your good and perfect will to do with what You have shown us.

Pray for messengers to be raised up to give this message to the Church, and bring them to repentance before it is too late!

Here are some additional thoughts from one of the brothers (Jon Feinstein) in the meeting:

Comments on the vision:

1. The baldness is itself an image of the separation of the wheat and tares. Once separated, they are not recombined. So, no, G-d would not repent of that separation.

2. The separation of the wheat and tares occurs within the Church, not just between the Church and the world. See the accounts of the last days in which those who are not truly of the Church will be revealed while the elect will remain. You may want to examine the Scriptures to see what causes some to be separated. Deception is definitely one cause. You may find others.

3. I was impressed that the path of the L-rd was out of the back of the church and not the front, where one would expect the leadership to lead the way. I think this is significant and has meaning that His ways are not our ways and He will be where we do

not expect. It may also signify the things we do not esteem are those G-d will select and esteem.

4.   I witness to the acceleration along the path.

We must become accountable to deal responsibly with what He gives us, as this will please Him.

> *Father, in Yeshua's name, we pray You will release this message to Your messengers in the Church and even some who are not yet born again, and fill them with this burden, raise them up to speak this word into Your Church so that it will be received. Let Your conviction be upon it so it will bring people to confession and repentance. Hallelujah. In Jesus's precious name we pray, amen.*

PLEASE CONSIDER THIS MESSAGE CAREFULLY BEFORE IT IS TOO LATE

The vision G-d gave us that day seems to show that not all will receive the Father's heart and support His end-time plan. However, I would not want to be one of those who are found to be against Israel and the Jewish people when our Messiah returns. For in that day, He is coming as a roaring Lion with the fiery judgment and wrath of G-d in His wings for all those who will not accept Him and who are still against Him—even those in His family.

This is one of the main reasons why it is so important now to get this message out, in order that the Church would have the opportunity to come into repentance before it is too late. For His desire is for all of us to be gathered unto Him and that none should be lost. But when that day comes, it will be too late, which was made clear to us in the vision.

THE RECONNECTION MOVEMENT

The veil being lifted over the Church toward Israel is not a sudden or immediate thing, but rather something that takes place more gradually, especially in its infancy. One could equate this lifting to a deep fog in the early morning hours. In the midst of the fog, none can see, but ever so slowly as the mist lifts, more and more can be seen until eventually it is completely clear to everyone. This is the way this crucial message will be received by the Body of Christ during these days.

This awakening and reconnection movement has already begun and there are others who are attempting to trumpet this message to G-d's Body, but much more is obviously needed. This is all the more reason, therefore, why those of us who are now receiving it, really begin to target the Church in our prayers. For we know that judgment begins in the house of the L-rd, and before He can truly begin to affect the darkness and strongholds over Israel, the Church needs to be dealt with first. This is so that we can go forth as a victorious army to trumpet the L-rd's causes in the earth, ushering in His return to establish His dominion throughout the world.

FIRST THE CHURCH, THEN ISRAEL

When the L-rd called us to begin to pray down the veil over the Jewish people in the Westchester area in New York, for the first five years He focused us almost entirely on the Church. He showed us that the Church would help rebirth Israel. He also gave us a deeper understanding about the veil over the Jews, and how the remnant of Israel was mirrored with a remnant of believers who understood G-d's heart for Israel and the Church. So to this day we continue to pray for His Body to awaken to this message so His power can go forth.

For while we must pray for the Jews as well as for all of the Muslims and the nations, the sleeping giant (the Church) must be awakened so that it can take up its intercessory position, its Ezekiel role, and push until our firstborn brethren come forth. Can you imagine when millions of us are praying and pushing for Israel to be reawakened, what will actually take place?

WE SHOULD SUPPORT JEWISH BELIEVERS FIRST

The next issue we need to take a more serious look at is how we properly support the Jewish body from within the Church. Over the centuries and up to this point we have basically told all Jewish believers coming to faith that they must become like the rest of us in the Church, following Gentile Church tradition.

Anything to the contrary has been met with great opposition and an immediate view to Judaizing. Although, as we have discussed already, Judaizing came about as a result of wanting to conform Gentile believers to Jewish practices, not the other way around. But this is not the same issue when it relates to Jewish believers practicing their own heritage.

The Messianic movement evolved and became separate from the existing Church because the new Jewish believers could no longer tolerate the Church's position toward them. Instead, they looked to create an environment that was more suitable to their Jewish roots and heritage, where they could have the freedom to do so without condemnation or disapproval from the Church who did not yet understand their call.

However, I do not believe that all Jewish believers are supposed to come out of the Church and belong to a Messianic congregation, unless the Holy Spirit leads them in that direction. Much is now also beginning to change from within the Church so that the two groups may find ways to coexist, which is very pleasing to the L-rd—that we dwell together in unity.

JEW AND GENTILE IN ONE ACCORD

The first church I was involved with in New York City, led by a Jewish pastor by the name of Richard Glickstein, was good proof of this as he properly understood Israel's calling and blessed separate activities to reach out to the Jewish community. In addition, the Jewish ministry I helped oversee at Times Square Church, under the Wilkerson brothers, really flourished as we focused much of the ministry around the feasts that Jewish people could more easily relate to than if they were in a traditional Church environment; we saw many Jewish people come to faith because of it.

MESSIANIC CONGREGATIONS

There is a most definite place in the world today for the Messianic body, which is also in great need of strengthening. What is really important at this time is that the Gentile part of our family begins to both acknowledge and support our rights to live as Jewish believers. This issue has been highly controversial within the Church, to say the least.

With the Father's heart, I believe we must come to fully accept Jewish believers' rights to coexist alongside Gentile believers; however, this may actually manifest itself in different ways. This may not be easy for us, even as it is in the Church attempting to be tolerant of all of the denominations because of our differences. While I am personally focused on finding this place in the Spirit in the One New Man, this does not mean I discard my association to my Jewish heritage. On the contrary, I look to uphold it. Nor should I only be accepting of those who see things in the Church or Messianic body the way I do.

Being raised as a secular Jew and wanting to reach my own, I look personally to reflect my New Covenant faith in Yeshua in the manner in which secular Jews practice or observe their faith. I do this so they can better relate to me and, as a result, I can be a light to them, hopefully demonstrating that it is quite normal to believe in Yeshua and remain Jewish.

JEWS HAVE LIBERTY TO PRACTICE THE LAW

On the other hand, if I was a Jewish believer called back to reach those more religious amongst my people (approximately 20 percent of Jews living in Israel today are religious), I would have every right to practice the law. Isn't this what the apostle Paul actually did when he returned to Jerusalem (see Acts 21:20-26)?

As Jews in the New Covenant, as long as we do not practice any association to salvation through the law, which is solely in Christ alone, do we not have the liberty as Jews to continue with the law? Didn't the apostles actually operate like this (see Acts 20)?

Let me also state quite clearly: while this is not my personal preference nor my calling, this should not exclude my tolerance of other Jewish believers who may want to practice it. Who am I to question the call and direction of the Holy Spirit in their lives? For I truly believe, like the apostle Paul, that I only know in part and cannot see the full picture until it is properly revealed to me (see 1 Cor. 13:12).

These Scriptures help me understand and tolerate the differences among us. I am just one part of the Body with my perceptions and views, but I will not allow my beliefs to wipe out the love and tolerance I should be showing other brethren who see things differently from me in the Body of Christ, including our Messianic brethren.

Of course, this is quite challenging for us do on a daily basis. In the same way, it is challenging for us to accept and acknowledge that many of our brothers and sisters in Christ belong to different churches, groups, and denominations, having several major differences in their theological positions, especially those in the Catholic and Protestant churches.

LOVE AND TOLERANCE

While we all may have our own individual perspectives and views within our different respective bodies, we must operate more in love and tolerance of one another to help eliminate the divisions that are among us without compromising the Word of G-d. For ultimately, there is a lot more for us to agree upon than not, and especially in this modern day where there is such godlessness in our world. It is as if the increased secularization of the world is naturally bringing us together, which is at least one good thing that can come from the crazy world we are living in.

LITURGICAL TO CHARISMATIC

This is also true of the Messianic body, which also has its ranges in faith and theology. Some are more traditional with liturgy and some are more charismatic, some practice the law and some focus more on the One New Man, and some do both.

While I may not be of the same mind as some of the more religious practices in parts of the Messianic body in their associations with the practicing of the law or even the way in which they see it, I must have tolerance for them. In the New Covenant, is there not liberty in the Spirit through the Word of G-d? Isn't this the heart of the teaching in Romans when discussing different measures of faith among us (see Rom. 14)?

THEY NEED OUR HELP

Relatively speaking, the Messianic movement is very young, especially when it is compared to the Church, which is over 2,000 years old. However, how long did it take the Church to really get established and organized? So to a certain extent, any new movement of G-d takes time. First, it is embryonic and then it is born. It then grows as a child and can even have an adolescent period before it grows up and becomes more mature in its thinking and approach.

This is certainly true of the Messianic movement in its beginnings. Perhaps it was a little unsure of itself in relationship to its continuity of Judaism in the New Covenant; it may have been too focused on Jewish issues rather than the intimacy and spirituality that the New Covenant brings to us from the Holy Spirit. On top of all this, coming from the Jewish side, they were being told that they cannot believe in Yeshua and still be Jewish. I'm not saying that focusing on Jewish practices is wrong, but rather that the Spirit of G-d would be first place in all things in order that our Jewish expression would be Spirit led.

This was true for me personally. When I first met Yeshua in 1984, the Messianic movement was still in its childhood. When I experienced it in those days, I often found it quite spiritually dry. And being so overwhelmed by my newfound relationship with the Holy Spirit when I first believed, I had difficulty with it myself.

At that time, however, more connection was encouraged on Jewish liturgy and practices than with the intimacy and spiritual connection with the Holy Spirit. To me, this was putting the cart before the horse. But as the Messianic movement has started to grow up, some of this is beginning to change, but a lot more is still needed.

MISUNDERSTANDING ON BOTH SIDES

A lot of misunderstanding still exists here on both sides between the Church and the Messianic body. As a result of this misunderstanding, we all need to continue to work hard to bring down the barriers that still exist and allow the Spirit of G-d to heal them. Just look at Jesus's statement in John 17 to confirm this, when He refers to Jew and Gentile in the Body of Christ being brought into complete unity, that the world would know that the Father had sent the Son (see John 17:20-23)!

There is definitely great power to be had by the fulfillment of Jesus's words in these verses. But until we can come to terms with the diversities and callings between us, especially as believers, this will remain a challenge. We are all in need of correction here and may that we have the humility to see it and make the changes that the Father's heart can so easily bring to us. This is so Gentile believers fully embrace Israel's calling to live as Jewish believers, and for Jewish believers to properly connect with their Gentile brethren, fully embracing them as co-heirs in the family of G-d.

NO PLACE TO REST OUR HEADS

The Messianic body is also in great need of being built up. As I have already mentioned in earlier chapters, most Messianic believers find themselves in somewhat of an unwanted space, rejected by their own and not properly understood by the Church either. Because of this, many Messianic congregations often struggle financially to survive. If the Church truly understood how significant they are to the fulfillment of G-d's end-time plan on the earth to reveal His glory, and for Jesus to return and take final dominion on the earth, then shouldn't our focus upon them dramatically change? Shouldn't we be trying to help them and strengthen them in their position in the community so that the Jewish people living around them truly begin to take note of their presence? Shouldn't we be lifting their hands up like Moses was supported in the desert so that the enemy will be defeated around them (see Exod. 17:10-12)?

WE NEED TO BLESS ISRAEL FINANCIALLY

Not only do Jewish believers need our encouragement in the Spirit, but they also need our financial support. Many Messianic groups could profit from the maturity some have in the Church, those walking in the power and intimacy of the Holy Spirit. This is where I learned these things from in my own personal walk with G-d, and I am extremely grateful for it. There is so much for us to learn and glean from each other.

Like the apostle Paul, who was never a burden to anyone, he always looked to raise funds for the local Jerusalem church because he knew how important it was to survive and flourish. He said:

> *Now, however, I am on my way to Jerusalem in the service of the saints there. For Macedonia and Achaia were pleased to make a contribution for the poor among the saints in Jerusalem. They were pleased to do it, and indeed they owe it to them. For if the Gentiles have shared in the Jews' spiritual blessing, they owe it to the Jews to share with them their material blessings* (Romans 15:25-27).

As we draw closer to the L-rd's return and G-d's firstborn are being awakened in this process, we must step in to help strengthen them in any way we can. Where would we be without Israel? It is the Father's heart for us to bestow our blessings upon them and to help His family become reunited in the Spirit of G-d.

If the message of this book has really started to break through and penetrate your heart, or if it has helped to strengthen the position you already have toward Israel's significance in the last days, then it should have a dramatic effect on your pocketbook. Again, I encourage pastors and leaders in this. You cannot make any better spiritual investment in the kingdom of G-d than by supporting some form of Jewish ministry, especially those of the remnant who are already believers. Please pray about supporting this ministry and helping to get this most crucial message out to the Church.

I WILL BLESS THOSE THAT BLESS ISRAEL

To the Jew first and then to the Gentile (see Rom. 1:16)—putting this principle into effect with our finances is of vital significance to the kingdom of G-d, as we are agreeing with the order that G-d has established among us. As a result of this, He will loose additional blessings on you, your family, your business, or your ministry in some form or another, whether materially or spiritually (see Rom. 11:15). May we be like the Roman centurion, who so surprised Jesus (see Matt. 8:5-13) because of his great faith in understanding how the authority of G-d was established in His kingdom, that in positioning ourselves to bless Israel first and applying this kingdom principle, G-d's additional blessings and power will come upon us. You should test it out for yourself and see what the L-rd will do on your behalf.

YOU MAY NOT LIVE AROUND MANY JEWISH PEOPLE

You may not live in an area where Jewish people live; however, you can still commit to prayer and intercession for them as well as beginning to support the Jewish ministries that are being effective around you, especially the ones in Israel that are in desperate need of our help and support. Pray about supporting ministries that are being effective in the most heavily populated Jewish areas, like Israel and the United States as well as some of the countries in Europe, but check them out thoroughly first before you start giving.

PLEASE USE WISDOM

We must come into a renewed understanding of how we financially support Israel. For until the Spirit of G-d has been breathed back into the Jewish people, we cannot always expect them to act righteously in all they do. We shouldn't be romantic about it either, thinking that whomever we send money to is necessarily a good organization.

As we discover our reconnection, let us use great wisdom in how we support the Jewish body. However, shouldn't Jewish believers and Jewish believing ministries be the first port of our call? It is to help strengthen them at their base—here, abroad, and in Israel—so that they may become like a shining beacon on the hill, able to bring life to all of those around them.

You may not be aware of this, but there are some Christian ministries giving money to and supporting Orthodox Jewish groups in Israel, who are actually the ones persecuting Jewish believers and Messianic ministries. We should put a stop to this as soon as we can!

Jews, who already believe in Jesus and who have already crossed over into the New Covenant, are now believers like the rest of us in the Church. They are in great need of our support, both here and in Israel; so please be prayerful and thoroughly research who you end up supporting.

MESSIANIC MINISTRY FROM WITHIN THE CHURCH

There are a number of things the Church can do to become more sensitive to this special calling in its reconnection with Israel and the Jewish people. I would like to point out a few of them for your consideration. But what is right for one group may not necessarily be right for another. So please be prayerful in whatever direction you may choose as I think you will find the Holy Spirit most willing to lead you in this direction; He knows exactly what is right for each group and church.

In addition, if you are not Jewish and sense the call toward Jewish ministry, please have no fear as it all can be learned. It only takes time and experience, like anything else in life, and we couldn't have a better teacher to guide us than G-d's most precious Holy Spirit.

DUAL EXPRESSION

Dan Juster's ministry, Tikkun, recently started a new focus to encourage the establishment of Jewish bodies from within the Church, known as *dual expression*. This is a great idea for churches that are located in more heavily populated Jewish areas. Simply put, dual expression honors both forms of Jewish and Christian heritage, allowing for the establishment of a separate leadership from within the church that focuses more on Jewish identity through the Word of G-d. It is somewhat similar to some Spanish-speaking churches that share space at many local churches today.

This has three distinct advantages in my mind: first, for the Jewish believer to continue their own expression of faith from within the New Covenant and still be part of a larger body; secondly, those Gentile believers in the church who feel called to help and foster Jewish ministry can actually carry out their ministry and still remain a part of the local church; and third, this focus helps foster much greater unity between Jewish and Gentile believers.

This is somewhat similar to the Jewish ministry we ran at Times Square Church, although ours was more evangelistically focused while dual expression allows for two separate bodies practicing on a regular basis.[4]

MESSIAH'S HOUSE: PARACHURCH FOCUS

Similarly, we have positioned the Messiah's House ministry that I manage and oversee in the Westchester area with a parachurch focus. It is as if we are an arm of the local church, assisting them with Jewish ministry. You may also find forming a partnership with a local Messianic ministry or congregation (if there is one in your area) the right way for you to go. The leadership of most Messianic ministries is usually Jewish and, as a result, is already naturally connected to their own roots and heritage, inherently carrying the sensitivities required to bring about this work amongst their own people. This will also create and foster more unity between both groups in your area, which is always healthy as well as pleasing to G-d. However, both groups need to be focused on G-d's heart to unite His Body so they are equally yoked in this work before you move in this direction.

At Messiah's House, we practice all of the main Jewish holidays, and, aside from enjoying G-d's presence in the center of these feasts, we also use them as outreaches for Jewish evangelism as well as further educating Gentile believers in the roots of their faith. We also put on events throughout the year that Jewish people may be interested in, while also bringing in different speakers and teachers who can help Gentile believers better equip themselves for Jewish ministry.

COMMUNITY-LED PRAYER

It is also our desire to help bring the local churches together for prayer meetings, praying over all the issues between Israel and the Church in the last days. In addition, I feel strongly that the Body of Christ is in much greater need of community-led prayer meetings to help break down many of the barriers in the Church, but also to come together more effectively in prayer, which has a much greater chance of helping all of us reach the lost.

It all starts with prayer, and perhaps causing church's to pray for end-time issues may become a good approach in this endeavor. This is one of our main ministry goals after the reconnection: to help establish community prayer and intercession. If we are open in our hearts to what the Spirit of G-d wants to do among us, He will lead us into several new and unique directions in order for us to more effectively reach heaven with our prayers, as well as reaching the lost through evangelism.

LIFESTYLE EVANGELISM

Once a solid foundation has been established in prayer and intercession, its natural outflow will be Spirit-led witness and evangelism. But it should never be the other way around as there is simply too much spiritual opposition in the heavenly realm. Evangelism without prayer often strips it of its real power. Ultimately, however, we cannot reach Jewish people with the Gospel unless we become willing to open our mouths and hearts toward them.

Evangelism is a crucial part of His plan to reach out to the lost and, in these cases, unredeemed Jewish souls. For this reason I have dedicated chapter 11 in this book to evangelism and witness among Jewish people. There is still a good amount to be learned in order to make us more effective in this area.

THE JEWISH FEASTS

There is one other area I want to address before closing this chapter, and that is in regard to the Jewish holidays. There is great significance in the connection of the Jewish holidays between the Old and the New Covenants, which is in need of greater understanding in the Church. In my mind there is no better way to connect with our Jewish friends around us than through the feasts of Israel.

For example, as a Gentile believer in a conversation with their Jewish friends, how do you think they would relate to a person who is explaining to them how they are participating in one of their own Jewish celebrations? *Ummm, isn't this person a Gentile, a Christian; so what are they doing celebrating and sharing in my feasts?* they may be thinking. You see, Christianity has become so foreign for Jewish people that they don't even think there is any connection between our faiths.

But as we think of participating and being more connected to the Jewish calendar in our witness and association with the Jewish people, it will naturally spark greater attention to our intimate relationship with their G-d. In this way, we can better draw them to jealousy as perhaps they may want what we already have, especially if it is presented to them in a Jewish manner—and the feasts can truly help us in this regard.

While we should have complete liberty in the Spirit of G-d in the New Covenant, the Jewish feasts are not just for Israel alone. Gentile believers, who have been grafted into the covenants and promises of Israel, may also choose to participate in the feasts if they want. In the New Covenant, many of these feasts take on more of a fulfilled focus while others are still pointing to Jesus's return. For all the characteristics of G-d are right in the center of each of them, so why shouldn't we celebrate them if we want to?

Yeshua is our Paschal lamb, whom we focus upon during Passover and who has taken away the sins of the world. Christ took two of Passover's main elements and made them eternal through His body and His blood. The Holy Spirit was loosed upon us on Shavuot (Pentecost), where Israel celebrates the giving of the law, which is now written upon our hearts in the New Covenant. Jesus is our *kippur*, meaning our atonement, who took away our sins and whom we celebrate at Yom Kippur. He is also the great light of the world, celebrated at Hanukkah, which makes for a great introduction to the Christmas season. In addition, won't all believers celebrate the Passover and the Feast of Tabernacles in the millennium, so why can't we celebrate them now (see Luke 22:16; Zech. 14:16)?

The Jewish feasts have been established for all of us to focus on and celebrate G-d, and each of them carries a special message that reveals much of G-d's plans to our world. Sadly, up to this point in time, much of this heritage has been lost because of the Church's disconnection to its roots. But as we look now to put this behind us, we will come into a fresh and new understanding of these feasts and how we should relate to them, aside from just wanting to evangelize the Jewish people. The feasts are rich in Christ and full of His presence as we celebrate them.

There are some really good books and teachings written about the Jewish feasts, one in particular by Valerie Moody, called *The Feasts of Adonai*. It clearly breaks down all of the different holidays along with their significance to us. In addition, there is a wonderful teaching by Dr. Renny Mclean on portals of G-d's authority and power through the feasts that I highly recommend as well.[5] G-d has something special waiting for us as we look to reconnect here.

THEOLOGICAL MISUNDERSTANDING REGARDING THE FEASTS

Before I go on further, let me address one of the theological issues here that may be in our way, in the hope that we can gain a better understanding of the apostle Paul's intentions with certain Scriptures, as there is some confusion that needs to be cleared up. It has to do with his writings to the Galatian church, where he challenges them about observing special days and months and seasons and years (see Gal. 4:9-10).

When one first reads this, as I did many years ago, its direction seems to lead us away from any observation of certain dates from the past, especially from the holidays associated with the Mosaic law. Was the apostle Paul really telling us to stay away from certain dates that caused us to focus and remember G-d's faithfulness? Then why is that we still have dates and special occasions in the New Covenant that also cause us to do the same thing, such as Christmas, Lent, Easter, and Pentecost? And why did the apostle Paul himself also celebrate certain Jewish holidays (see 1 Cor. 5:8; 16:8; Acts 20:16)? Or was he raising this issue to the Galatian church because of what they were being challenged with, which most Bible commentaries seem to point out?

Some theologians suggest that the Galatians were being pulled back into the habits of their past and becoming dependent on them once again. However, most other theologians write that the Galatian church was being challenged by certain Judaizers who were attempting to bring them back into the law, which the apostle Paul strongly refuted, being the main reason for his writing.[6] Not that celebrating certain holidays is bad, but if we are becoming dependent on them, that is another issue entirely.

"It is for freedom that Christ has set us free. Stand firm, then, and do not let yourselves be burdened again by a yoke of slavery" (Gal. 5:1). The apostle Paul's teaching is clear to us, that nothing should cause or allow any form of legalism to shipwreck our faith. Do's and don'ts are good but not when they come before G-d. The New Covenant has set us free from ourselves, hopefully bringing us into a personal and intimate relationship with G-d where we are distinctively directed from within by His most precious Holy Spirit through the Word of G-d (Spirit and truth [see John 4:24]), where nothing religious should stand in the way.

Wasn't that the main problem with the Pharisees, that legalism in their faith had taken complete control? We always need to be cautious when it comes to spiritual pride that so easily creeps in. Even when we are attempting to walk in righteousness, we all need to be on the alert because it can affect us all. For there is a subtle balance between the grace and works of G-d that only our continued dependence and humility in Christ can truly find.

FREEDOM IN CHRIST

This freedom that has been granted us in Christ should also provide us the liberty we need for participating in our heritage and our past without getting wrapped up or entangled with it. For we have been grafted into a Jewish vine and, as a result, the feasts are just as much for Gentile believers to celebrate as for Jewish ones. In addition, there is not much legalism to be had from enjoying the feasts when we are celebrating Christ through them.

It was a sad day when the Church looked to move away from its roots and heritage, creating a Gentile faith that was severed from its past. The Father's heart looks to correct that move without any judgment or condemnation, but with the Father's love wooing us to help reconnect to His full family so that they can be won to faith. All this happens while Gentile believers also have the freedom to enjoy the richness of our heritage.

There does not have to be any legalism in participating in a Passover Seder, or a Shavuot service that actually celebrates Pentecost. When experiencing Yom Kippur, we can be reminded of the holiness of our G-d, who sent His one and only Son to tear the veil in two, for both Jew and Gentile to experience G-d for themselves, which is exactly what the New Covenant is all about. For there is something special and extremely dynamic about these High Holy Days, and they are not just for the Jews but also for the rest of us. In addition, what better way to help bring your Jewish friends to faith than through their own feasts?

THE FEASTS THROUGH EVANGELISM

In my first book, *The New Covenant Prophecy,* I tell the story about the ministry I was involved with in the former Soviet Union shortly after the Berlin Wall was brought down in the early 1990s. I tell how we used the Passover story to reeducate the Russian Jews about their heritage, and then preached the Passover's fulfillment in Christ, witnessing thousands upon thousands of Jewish people coming to faith in that part of the world. You can watch the video on my website and see for yourself how powerful it was.[7]

There are no better connections to have between the Old and the New Covenants than through the Jewish feasts. They are G-d designed portraits of Himself and His salvation plan, as well as His plan to return to us as we reconnect to the family of G-d. Please feel free to enjoy them.

FASTING THROUGH THE FEASTS

When I became a believer, I was set free from the old system to embrace the new one; and so for the first few years of my faith, I had no need to fast anymore on Yom Kippur, or even abstain from eating bread during Passover. It was in the Church that I truly learned the principles of fasting and was led to fast for many other issues in my life that needed more of G-d's attention. However, as the L-rd began to lead me back to my people, I started to use the feasts to better relate to the Jewish people. And now I use both the feasts and fasting to intercede for their awakening.

ENDNOTES

1. Judaizers are those of mainly Jewish descent in the first century, who believed all believers in Christ had to also observe the law of Moses to obtain salvation. They were essentially tying together faith in Christ and observance to the law in order to be saved.
2. This is a form of legalism and was talked about on page 50.
3. You can find out more about Art Katz and his ministry at his website: www.artkatzministries.org.

4. For more information on dual expression, please visit the Tikkun Ministry website, www.tikkunministries.org.

5. "Portals through the Feasts: Discerning Portals," available on YouTube.

6. H. D. M. Spence, *The Pulpit Commentary of Galatians*, (188-191); David H. Stern, *Jewish New Testament Commentary*, (557-558).

7. For more information about this, please visit my website, www.reconnectingministires.org.

10

Prayer and Intercession

Prayer does not fit us for the greatest work; prayer is the greatest work. —Oswald Chambers

Personally in Touch

In my understanding, personal prayer is a must for any New Covenant relationship with G-d. In Jeremiah's prophecy about the New Covenant, an intimacy is promised to each of us in the Gospel where we would know G-d for ourselves. For it is here, in personal prayer and relationship, that we begin to connect with the Spirit of G-d now living inside us, which is essential for us to develop in strengthening and building our faith (see Jer. 31:34).

Personally speaking, it is in this place that I receive my guidance and direction, and sometimes discipline and correction if I have somehow gotten off the path. It is here, after I have connected with G-d, that I feel His love and His peace and can tap into His strength and will for my life, usually intertwined with His Word that I so greatly need for my day. It is that great balance of Spirit and truth (Word) that Jesus spoke of when referring to the New Covenant (see John 4:23-24).

The fullness and intimacy of the New Covenant cannot be had through our priests and pastors alone or without developing a prayer life with G-d, for we now worship G-d in Spirit and truth, which no one building can completely hold. Reconnection is not just about Israel and the Church coming together, but for those of us who do not yet have this intimacy, we must first connect with G-d through the Spirit so that we will ultimately know Him for ourselves. It cannot come only through a religious system, which was one of the mistakes of the Jewish people who left their spiritual guidance to their priesthood, but rather through a circumcision of the heart where our spirits have been reborn and set free from the curse of sin and death that is upon humankind. For Christ did not come to condemn the world, but rather to save it from its sins (see John 3:16).

WHERE TWO OR MORE ARE GATHERED

This chapter however is not focused on personal prayer, but rather the prayer gatherings where two or more are present, causing G-d to deeply move in our midst. The way G-d moves in our midst when we pray with others is quite different to the way He will move when we are on our own with Him (see Matt. 18:20). Most people refer to this type of prayer as *corporate prayer* or *intercession.*

Both are good and necessary, but G-d cannot fully bless lone rangers who tend to avoid connecting with the Body, which is not His perfect will. The Spirit of G-d will work differently among us, doing things in a group that He will not do with us on our own, and vice versa. If you are a believer and follower of G-d, I would strongly encourage you to get into a prayer group, especially one focused on Israel and the end times. For it is here that the battle will be fought and won; and it is here that you will learn to draw closer to G-d's heart.

PRAYER MAKES ALL THE DIFFERENCE

It was not long into my walk with the L-rd that He taught me the significance of prayer and intercession. As a young man attempting to bring the Gospel to the streets of the East Village of New York City, as well as beginning to share my faith with my own people, I quickly encountered all types and forms of resistance to Jesus. It deepened the need for prayer in my life to help me break through. In addition, I was also exposed to some great teachers of the faith who knew that prayer made all of the difference in the world.

For example, Billy Graham, who is perhaps the greatest evangelist of the 20th century, could almost immediately recognize after entering a new city or town where he was about to preach the Gospel, if the outreach had been bathed in prayer or not. He often commented how different it was for him to speak if there had been a lot of prayer, as if the spiritual skies had become more open and he could feel his gift flowing much more powerfully as the Spirit of G-d moved through him.

These teachings had a great impact on me and truly emphasized the significance of prayer and intercession. So it wasn't long before in my own experience with the L-rd that I started to apply these principles, which had a dramatic effect on my life. I quickly learned that true success in ministry was a result of the effectiveness of prayer and intercession that preceded any work I was involved in. After that time, I never looked to be involved in any type of spiritual work until it had first been bathed in prayer and I had a release from the Holy Spirit to move into it. As for sure, G-d's timing is not always the same as ours (see John 16:13).

It was not long after I joined Times Square Church in New York City that I began to teach on prayer and intercession. In addition, Messiah's House was started as a prayer meeting—we prayed for five years before anything else transpired. The works we are now involved in came as a result of the direction of the Holy Spirit through prayer and intercession.

PRAYER AND INTERCESSION

Prayer and intercession are absolutely crucial to our role in reconnecting the Church with Israel. It is our prayers that not only lay the foundations for effective ministry, but also empower the heavens to break through the natural realms and that make us effective. *It is from prayer and intercession that all of our good works should come, never being the other way around.*

It is prayer and intercession that will change the hearts of those in the Church toward Israel and remove the veil that still exists between us. It will release the mercy and love of G-d, the evangelism required, and the power of G-d unto G-d's salvation and Jesus's return. It is prayer and intercession that will lift the veil over Israel, bringing the children of Israel into their true destiny. Prayer and intercession will also affect the veil over Islam to release G-d's children from that stronghold.

It goes without saying that it is G-d's Spirit and His heavenly hosts who will move to make these things happen. I believe, it is prayer and intercession through us that causes and empowers them to move; therefore, we cannot discount their significance to the kingdom of heaven upon the earth along with our role and agreement in the process.

Nearly every great revival has been preceded by prayer, not only from the leadership but from the Body as well. English preacher Sidlow Baxter, when he was 85 years of age, said:

I have pastored only three churches in my more than sixty years of ministry. We had revival in every one. And not one of them came as a result of my preaching. They came as a result of the membership entering into a covenant to pray until revival came. And it came every time.[1]

And Frank Beardsley said, "Prayer is the fountain from which revival springs. The key to revival in every age is prayer. It is possible to have revivals without preaching, without churches and without ministers, but without prayer a genuine revival is impossible."[2]

PRAYER AND INTERCESSION: DISTINCTIVE ROLES

Prayer is like the fuel that runs the car and keeps the engine going. It is like putting money in the bank that keeps the business moving forward. But intercession can hit targets and break down doors. Both are needed and both serve their unique purposes within the Body of Christ. Prayers are like petitions or guided requests going up to the Father, whereas intercession are prayers that He is guiding through us—there is a difference between the two.

Some say that prayer or intercession is not their gift and there are definitely those in the Body who have a deeper calling in this place. But I believe we are all called to prayer, and, in my humble experience, any believer who wants to learn to pray and intercede can. All G-d needs is a willing heart and a teachable spirit while remaining humble along the way.

THE ENEMY'S DEVICES

The enemy is always looking to throw in his wrenches to stop this power from flowing and to stop us from praying; but we must not be ignorant of the enemy's devices (see 2 Cor. 2:11). All the power we ever need comes through prayer!

There are some wonderful books on prayer that we would do well to read. I would recommend you read the ones that your church group is most comfortable and familiar with, equipping you to flow better with those whom you are praying with, which can make a major difference.

Those currently in the Body from a Charismatic and Pentecostal background have tended to be more comfortable than others when moving from prayer into intercession, as moving in the gifts of the Holy Spirit can really help in this regard (see 1 Cor. 12). However, we do not have to speak in tongues to intercede, although tongues can oftentimes help.

I have found our most loving G-d to be a great respecter of persons, along with our different beliefs and interpretations in this regard, whether we believe in tongues or not, and how we flow in the gifts of the Holy Spirit. But we should not allow our theology to interfere in this area by restricting us from moving deeper into the Spirit in prayer and intercession, which is definitely G-d's desire for all of us.

The world is getting darker and the attacks against us in the Body are definitely on the increase. It seems as if evil and righteousness must come into their fullness before the harvest comes in (see Matt. 13:24-30). That's why we must not fight these battles in the flesh alone; otherwise, we will lose. This is all the more reason we must fight these battles with heavenly weapons; that way the enemy is no match for us, and we can have victory over him. Satan wants us in the flesh, where he can have power over us; however, if we focus the battle in prayer and intercession, we have power over him. The apostle Paul wrote:

> *For though we live in the world, we do not wage war as*
> *the world does. The weapons we fight with are not the*

weapons of the world. On the contrary, they have divine power to demolish strongholds. We demolish arguments and every pretension that sets itself up against the knowledge of G-d, and we take captive every thought to make it obedient to Christ (2 Corinthians 10:3-5).

UNITY IS KEY

The key element of effective and fervent prayer in any group is unity. Getting comfortable with the people you pray with is essential. Every prayer group has its own characteristics as every group is full of different people, resulting in different gifts being represented. It is a good thing to learn and appreciate each other's gifts and give the people the freedom and space to move in them, even when they make mistakes, because we learn in the New Covenant through trial and error. Let us fully allow the Holy Spirit to be our teacher in such circumstances.

In addition, we may not agree on everything theologically with those whom we are praying with. However, in this case, it is important to respect one another's perspectives and agree to disagree. Assuming we are not talking about the fundamentals of our faith, many of us have different views and perspectives on certain doctrines in the Word.

What I have come to learn is that while G-d definitely knows the truth, He can tolerate our different viewpoints on some of these issues without it breaking the fellowship and love that we should have for one another. Let's not forget that at best we only see through a glass dimly (see 1 Cor. 13:12). It is only when He comes that we will see and understand the fullness of His Word in every respect. That is why up until that point, it is good to be able to respect each other's viewpoints and see how it will ultimately play out. It is actually rather freeing when we look at it in this manner, because it enables us to be more tolerant of one another, which is extremely vital to the kingdom in these days. This is why Jesus said, *"By this all men will know that you are My disciples, if you love one another"* (John 13:35).

Next to love what counts to the Spirit of G-d in prayer is the element of faith and agreement amongst us that is necessary for Him to move in our midst. It is also necessary for Him to lead us into heavenly places that can alter and affect the natural ones. But without our acceptance of each other's viewpoints, we empower the enemy's divide; and we must not be ignorant to his schemes to divide us (see 2 Cor. 2:11).

PRAYING BY FAITH

Whether we are praying or interceding, one thing is for sure: we must begin to see Israel and the Jewish people from a position of faith. We are not to see them as they are currently, but what they will become when the Spirit of G-d is breathed into them, as the Word of G-d foretells. We must see them spiritually restored, back in their priestly role, dwelling in the land with Yeshua sitting on His throne running the kingdom of G-d with the rest of us in the Church. This is where we are now heading and, indeed, where we need to go with our prayers.

This also applies to how we currently see the resistance in the Church as well as every other obstacle that stands in the way of G-d's plan for the end times and His return. For example, while we may need to accept the current spiritual condition of the Jews and the Muslims in the natural so we can still love them, we should never accept it in the Spirit. Our prayers should be pressing on into the changes we know G-d needs to bring about through us. That is what faith is all about: *"Now faith is being sure of what we hope for and certain of what we do not see"* (Heb. 11:1).

My experience with the awakening of the Russian Jews to faith back in the 1990s really helped me in this regard as I witnessed the very fulfillment of prophecy before my eyes (see Jer. 16:14-15).[3] I knew then that it was only a question of time when the rest of us (Jews) would awaken from our sleep.

We already know the end of the story and how it all falls into place, so the only question is that of His timing. G-d *will* heal the divide and separation that currently exists in the Church toward Israel, for we are His conduits to help rebirth them. But He needs our prayers and intercession to help bring these changes about. He *will* lift the veil from the Jewish people, but He will not do it by Himself; so our prayers are vital in the process.

In addition, the position we take in faith toward the Word of G-d and our agreement with it is absolutely crucial to bring these changes about. There are already streams of prayer flowing in this regard. But the heavenlies are in need of torrents to bring this baby forth, torrents that only His Church can provide as His intercessor. And the same goes for the veil over Islam. The apostle John reminds us, however, *"Greater is He that is in you, than he that is in the world"* (1 John 4:4 KJV).

G-d has given us all we need to help bring these things to pass. But we must respond to the call to pray and intercede to release our faith, so that His Spirit can guide us into heavenly places to target the strongholds of the enemy and crush the opposition. For we have divine power and authority, and if we are willing to move into these places for His kingdom purposes, He will give us both the guidance and the protection necessary to get the job done.

INTERCESSION CAN BE LEARNED

Many of us know how to pray, but fewer of us have learned how to intercede. Perhaps the greatest difference in my mind between prayer and intercession is who is leading it. For while many of our prayers can be Spirit led, in intercession we do not look to pray until His presence and leading are evident.

Intercession can be equated to a fine orchestra—the Holy Spirit being the conductor and we the instruments, being gently guided into His perfect harmonies. The art of intercession has to be learned, which is often through trial and error as we learn to sharpen our spiritual antennas in hearing His voice and guidance from within. However, He willingly gives it to any who may be eager to learn.

INTERCESSION MUST BE SPIRIT LED

In intercession, we look to get out of His way so He can lead and guide us into His prayer purposes. In this way, we also have His power and guidance to effect the change He is looking to bring about. As a caution, we should not move without it because we are no match for the devil and his strongholds in our own strength.

I *never* go up against a stronghold in prayer unless I sense His leading first, in which case I am under the shadow and the shelter of His wings, being protected by Him. Please keep in mind that just with the Jews and Muslims alone, the spiritual forces aligned against the kingdom are huge, and we know from Scripture that there are spiritual battles in the heavenlies that have to be fought and won. In intercession, He can take us into those places, and, with our faith and prayer, He can use us to defeat them and help bring them down. Praying in tongues in this place can make a major difference as the Spirit is praying through us and we are free to enter warfare through the leading of the Holy Spirit.

INTERCESSION CAN HAVE A MAJOR IMPACT

Our prayers provide strength to the spiritual and angelic forces that take on these fights. It is our intercession, however, that can help bring them completely down. And as I have already stated, both are of great significance in the kingdom of G-d.

It is also through intercession that we can receive additional insights and revelations as to G-d's direction and purposes in a matter that we may not necessarily receive in prayer alone. As a result, we must learn to move more effectively in the intercessory realm to help the L-rd better achieve His plans and purposes in this area.

When I look back at all that we accomplished with our tiny group—in bringing the Gospel to thousands of Russian Jews through the Abraham's Promise ministry I was involved with—it was always prayer and intercession that made the difference. We fasted, prayed, and interceded weekly for months and months prior to our actual visits to the land; it was actually in our little prayer and intercessory meetings that the battles were fought and won and the spiritual skies were cleared. We prayed so much beforehand that when we actually went into the land, all we needed to do was harvest the work.

INTERCESSION THROUGH THE EZEKIEL SPIRIT

Similarly, G-d is calling us in the Church into the place of intercession, to be the Ezekiel of G-d and to breathe the breath of G-d back into His children who do not even want to receive Him. It is a momentous task that only can be achieved through His guidance, but also our willingness to step into this role. Remember the story of Joshua's birth, how Donna was in labor and pain to bring him forth? Our fight and struggle will be similar in order for these things to take place.

Do not be intimidated by intercession, just be open to His leading and guidance and He will show you and your group the way through it. I can tell you from personal experience that when He moves through you, it is actually one of the most exciting things that you can do.

Intercession can often be experienced in the midst of prayer. So as you gather to pray for Israel, allow Him to take the lead by His Holy Spirit and you may be quite surprised by the outcome.

INTERCESSION NOTES

The following are some helpful guidelines from my own experience of intercession and prayer, and the difference between the two. To help distinguish between prayer and intercession, I often use the term *pure intercession* as opposed to just intercessory prayer.

Pure intercession can take on a different focus than a regular prayer meeting. In a traditional prayer meeting, we all take turns lifting up our individual requests to the L-rd, which is most acceptable for this type of prayer format. And it is important to note that intercession can be experienced through traditional prayer.

LET THE SPIRIT LEAD

However, in pure intercession our focus shifts. Although prayer and intercessory meetings can both cover the same topics, in pure intercession we take on a different position by allowing the Holy Spirit to guide our prayers. In this way, we truly want to give control of the meeting over to the L-rd, and through it He begins to teach us how to move more effectively in this area by further developing our spiritual senses from within.

Before we begin a pure intercession prayer group, we must have agreement between the people we are praying with and the direction we now want to move into with more of the Holy Spirit's leading and guidance. In addition, how we move in the Spirit together along with our different giftings should be discussed openly. It is important in this type of prayer group that we are all comfortable with each other and that we are all working together at a certain level of understanding in the Spirit.

Listening, sensing, and *seeing* are just a few of the spiritual muscles He desires to develop within each one of us for intercessory purposes so that He may lead us into deeper places in His Spirit. It is as if we defer both our prayer burdens and timing to His guidance and do not move with it until we sense a release to do so. I often think of developing a spiritual antenna here that helps me visualize His sensitivity from within my spirit.

In pure intercession meetings, we also do not switch praying for subjects until we sense a completion; so much so that if our current prayer burden does not fit within the current context, then the timing of it is not right. G-d may have given it to us to move the group on at a later time in the meeting or after the current topic is completed. So again, deferring back to His guidance and timing is vital in how we move from prayer to prayer and issue to issue in pure intercession.

The best way to learn is through trial and error, because as we further develop these senses, we will know when it feels right or wrong. And we could not have any better teacher than the Holy Spirit, who helps guide us into all truth from within.

If we are open to it, the gifts of the Holy Spirit can also play a key role in how the L-rd can move among us in pure intercession. Some see things in the Spirit known as visions, and often the L-rd will give the group a picture that He wants them to focus on. In addition, sometimes the pictures come in parts; He takes pleasure in speaking to us in this manner as He enjoys us searching and looking for the hidden meaning that He may want to impart. Similarly, some prophesy, and He can give words of direction and/or encouragement to lead the group in a particular direction. He also often moves through His holy Word and may lead each of us to certain Scriptures that confirm His heart and direction for the meeting. Sometimes He moves through silence while at other times He wages war.

The key in pure intercession is to allow Him to take control and go wherever He may want to lead. In every intercessory prayer group I have been involved with, He often chooses to minister to each of us in the group who may be in need at the time. He is always interested in the hearts of the intercessor because sometimes our personal lives can play significant roles in the intercession itself, which is perfectly fine.

WE WERE PRAYING FOR ISRAEL—G-D WAS PRAYING FOR HIS CHURCH

When we first received the call at Messiah's House to pray down the veil over the Jewish people in our area, for the first several years G-d focused us mainly upon the Church. In time, this became challenging for some in our group as they wanted to pray for the Jewish people and for Israel. But every time we met, the L-rd began to impart more and more of His purposes to us through the use of the Church to rebirth Israel in the Spirit, which ultimately affects the ones He has called us to pray for.

His ways are not our ways and His purposes are not our purposes. So the key with intercession is to be obedient to His leading, wherever He may take us, even if it seems abnormal. An obedient soldier always fully obeys the commands of His superior officer, and so it is with the guidance and leading of His Spirit in pure intercession. Sometimes He will even test us in this regard to know if He has our trust or not.

ENTERING IN

In order to enter into pure intercession, we must first be able to enter into His presence so we can sense His leading. Again, the characteristics of your group are important here and exactly what you are comfortable with in your faith. Most enter into worship

256

to find this place, others move in silence, some move into tongues, while still others move through all of them. The key, however, is to sufficiently lift Him up so that His presence will come into our midst. Directional prayer should not start until we sense His presence and leading.

COME PREPARED

We need to be spiritually ready before we start in pure intercession. Any problems from the day, struggles, or sins should be confessed privately or to one another (whatever is most comfortable) so we are ready to be used by Him. Faith is obviously an important operative in our prayers, and it is okay if we don't yet have it in a particular area of prayer, in which case we should ask Him to release it to us so we can move into agreement with Him.

BE COMFORTABLE WITH EACH OTHER

We also need to be comfortable with each other so that we can learn from Him. It is always good to review and discuss how the meeting went afterward in order to be more effective the next time we meet. Humility and a teachable spirit go a long way in learning to intercede, and I always encourage openness.

The truth is that we can all make mistakes in intercession, just like in an orchestra. The sound will still be heard and felt when it is out of sync, but it is here that we learn to improve. So don't be oversensitive or defensive when something goes wrong or you feel like you missed the mark. The truth is that from time to time we all do. We only need to learn from it and remember there is no condemnation in our L-rd.

BE EXPECTANT WITH UNITY

Once we have hopefully entered into His presence, expect the L-rd to move and for His guidance to come. Unity of the people in the group is another vital ingredient to effective intercessory prayer meetings.

The enemy will often try to attack in this area in order to reduce the group's effectiveness, and this should not surprise us. When we start to get closer to the things of G-d, we can always expect resistance. It is actually a good sign. Differences in theology and/or any misunderstandings can interfere or interrupt with the flow of the Spirit. Sometimes we may need to talk things through so that any disagreements are brought into the light, where members of our group can clear the air.

We should always look to protect the unity of the group, as the slightest division can disrupt His purposes. This is one of the main reasons why I always keep pure intercessory prayer meetings closed. It is not as if we want to turn away new people from our group, but when our group starts to move on a certain spiritual plain, the unity needs to be protected. So when inviting new people into the group, let them first be prayerful as to its commitment and, secondly, make sure they are properly schooled in how you are moving in the Spirit so that when they join they can flow with you.

Otherwise, if they are not properly prepared, they can easily bring the level down that your group is already moving in. This can be a setback if it is not addressed properly in the first place with effective teaching and training through discussion. Trust me here: I have learned through my own experiences.

If new people joining the group have not been prepared or taught your group's regular disciplines, how would they know to move in them? This alone can disrupt the flow of the meeting; so good training and communication are healthy for any pure intercessory prayer group.

COMMITMENT AND DISCIPLINE

Commitment to a regular time is important with all prayer, but especially with pure intercession. The Holy Spirit will work His majestic guidance through those people who regularly attend the meeting and, more importantly, through each person's gifts in the Holy Spirit. So when someone is missing or in and out, it can affect the group.

It is important when starting an intercessory group to let people know this and that a commitment of their time is required, whenever you choose to meet. I have always found each intercessory group that I have been involved in to take its shape and characteristics through the different people who attend the meeting. This makes perfect sense considering we are all part of a Body with different gifts. It is also important to be punctual and to start and end the meeting together because this helps to strengthen the unity.

Of course, it goes without saying that our G-d can always work around these issues and interruptions, so we should have the same flexibility with however the circumstances may change. But consistency and discipline can definitely help any group that is looking to intercede.

SELF-CONTROL

Remember that the spirits of the prophets are subject to the control of the prophets (see 1 Cor. 14:32). In other words, we have control of ourselves as well as our gifts. While we will have the floor as the Spirit leads us, we should be conscious that others might want to add to the issue and topic of prayer, so we cannot monopolize the time. Some of the more experienced intercessors, who are completely comfortable with His guidance and leading, can have this challenge and can go on for far too long. This can prevent the strings or the percussion from adding to the same melody, so we need to be sensitive in this area.

I often find the best way to address this personally is to yield while in the midst of a prayer topic in order to allow others to add to it if they are so led. If no one picks it up, then I feel free to go back to it; or if they do and I still feel I have something to add, I can easily pick it up after that person has finished. We should not be moving on from a topic until it is completed, so there will always be time to pursue what G-d is laying on our hearts.

When reading from Scripture, we shouldn't read long sections of text, but rather the ones that more specifically tie into the subject at hand unless the whole text is relevant. It is always a good idea to scan the Scripture first so we know what sections to read beforehand. The more we are conscious of the flow and leading of the Holy Spirit, the more effective we become for Him and His purposes.

I also like to think of a pure intercessory group like the grip of G-d's sword, with the Holy Spirit's hand firmly in control of the weapon, which, of course, can take time in any group to develop. But the more refined we become for Him, the more effectively He can use us and target us for His purposes.

For a moment, just think of the millions upon millions of well-trained prayer and intercessory teams from all over the world, from all types of churches, pounding the heavenlies in order for His end-time plans to manifest. *This is our goal and aim in this regard: to stand in the gap as His Church, and to pray and intercede that Israel would be born and that His kingdom would come upon the earth.* What a mighty call we have!

FAITH

Praying in faith is vital to G-d as I have already mentioned above. However, there are also positions of faith that can be attained in intercession that we especially need for Israel and the end times. We know far less about this kind of faith. But I believe G-d wants to impart more of it to us, as it is this type of faith that can truly move mountains and is a weapon in the heavenlies.

> *Father, we ask You to impart more of Your supernatural faith into our spirits and into our meetings, that we can come into agreement with You in special places of Your leading and guidance. In Jesus's special name we pray, amen.*

AGREEMENT

It is important to agree with what is going on and what is being prayed in the meeting. If the L-rd is leading, then He is also working through the others in the group; we should agree and support what is being prayed and get behind it, even while the L-rd might be showing us something else. Again, this is all part of the unity that is essential for effective, fervent prayer.

WARFARE

Warfare can often be in tongues, and comes and goes in waves (it can also be in whatever natural language you may speak). When one member of the group leads off in this area and we sense it, go with them, for the agreement is vital to how the L-rd will lead us in this area. It is important to loose our faith in agreement.

Sometimes it feels like we are transported in our spirit into the heavenly realm as in a military charge, like we were on the front lines and the commanding officer has launched an attack. Would we let them go on their own? No, we would be right by their side. And this is where we need to be as He leads us in warfare, strongly supporting those in our group who may have received this prayer burden and direction, which will also fall upon us as we come into agreement with it.

It is this type of intercession G-d uses to crush demons and break down strongholds in the heavenly realms. In this way, the spiritual air can be cleansed to make way for the L-rd's work, which is extremely exciting. As a caution, however, one never wants to go into spiritual warfare in our own strength, and we should use wisdom here as we are no match for the enemy by ourselves.

We must be led by the Holy Spirit into these types of spiritual prayer battles, in which case we will have His covering and protection when we do: *"Because greater is He who is in you, than he that is in world,"* so we should not be afraid (1 John 4:4 KJV). Similarly, one never wants to finish this type of prayer until we sense His direction and calm.

SEAL THE WORK

When praying in warfare, after the victory, it often feels like spiritual land has been taken, which is why we always pray and ask the L-rd to seal the work so that the enemy cannot return to it. We also want to pray for His protection upon our families and ourselves, praying protecting prayers when we come out of this place. It is wise to do so that we will be properly covered.

CHRIST'S CHARACTER

While G-d is interested in using us to intercede with Him, He is always interested in those who are interceding. So be open to His personal ministry in this regard, and know that as you have offered yourself in this place, He may also use parts of your life and walk to help you further identify with those you are standing in the gap for. While none of us are perfect, as we draw closer to Him in prayer and intercession we always want to develop more of His character within our lives, especially as we move in the gifts of the Holy Spirit. These, of course, are more for His service than anything else, and it is healthy to have a sober attitude in this regard.

TAKE GOOD NOTES

Good note taking is extremely important in pure intercession, otherwise we too easily forget what G-d may have shown or told us in the future. Usually, there is always someone in the group who has a particular gift for this we may want to encourage. It is good to capture His direction through properly recording what the Spirit shows through the Word, through visions, and/or through prophetic words.

REVIEW AT THE END OF THE MEETING

It is important to review the meeting to understand and agree what has gone on and what the L-rd has done in your midst—talk about it with your group. At the end, you always want to take a step back and see how the conductor led and guided the meeting. Your achievements, the ground gained, words given, etc., as well as failures and missed opportunities can be discussed. But be sensitive when sharing any of the negative issues. You may be better off just praying them through rather than bringing them up. So make sure to listen to the L-rd during this time.

DON'T BE AFRAID TO PRAY FOR G-D'S WILL

Even if it is difficult for us to fathom or wish on others, G-d uses all things for the good of those who love Him and are called according to His purpose (see Rom. 8:28). Shakings will come, especially in these last days, and we must pray G-d's will through them, that as the world comes into judgment, we would continue to petition Him to loose His mercy from within it.

THE QUIETER ONES

One final note to those of you who will be interceding regarding those who are quieter than others: while listening is good, if you are going to be a part of a pure intercessory prayer group, you must learn to step out when you are supposed to so that the Spirit's flow does not get missed through you. Be bold when you need to be, and if you need help in this area, please pray and ask G-d to help you as you could turn out to be a major blessing to the group as well as to the kingdom of G-d.

If we do not step out when we are supposed to pray, the harmony in the orchestra can be affected; this principle applies to every one of us. All of our battles in the kingdom are fought and won on our knees, and the service of prayer in the kingdom is of the highest calling, with great spiritual blessings and rewards to follow.

PRAYER AND INTERCESSORY TOPICS

To help with prayer and intercessory topics, I have made a list of the following. But please note that this list is not exhaustive by any means. Please be open to the many more items and issues the Holy Spirit will give to you as you seek Him and look to stand in the gap for the Church, Israel, and the world in the end days. I feel confident that you will be pleasantly surprised.

TOPICS ON ISRAEL AND THE CHURCH FOR INTERCESSORY PRAYER

- Understanding G-d's plan through Israel and the Church

- G-d's covenants to Israel and the Church

- The roles of the Church and the roles of Israel

- Receiving and loosing the Father's heart for His lost son and the family of G-d

- Releasing the mercy of G-d

- Strengthening the Ruths and Corneliuses

- The darkness of the Church toward the Jewish people

- The Church's disconnection from their roots

- Anti-Semitism

- Cleansing the bloodline through generational anti-Semitism

- Confession, renunciation, and repentance

- Lifting the veil over the Church

- Pastors and church leadership receiving this revelation

- The Church's reconnection

- The Messianic body's disconnection

- The Messianic body's reconnection

- Holy Spirit led reconnection

- One New Man

- To the Jew first and then the Gentile; kingdom positioning

- The Ezekiel of G-d

- Strengthening and blessing the remnant of Jewish believers

- Celebrating the feasts of Israel

- Drawing the Jews to jealousy

- Adjusting and balancing our theology

- The spreading of this teaching to ignite the Church in Jerusalem, Judea, Samaria, and to the ends of the earth

- Prayer and intercessory groups everywhere, praying for the Church, Israel, and the world

- G-d can cause that which is evil to work good

- Lifting the veil over the Jews

- Orthodox Jews

- Secular Jews

- Lifting the veil over the Muslims

- Lifting the veil over the rest of the world

- The land of Israel

- G-d's protection over the land

- The Jewish people in the land

- The Jewish people in the Diaspora

- Lifestyle Jewish evangelism

- How to share the New Covenant with Jewish people

- Spirit-led evangelism

- G-d's love, patience, and timing

- The Holy Spirit's power to be loosed

To close this chapter, I would like to leave you with a vision and word that one of the members from the Messiah's House intercessory prayer group had recently.

> As we were standing in the gap for Israel and the Middle East, the Holy Spirit said to me in a vision, "Look and see." When I looked, I saw an immense camp; and in the middle, there was a little tent with a little light on top. The L-rd said, "The little tent is Israel." Suddenly, darkness covered the camp, but I could still see the little tent for there was a light right on top. The darkness turned into a huge army, soldiers armed with all kinds of weapons, ammunitions, etc.
>
> Next, I saw an enormous white canopy covering the camp. On the canopy there was a multitude dressed in white. I could hear their voices crying out for mercy, praising and exalting G-d's name. And I saw the armies going toward Israel—Israel looked so tiny, defenseless, and forsaken. As the armies were getting closer and closer, I saw them pull back all at once. They tried to attack Israel again and again, but every time they tried, they were pulled back. I was astounded, and heard the voice of the L-rd saying, "The prayers of the saints have been heard in the heavens; it is the prayers of the saints that are keeping and protecting Israel." I kept hearing

an echo, "The prayers of the saints...the prayers of the saints..."[4]

G-d wants to powerfully use us in pure intercession for the Church's reconnection to Israel.

ENDNOTES

1. Sidlow Baxter quote from *Revival and Prayer* by Louis Bartet.
2. Frank Beardsley quote from *Revival and Prayer* by Louis Bartet.
3. See chapter 18 of my first book, *The New Covenant Prophecy*.
4. This word is from Pastor Ruth Diaz, Harvest Time Church, Greenwich, Connecticut.

11

LIFESTYLE JEWISH EVANGELISM

Many who read this book may not even know a Jewish person, considering that there are only approximately 18 million Jews and 7 billion Gentiles in the world. You may be surprised to find out that there are Jewish people in almost every nation throughout the world, which is actually a fulfillment of a prophecy from the Torah (see Deut. 28:64).[1]

Most Jewish people are usually found in the more cosmopolitan areas of Western culture and obviously in Israel, which now has the greatest Jewish population in the world—close to 6 million, while the United States is not very far behind that number. It is also fair to state that while we are all called to pray and help in this spiritual rebirth for the Jewish people, which will have its effects on us all in one way or another, those of us who live in places and countries where there are greater Jewish populations have an additional responsibility to reach out toward our Jewish brethren.

ALL THINGS TO ALL PEOPLE

The apostle Paul became all things to all people so that he might win some of them to the faith. This was his evangelism focus,

thereby giving us more information on how we should position ourselves to reach various groups of people around the world:

> *Though I am free and belong to no man, I make myself a*
> *slave to everyone, to win as many as possible. To the Jews*
> *I became like a Jew, to win the Jews. To those under the*
> *law I became like one under the law (though I myself am*
> *not under the law), so as to win those under the law. To*
> *those not having the law I became like one not having*
> *the law (though I am not free from G-d's law but am*
> *under Christ's law), so as to win those not having the*
> *law. To the weak I became weak, to win the weak. I*
> *have become all things to all men so that by all possible*
> *means I might save some. I do all this for the sake of the*
> *gospel, that I may share in its blessings* (1 Corinthians
> 9:19-23).

The main point here is that the apostle Paul did whatever he
needed to do in order for the Gospel to be promoted. Many mis-
sionaries could better relate to this teaching than most of us, as the
more successful ones have found ways to adjust and compensate for
the different cultures that G-d had called them to. However, this
Scripture can also apply to all of us as we try to reach out to the
different people groups around us, always learning to be sensitive to
their cultures.

As my family felt G-d's leading to refocus on our own people as
Jews, we naturally started to reflect much more of the secular Jewish culture and traditions we were raised with so that those people
around us could better relate to us as Jews. As a Jew it was natural
for the apostle Paul to make this transition just as it would be for all
other Jewish believers.

But the point here for those of us who are from a Gentile background, is not necessarily that we should become like Jews, because

we are not, but rather as believers in a Jewish G-d we reflect our beliefs through their vine, their covenants, and their heritage. And we do this in a way that is more sensitive to their background, in a way that may help them more easily connect with their own G-d.

The lady who brought me to faith never even mentioned the New Testament and always presented the Gospel to me in a Jewish manner, in a way that I could better relate to. This shouldn't be too difficult to do as everything we now follow and believe in has its origins with the firstborn. So why shouldn't we relate to the Gospel in a Jewish manner when we are sharing it with Jewish people? Because, in reality, it belongs to them anyway. For wasn't it the apostle Paul's main point here, that we would break down the barriers that exist between us that prevent the Gospel from going forth? I think that is exactly what he was conveying.

As more of us look to reconnect with Israel, let us focus upon its people rather than the actual land and its history. While the land obviously has great spiritual significance, it is nothing without its people or G-d's covenant and promises to awaken them. This must become our central theme with our Israel focus, as it is G-d's plan to establish His kingdom upon the earth through their spiritual reconnection.

As the Church fully embraces this role to help rebirth them in this regard, with a huge emphasis on prayer and intercession, the natural outflow and workings of the Spirit will lead those of us who live in more Jewish populated areas to begin to reach out more effectively in witness and evangelism.

JUST ONE JEWISH PERSON OR ONE FAMILY

If we only look at the basic mathematics when we compare the Gentile population to the Jewish one, how long do we really think it would take to really make an impact among them if every

Gentile believer living in a Jewish area committed themselves to just one Jewish person or family? Consider this especially when we are beginning to enter into conversations about G-d and conveying the message in a more connected manner. In G-d's timing, with a lot of love, patience, and prayer, the Spirit will be able to break down the barriers that exist between us so that He can begin to penetrate their spirits and bring them to faith. Please begin to pray and ask the L-rd for guidance here in whom you could reach? It is only by stepping out that we can make a difference; just one prayer can change everything!

In my mind, however, until we see a greater movement of G-d's Spirit in awakening the Jewish people, without a shadow of a doubt the most effective way to reach out and share our faith is through friendships—what I call *lifestyle Jewish evangelism*. I am by no means suggesting it is the only way to reach out to Jewish people, because G-d can use anything and we should never look to limit Him in this regard. However, most traditional forms of Christian evangelism are usually not effective with Jewish people, owing mainly to the great divides that exist between us.

Most Jews see Christianity as a totally separate religion to that of their own faith, one that they should definitely stay away from, owing to all of the persecution that has come from it toward the Jewish people. While we obviously need to work on breaking down these barriers in our witness to them, I cannot stress this point enough in the hope that it will be firmly established in our minds and spirits so we are more sensitive to the Jewish psyche.

They also have little understanding, if any at all, of the connection that actually exists between the two faiths. And who could blame them when we think of how separate Christianity has been presented from its Jewish heritage up to this point?

THE CHURCH HAS AN EDICT
TO THE JEWISH PEOPLE

The apostle Paul gave us a command, one that we should not take lightly:

> I am talking to you Gentiles. Inasmuch as I am the apostle to the Gentiles, I make much of my ministry in the hope that I may somehow arouse my people to envy and save some of them (Romans 11:13-14).

If the apostle to the Gentiles spent a majority of his time trying to reach the Jewish people, always going to them first, then why shouldn't we? And especially now that we have realized we are actually the vessels chosen by our Father to release mercy back to them (see Rom. 11:30-31).

CAUSING JEALOUSY

How can we make them jealous? We are attempting to promote something that actually already belongs to them (without most of them even knowing it), yet appears so foreign from their own faith. While the Gentile branch of Christianity may work for the nations, it does not work for the Jews and we must look to reconnect our witness back to them from their own vine (see Rom. 11:16-18). This is one of the main reasons why presenting Christianity in its current form does not work and loses much of its effectiveness toward the Jewish people, as it has been separated from its Jewish roots.

If you have read this far in this book, then you have already been confronted with many of the bloodline issues that have caused the divide between us and hopefully dealt with them in your heart, now praying for your church and the Body at large to do the same. As a result of this, I am not going to readdress these issues, except to say that in regard to our Jewish witness, if we can learn to present the New Covenant from a Jewish perspective in a reconnected manner, it will make a huge difference in our effectiveness in arousing jealousy. This is one of the main reasons why our spiritual reconnection is so vital.

The apostle Paul wrote, *"Salvation has come to the Gentiles to make Israel envious"* (Rom. 11:11). What exactly did he mean by this term anyway, and what should they be envious of? They should be envious of our New Covenant relationship with their G-d. For when we accept Jesus and give our lives over to Him to live by faith, are we not supposed to come into a personal and intimate relationship with G-d where we know Him for ourselves? And wasn't this the covenant that was promised to them first through the prophet Jeremiah (see Jer. 31:34)?

IT'S OUR PERSONAL RELATIONSHIP WITH G-D

It is our relationship with G-d, the intimacy and personal connection that we have with Him, that the apostle Paul was referring to when he challenged us to draw them to envy. For in reality, we in the Body of Christ are now the ones who have this connection with Him. But it makes a huge difference when we re-present the Gospel back to them as being theirs in the first place, showing and expressing great gratitude for all their people have done for us as well as giving us Jesus. This will ultimately cause them to question more when they personally witness the dynamic of our own relationship with their G-d, claiming and fully associating it to their Jewish heritage.

MARIA: RELATIONSHIP WITH MY G-D WAS REAL

This will naturally give them a lot more to think about and is exactly what happened to me when Maria (the person who led me to the L-rd) shared Yeshua with me. After a while, I knew that her relationship with G-d was real and that there was a legitimate exchange going on between her and G-d. "How come this Gentile girl knows my G-d and I don't?" was the question I eventually asked myself.

Maria presented Yeshua's message to me as if she had a relationship with the Jewish G-d, the G-d of Abraham, and in a completely Jewish light. She also presented it with such a deep love and a sincere respect for my people and our heritage, that over time I was naturally drawn to jealousy because she knew my G-d and I didn't, if I was willing to be honest with myself.

Maria never even spoke of the New Testament because she was already aware of the resistance that we Jews had to anything Christian. She was also grateful for all of the contributions my people had made and was conscious of all that we had suffered. Instead, she focused on the prophecies in the Hebrew Scriptures and spoke the words of Yeshua and the apostles through her own speech as if they were just an extension of Judaism itself and the other covenants given by G-d.

She also explained the New Covenant that was promised to us through the Jewish prophet Jeremiah (see Jer. 31:31-34). She explained that through the Passover, Yeshua had laid down His life for all of us and, as a result, she had been grafted into the same covenants that G-d had given to me. She was now also a child of Abraham (see Rom. 4:16-18; 11:17; Gal. 3:6-14).

Despite my current rejection of the Gospel, Maria saw me as the other half of G-d's spiritual family whom G-d still loved and had covenanted with, His love flowing through her. Can you see the connection in how Maria presented the Gospel to me? In this way, the Word of G-d was still going out, but it was being presented in a different form, in its Jewish light, in a reconnected manner. And because Maria worked through the connection from the Old to the

New, I was brought to envy in the process. And I thank G-d that I was.

Maria was no expert either, she just learned through experience because G-d had given her such a deep love for the Jewish people that she couldn't stop sharing the message—and she was bold about it too. In so doing, I am sure G-d taught her through her trials and errors to become an effective witness to the Jews as she quickly learned what and what not to say in order to promote her King back to His firstborn.

The key for Maria is that she always had the *boldness* to step out. If you don't have boldness, pray and ask G-d to give it to you, for He willingly provides for all of our needs according to the riches of Christ Jesus (see Phil. 4:19).

WE ARE ALL CALLED TO BE WITNESSES

While we may not all be evangelists, we are all called to share our faith with those who G-d puts around us. We should be Spirit led here, for He gives us liberty and wisdom in this area. What was it that Jesus taught the apostles right before He ascended into heaven? He said, *"Go and make disciples of all nations..."* (Matt. 28:19). If we are willing, the opportunities will always come as there is a lost and dying world out there in great need of the light He has placed in each of us. There may be people around you that only you can reach because of your life and your experience, which G-d may have tailored for that particular person. If we are fearful or nervous, we risk the chance of losing great blessings in our lives by not opening up and stepping out. So if you struggle in these areas, pray and ask G-d to help you, confess any obstacles in your heart, and He will take them away so you can become more free to share your faith.

Please also keep in mind that I am not presenting a formula for Jewish evangelism here, but rather a position in which to bring the message of salvation back to the Jewish people. For despite all of Maria's efforts to win me to faith as well as her own experience, I still did not come easy. And like every Jew from the West who comes to faith in Christ, we had to work through the *inherent barriers* in our bloodline that are there to keep us away from Yeshua.

Without Maria's prayer and intercession for me, however, I am not sure I would be where I am today. It was G-d's sovereignty that led her to pray and push in the Spirit, causing the walls to fall down and the grace of G-d to be loosed upon me, ultimately bringing me in. But without Maria, whom would G-d have worked through? *She was my Ezekiel who prophesied for the breath of G-d to breathe into me so that I could live* (see Ezek. 37).[2]

LIFESTYLE JEWISH EVANGELISM

So what is lifestyle Jewish evangelism? With the Holy Spirit's leading, it is using our life and our time to develop sincere and genuine friendships with Jewish people so that the Gospel can go out to them through us. It is committing ourselves to them to reflect the love of G-d through our friendships and day-to-day life, developing trust and sincerity before anything else with no other strings attached.

DEVELOP TRUST FIRST

At the beginning of many of these new friendships, the open door to conversations about G-d and Yeshua were more limited because the love and the trust that friendships often develop was not in place enough to share more freely with our Jewish friends. At that time, they also may not have been able to handle it and it could have cut off our relationship with them if the timing was wrong.

In the New Covenant, we also *learn through trial and error*; and in being overzealous about sharing our faith, we most probably frightened some away in the process. However, the key is to learn from it in the hope that it will make us wiser the next time. I love the Scripture from the apostle Peter that says we should always be ready to give an account for what we believe (see 1 Pet. 3:15).

LOOK IT UP IF YOU DON'T KNOW

We don't always have all the answers and cannot explain everything (see Deut. 29:29). However, when an issue comes up that Scripture does shed light upon and we are unable to explain, it always helps to do some research and study so we are ready the next time the question arises. This is how we learn. So don't be afraid to make mistakes or to tell people that you don't know something.

BE SENSITIVE TO HIS LEADING

Being led by the Spirit helps provide continuity and balance in what we should say and even when we should say it. Our ever-increasing dependency on His voice from within us and the personal connection we share with the Father and the Son through His Holy Spirit will give us all the help we need in reaching out, for it is His pleasure to lead us. There is a similarity here in how we listen in prayer and intercession and how we share our faith, as the Holy Spirit loves to guide us if we can only become better listeners to that gentle voice from within.

We will also not be able to properly move in lifestyle evangelism without having the Father's heart first. Our love must be genuine. Most Jewish people are extremely smart, and if our love and friendship is not sincere, or even if they see we are looking to awaken them more than anything else, the doors of opportunity will quickly close and may not reopen again without a lot of prayer.

If we are in G-d's timing to help draw them to the faith, they will also quickly get over it once we have reestablished the sincerity of our connection and friendship. Loving our Jewish friends and neighbors through the power of His Spirit makes all the difference in how we both relate and respond to them with His heart, for it is difficult not to be sincere in our approach as the Father is love.

It is a good thing to pray for this sensitivity, and also how to move and operate in His heart. As we do, we will naturally find more of His qualities leading and directing us. If we make a mistake, or when our own nature or will gets in the way, it is also good to remember our humanity and to be open and honest about it, always with G-d and sometimes with our Jewish friends as well. Humility can go a long way in establishing and demonstrating our sincerity and love.

There is so much misunderstanding from the Jewish side about Jesus, and their perception of Him has far more to do with curses than it does with blessings, so one has to learn to tread carefully in this regard. Once the friendship has been built, there is already a foundation in place in which we can build upon, and it is here that the conversations can begin to flow more freely because they will feel less threatened or intimidated. This happens as they know how much we already accept them for who they are, which is very important. Try to understand that because of the past there are deep chasms of fear in the Jewish mindset when it comes to Jesus, much of which needs to be broken down through prayer.

ABOUT JEWISH PEOPLE

For evangelistic purposes, we can divide Jewish people into two main groups: *religious* and *secular*. Of course, there are numerous differences within both groups. Religious Jews (Orthodox) hold rigidly to their interpretations of the law in every aspect of their lives; the less Orthodox, who are also known as *Conservative* or *Reformed,* are more accepting to the world around them.

While the extreme legalism amongst the Orthodox was a major turnoff to me, as it is to most secular Jews, let's try to keep things in perspective. If it was not for these G-d-fearing folk holding rigorously to their beliefs, it would have been difficult for Judaism to have survived into the modern day as secular Jews do not always marry in the faith. In addition, wherever the Word of G-d is kept and honored, there is always a measure of light. Please keep in mind that despite being misguided, they are extremely dedicated to serving G-d through their rabbinical laws.

Most Jews are actually secular (Reformed) and are mostly liberal in their approach. They hold mainly to the basic traditions of the faith, with little knowledge at all of their own Scriptures, except for the more famous Bible stories. Most Christians are actually surprised by this when they first encounter a Jewish person and engage in conversation. Their connection to their faith is not based upon the Word of G-d, but rather on its traditions and heritage. Most secular Jews only really attend Synagogue on the main Jewish holidays (Rosh Hashanah and Yom Kippur), or when one of their family or friends' children are being Bar or Bat Mitzvahed (Son or Daughter of the Law).

Nearly all secular Jews attend at least one Passover Seder service with their friends and family. They are comfortable in the worldly system, often excelling in many different areas. They have also made some incredible contributions to our modern society and definitely excel in leadership in light of their gifts from G-d that are irrevocable (see Rom. 11:29).

Most secular Jews are agnostic, acknowledging some sort of a spiritual world and/or G-dhead but not really knowing it, and a good number of Jews are atheists. But nearly all Reformed and Conservative Jews live very much in the world along with its principles and, for the most part, are comfortable in doing so. There is also a strong drive amongst Jewish people for success, which is extremely important to them in how they relate to one another.

A TIME TO BECOME
MORE CONFRONTATIONAL

I have a Jewish friend whom I have been sharing with for years, and it was only recently that I became more confrontational in my witness to him. All of a sudden, I found myself speaking stronger, more challenging words. As I did this I could feel his discomfort, but I also knew how close we had become, and because of our friendship he could deal with it. I was personally witnessing the Word of G-d cutting into his heart. I knew the Word of G-d was going out to him and that it would not come back void.

At the same time, the Holy Spirit was confirming and encouraging me in this like I had almost earned the right to be more confrontational. And despite his discomfort, it was perfectly okay. We don't always know G-d's timing and that's why His leading and our agreement with it can make such a difference in the lives of the people around us.

In lifestyle Jewish evangelism, we are committed to our Jewish friends whether they believe or not; for their awakening is not within our control, but rather in the hands of our most loving and patient G-d, who actually loves them more than we do. However, He certainly uses our prayer and discernment along the way to help in the process; so *listening* to many of their responses and objections is important in how we should actually pray for them. The closer we get to the heart of people with the Gospel, the closer we get to hear and see their objections and defenses to it.

LIGHT PIERCES THE HEART

Think about the Samaritan woman at the well with Jesus as He told her about her life (see John 4). As He touched her heart and began to get closer to her, her defenses came up in what she believed in. She said, *"Sir, I can see that You are a prophet. Our fathers worshiped on this mountain…"* and then immediately she explained her differences in faith to that of the Jews (John 4:19-20).

It is here, with our friends' responses and objections, that we listen with our spiritual antennas so that we can immediately take them to prayer. Then we should ask G-d to deal with whatever is in the way in order to break through these resistances so His Word can go forth. It is here, as their personal intercessor, that He may lead us into more focused intercession for them to bring down certain spirits or strongholds that may be attached to these obstacles and defenses. This is so they can be dealt with in the spiritual realm, thereby breaking them off in the natural realm.

Connecting the dots from what we are hearing to what we are praying is essential in the overall process. Otherwise, we can miss out on the power of prayer to intervene and bring about change, which will come about in G-d's timing.

COMMON BARRIERS

There are a number of common barriers that exist when sharing our faith with Jewish people: fear, anger, and even hatred are some of the emotions they can feel when first being confronted with Christ.

However, one of the good things to come from our modern humanistic world from the Jewish side is a greater tolerance toward other religions and faiths. "As long as it works for you, it's okay with me," is a common response from most secular Jewish people today. But as you get closer to them and lead them to their Messiah, usually one of these emotions surface, the most common of which is fear.

As we begin to share our faith and the Word of G-d goes out through us, some Jewish people will actually feel threatened. This is just not a place that any Jew will ever consider at first in light of their own inherent bloodline against Christ because of persecution.

For most Jews, especially from their ancestry, anything "Christian" has been used against them. As a result, there is an invisible line between our faiths that they should never get near to and definitely should never cross. So don't be surprised if their heart quickly closes and they look to shut you down in conversation or change the subject.

Please understand that this a normal response from a Jewish person, something we just need to pray through until the next time when the door opens again, which it will in time. We must not try not to take it personally either. We must continue to be patient and sensitive to the Holy Spirit's leading and continue to love them as our friend.

Fewer Jewish people today will actually express their anger than in the days past—but they are more likely to do this with a Jewish believer than with a Gentile one. Gentile believers actually have more grace here, especially when sharing their faith from a reconnected position. Jewish people are more likely to be led quicker into deeper conversations with their Gentile friends than with Jewish believers, as they are naturally less threatening. I can attest to this from my own experiences.

The same love principles apply to Jewish believers here when sharing their faith, as love never fails! It is one thing for a Jewish person to try to understand Yeshua's message coming from a Gentile, but when it is being presented from one of their own, it is much closer to home and too close for comfort. I have often experienced their fear more easily as a result.

IT BECOMES EASIER WITH MORE FUEL

Regarding other heart issues: Jewish people are just like everyone else. And just by listening to where they come from and how they operate, they can tell us what we should be praying about for them.

Bringing the Gospel to our Jewish friends can definitely be a lengthy process, which is why our friendship with them is so important. But this is going to change as the heart of the Church looks to reconnect with Israel in the Spirit. As the Church begins to push and cry out in prayer for this baby to come forth, the present barriers between Jew and Christian will not only soften but ultimately be brought down so the Word can go forth with power. The *heart of stone* among the Jewish people will be *transformed into a heart of flesh* (see Ezek. 36:26). This is much more complicated than it sounds; however, the process is still the same.

To a certain extent this is already happening, and much more is needed to help us get the job done. I think of some of the stories that are happening now to the Gentile intercessors in our prayer group at Messiah's House: how the Holy Spirit is opening doors to rather unusual circumstances in their own lifestyle Jewish evangelism, and how they are more effectively impacting Jewish lives when sharing from that reconnected place. And this is not only among secular Jews, but among the Orthodox as well. The more we sow into this place, the more we will reap!

New movements take time, especially this one, because it is extremely complex and has so many nuances. But as it catches on in the Church, there will come a point of flooding and major breakthrough when G-d's Body will open to His plan. So please be patient and remember that G-d is ultimately in charge. Know that as the prayer and intercession increases around the world for Israel's spiritual awakening, we will begin to see more and more Jewish people coming to faith. It is only a question of G-d's time and plan.

THROUGH THE FEASTS

Another great way to reach out to and connect with our Jewish friends is through the Jewish feasts and calendar. As I have already mentioned in earlier chapters, Gentile believers can fully enjoy their own participation in any of these Jewish holidays without legalism. And what better way to connect to our Jewish friends than through their own events that also now belong to us.

In embracing the Jewish feasts[3] into our church calendars, we can find tremendous reconnection, not only in the Spirit but also in our theology. More importantly, though, as we look to rebuild the bridges from the new to the old in order to awaken Israel, the feasts can be used as common ground between us to better reflect the intimacy of our New Covenant connection. I have conducted so many Passover Seders for the Church that I can tell you personally what a thrill it is for all Gentile believers to share the wonderful connection of Messiah through the Passover meal and its remembrance. It is also a thrill for me to see my Gentile believing family enjoying the feasts of the L-rd.

Just recently, however, I attended my first Passover Seder, which was run by Gentile believers; very good friends of mine, Kent and Josephine Johnson, who are part of the leadership in Messiah's House. Even though they had been to numerous Seders, they had never done this before and were a little nervous. But it was one of the best Seders I have been to in years. Kent invited the Holy Spirit's leading into the night and the rest was history. It was just so full of fun, excitement, and the richness of the Word of G-d. And here my Christian friends were actually leading it; what a blessing it was!

This is one of the main purposes of the reconnection for this day and hour of the time in history we are living in. It is a time G-d has chosen to unite His family once and for all so that the new era may come, which I believe will be quite Jewish in its characteristic—a Jewish L-rd returning to a Jewish city, sitting on a Jewish throne, and celebrating Jewish feasts. I think we need to get prepared, don't you? What a blessing G-d is actually bestowing on us in the Church, one that we should also be extremely grateful for—to live in the time that is close to our L-rd's return and also to be able to play a major role in this occurrence to help bring it all to pass!

PRESENCE EVANGELISM[4]

I would be remiss if I did not make mention of power encounters. Jesus's experience with the Samaritan woman at the well is a great example of this in how He operated in the gifts of the Holy Spirit to bring her to faith (see John 4:16-17). With just one word of insight (a word of knowledge [see 1 Cor. 12:8]), Jesus was able to open the door to her heart. It enabled Him to effectively break down any barriers between them. And look at the fruit of the ministry toward her—how it ended up affecting a whole town of people.

If we are willing to move out into the spiritual realm more, the Holy Spirit is always there to help us reach out to others. In addition, let's not forget that His desire to win souls is always greater than our own and we could never find a better partner in this regard. If we are willing to learn to listen more to that inner voice of G-d within us, we may find that the results can be encouraging in helping us to be more effective as we reach out.

Greater dependency on the Holy Spirit is all that we need for this to happen. He will always guide us; we just need to learn to listen better. In addition, any example to demonstrate our spiritual connection with G-d toward others will always help further establish the kingdom dynamic between us and those we are trying to reach. This is good as it is the relationship that we have with Him that can ultimately make them envious.

OFFER PRAYER WHEN APPROPRIATE

We may sometimes have the opportunity to pray for our Jewish friends that we are sharing with. What may be natural to us—to pray for things and different circumstances as we are living a life of faith—is most definitely not natural to them. I am not suggesting that Jewish people do not pray or talk to G-d; however, our experience in prayer as believers in the New Covenant is quite different to most secular Jews, and most of the time they will be grateful that we offered if the opportunity called for it. When you pray with them, it is important to use intimate terms between you and G-d that demonstrate your relationship with Him; but also be careful to choose the right words, using more Jewish references for Christian terms.

During our Hanukkah celebration recently at Messiah's House, I asked one of my closest Christian friends, Al Sanchirico, who is also one of our board members, to say the blessing over the food. His prayer was beautiful and connected, and I know some of my Jewish friends were touched by it. It demonstrated a spiritual relationship and intimacy with the Father, which actually caused one of my Jewish friends to become uncomfortable (which is okay by the way). If we don't rustle their feathers occasionally, how will they ever see the difference between us?

Al made a number of errors, however, which would have been fine in the normal Christian circles. But Al was not just with believers, he was also with a number of Jewish people at the party who had not yet come into a relationship with Messiah. Al immediately picked up on this when we discussed it at a later time and he truly learned from this experience, which is why we both think it is a good story to share in this book.

First, he prayed in Jesus's name instead of Yeshua's, and then he mentioned the Trinity in his prayer, except he did it in a normal Christian way. The problem is that most Jewish people think that Christians worship three gods, so instead of reinforcing reconnection here, his prayer actually perpetuated the separation between the two faiths. The lesson learned was this: we obviously all need to be more sensitive in the words we choose to use when around Jewish people.[5]

DON'T BE FEARFUL TO
MOVE IN THE SPIRIT

I truly believe, in this last era before the L-rd returns, moving more in the gifts of the Holy Spirit is an essential part of G-d's plan to better equip us for the increased spiritual climate that is coming. It is also important to be able to better discern the counterfeit and the works of darkness that are only going to increase during these times.

The book of Revelation speaks about a strong spiritual climate on both sides of the fence. From my own experience, as one who may have gotten carried away in the gifts earlier on in my faith, there is definitely a healthy balance that can be had in this area, especially when we are focused on using them for G-d's glory. The gifts of the Holy Spirit do not make us any more spiritual, as only His character can make us godlier. This is the greatest danger of the supernatural—thinking we are more spiritual by moving in the gifts as can be clearly seen from the Corinthian church. But let's try not to discount the gifts either, because we cannot necessarily control them. After all, who is the boss anyway?

Power encounters can be a real blessing in our witness to our Jewish friends. Dependency on the Holy Spirit is vital for power encounters to take place—they go hand in hand.

We will most often find doors of opportunity opening up in our various conversations with our Jewish friends, and we'll probably notice when the door is closing as well. Most of the time in the beginning they can usually only handle so much talk about G-d anyhow. So please try to remember that the Word of G-d cuts into the heart, so we need to learn to be sensitive here and not be too pushy.

HEAVENLY DOORS

Heavenly doors are the doors of conversation that will open up in lifestyle Jewish evangelism, or any type of evangelism for that matter. We need to be sensitive to these doors and learn to flow with them, as at the right time we put the Word of G-d out there to do its work upon our friends' hearts.

Listening is also key here in how to respond to them, *if* we respond at all at first. Then we can take what we hear to prayer so G-d can deal with it in the spiritual realm. But the more we explain our faith from our reconnection, the more effective we will be for G-d to begin to penetrate their hearts and help lead them to faith.

DOS AND DON'TS

It is not my intention in this book to give you a long list of the dos and don'ts in Jewish evangelism, as there are already some good books on the subject, which could always be referenced as you enter into this experience.[6] But I do want to share some guidelines to keep in mind when evangelizing the Jewish people.

SHARE FROM THE RECONNECTION

I want to emphasize the significance on reaching out in a *reconnected manner* that will make all the difference in reaching our Jewish friends. If we can refocus on the fact that Christianity is a Jewish faith, fully understanding our Jewish friends' disconnection as well as their objections and resistances due to our past history, then it will go a long way in becoming more effective in our witness to them.

We should show our love for them, our sincerity, and how grateful we are to them and their people for all that they have given to us. We should acknowledge the call on them when it comes up, that they are His firstborn with a special calling; and because of Yeshua we are now connected to them as well as being grafted into their covenants and promises.

USE JEWISH TERMS INSTEAD

Use Jewish terms and focus on the Hebrew Scriptures when witnessing to them. Do you know that He was never called Jesus once while on the earth (of which my Jewish evangelist friend Jeffrey Bernstein always reminds us about this)? Nor was His mother called Mary, but rather Miriam. So use His Jewish name (Yeshua) and be sensitive to the signage and emblems of our faith that have been used against the Jewish people.

Refer to Jesus as Yeshua, Christ as Messiah, the cross as that tree, the Church as congregation, and the Gospel as the New Covenant, which we can tie into their own Scripture through Jeremiah's prophecy (see Jer. 31:31-34). You can also relate to the trinity through the Shema and the plurality of G-d which is spoken of in the Torah (see Genesis 1:2; 1:26; Deut.6:4). In addition, whenever we refer to the Jewish people, we should not simply use the word "Jew" or "Jews," because most of the time it automatically pushes a memory button in association with anti-Semitism amongst Jewish people.

CHRISTIANEEZE

Also refrain from *Christianeeze*. If every word out of our mouth is hallelujah, praise G-d, and amen (which is okay when around believers), they will quickly think we are strange and causing more separation, which we have to work hard against in our witness. We should be wise in the way we act toward outsiders, making the most of every opportunity (see Col. 4:5-6).

Hopefully I've given you some good tools and guidelines to keep in mind while witnessing to the Jewish people. But remember that these are only guidelines, and listening to the Spirit speak to you about each individual is the key in seeing them come to faith.

ENDNOTES

1. Please refer to www.jewishvirtuallibrary.org for a thorough listing of many of these countries with each of their respective Jewish populations.

2. You can read more about my awakening experience in my first book, *The New Covenant Prophecy*, which goes into much greater detail about my personal testimony.

3. The Jewish feasts are: Purim—the Jews deliverance from Haman; Passover and Feast of Unleavened Bread—Israel's deliverance from Egypt; Shavuot—celebration of the giving of the law, which is the same day as Pentecost; Rosh Hashanah—The Feast of Trumpets, the Jewish New Year; Yom Kippur—the Day of Atonement; Sukkot—Tabernacles; Hanukkah and Feast of Dedication—the celebration of light. Some of these feasts were not written about in the Torah, but rather came later. For a great read on the explanation of Jewish feasts for Christians, see *The Feasts of Adonai* by Valerie Moody.

4. I got the term "presence evangelism" from Art Katz, who is one of my mentors in the faith.

5. There is a great way to discuss the Trinity in a more Jewish sensitive manner based around the Shema, the oneness of G-d (see Deut. 6:4). And if you go to www.reconnectingministries .org and click the *What We Believe* tab, there is a great definition of the Trinity in more reconnected terms. But I bless my dear brother for his humility, as honestly this is how we all learn.

6. Some good books on Jewish evangelism are *The Olive Tree Connection* by John Fischer, *You Bring the Bagels, I'll Bring the Gospel* by Barry Rubin, and *Yeshua, the Messiah* by David Chernoff.

12

SIGN HERE

I have not written this book to just raise our awareness on the issue of Israel and the Church, but without a decent explanation, it would be impossible for us to go to the next step. Any foundation we look to in the New Covenant should always be firmly rooted in the Word of G-d, which I hope I have fully demonstrated with the Father's heart in *The Ezekiel Generation*.

The question I have for us all is this: What will we now do with this information? Will it be business as usual or will we look to take the truths and revelations of this book and apply them to our faith? Will we allow the Father's heart to change us and bring about the corrections He desires so that His family can finally be united and His end-time plan be fulfilled?

G-D HAS GIVEN US A COMMISSION

G-d has given us a commission in the Church to draw Israel to envy and to release His mercy back to them. This must be considered carefully in this time of transition in the family of G-d between Jews and Gentiles. Like Jonah, who did not understand

G-d's timing and never thought the Ninevites would repent, Israel is being prepared by G-d for this time of reconciliation, and their spiritual awakening is coming. Which is all the more reason for us in the Body of Christ, who have received the prophet's call, to ready ourselves for the time we are coming into so His plan to glorify His Son upon the earth will come to pass.

We will never see this through our natural eyes, but only through the Father's heart. This family connection can only come through the Spirit of G-d and through His revelation to us. It is definitely a heartfelt issue, as G-d desires to make Jew and Gentile one at this time.

WE MUST BE SPIRITUALLY LINKED TO ISRAEL

In order for this to take place, we must spiritually reconnect to Israel and reestablish the kingdom principle of putting the Jew first, as per Christ and the apostolic foundations of our faith. This in itself will dramatically change how we go about presenting the kingdom of G-d and our overall witness to the Jewish people, opening the door more fully to their return. This is inclusive of how we will embrace Jewish believers as they come to faith, releasing and empowering them into their calling to be a light to their own people.

When we fully embrace the Father's heart message and the reconnection to our Jewish brethren, we will invite the power of G-d to transfigure the end-time Church into its full destiny—into the fullness of the Gentiles and the Jews upon the earth. This message is so highly significant to us that placing the golden key into the heavenly door through the will of God, will change this world forever—and let it be so that the kingdom can come upon us!

By blessing Israel and taking on the role of helping to rebirth them into the kingdom of G-d, we have everything to gain and absolutely nothing to lose. As I have discussed throughout this book, neither of us can actually come into our inheritance without the other, which is the perfect plan of our Father: to unite His children before He returns by breathing the breath of life back into the Jewish people through the power of the Holy Spirit. Not only will they receive their full inheritance, but we will also receive ours—ruling and reigning together with Christ on the earth. These are the times we are coming into, the glory of the L-rd upon the earth, amen.

THEY ARE SPECIAL, AND SO ARE YOU

In addition, I hope by now that in looking to reestablish kingdom positions, we do not in any way overexalt the Jewish people but rather honor them in the role they have been given. I hope that we can see their final journey by faith, which will actually help us overcome many of the obstacles in the natural that currently stand in the way of them receiving the Messiah. We must also keep in mind that in loving them at this point, they still are in great need of G-d's redemption without even knowing or wanting it. But there is no clearer word for us than in the letter written to the Hebrews, that *"faith is the substance of things hoped for, the evidence of the things not seen"* (Heb. 11:1 KJV).

With the Father's love we *must* see them through His eyes and words, not as they currently are but as He has called them to be, and pray for them to the point of their own redemption through Christ. This will only come through the New Covenant that was given to them before it was given to the rest of the world. Indeed, the first truly shall be last!

LET OUR LIGHT SHINE

This world is getting darker as has been foretold (see 2 Tim. 3:1-5), which is all the more reason for our righteousness to shine and for the Body of Christ to come together despite our many differences. We must let love and faith so shine in our hearts that it will win the balance of G-d's children, both Jew and Gentile alike, before it is too late. We must let the power of G-d be loosed upon us to heal our divides, so that His kingdom will be glorified upon the earth; and we must prepare ourselves for the great battle that is ahead of us in order for the kingdom of G-d to fully come.

CHALLENGING BUT GLORIOUS

I would be remiss in this book if I did not make any mention of the time to come, as I personally believe there are challenging times ahead for all of us. These times will be extremely exciting for the kingdom of G-d, and I think it is important for us to properly prepare ourselves. Like the five virgins who had enough oil to wait for their bridegroom, we really need to be serious about our faith in these coming days (see Matt. 25:1-13).

As the power of darkness thickens upon the earth, there will be no room left for lukewarm believers—we will either be hot or not! We know judgment is coming and have already received a number of warnings. However, within the acts of judgment against humankind's sins, there are always cries from the G-d of mercy for our hearts to come into repentance. G-d said in the Old Covenant:

> *If My people, who are called by My name, will humble themselves and pray and seek My face and turn from their wicked ways, then will I hear from heaven and forgive their sin and heal their land* (2 Chronicles 7:14).

This is a time for us to make sure our walk with G-d is where it is supposed to be, and for us to earnestly pray for our countries, our world, and its peoples. We are to earnestly pray for the kingdom of G-d to be glorified on the earth and that many of G-d's children would be saved out of it.

At the end of the day, when you think about it from an eternal perspective, what counts in the end is who will be there with us and who will not! This is why Jesus told us to fear the One who has the power to give life to our souls (see Matt. 10:28). Yet the world is blinded to these warnings because of sin, so their adverse reactions should not be surprising to us.

WE MUST NOT BE IGNORANT OF THE ENEMY'S SCHEMES

As we enter into this time of shaking, let us hold tightly to the tenants of our faith and to the Word of G-d so that His light can shine so brightly through us to a world that desperately needs Him. Let us be more loving, and full of His mercy and understanding during these times.

Let us cross over into the world with a greater understanding of humankind's blindness because of sin and the devil's schemes to keep them that way, knowing that it was only His grace and His mercy that enlightened us in the first place, opening our eyes to the truth, for His sheep know His voice. Without Jesus we would be blinded like the rest of the world. So we must have more compassion for them instead of treating them like they are the enemy themselves. Think for a moment how free Christ was to be around sinners, and we must try to do the same without compromise.

Let us rather expose the trickery of the devil in prayer that is so deceptively turning the world against us, making us out to be the weird ones. For our battle is not with flesh and blood, but with spirits and with principalities (see Eph. 6:12). Let us plunder the heavenlies in such a way through prayer and intercession that the power of G-d would be more greatly manifested upon the earth and more clearly demonstrate the kingdom when we present it. This is so that His peace, which surpasses all understanding, would be manifest to those He is calling out at this time, and that many more souls would be made ready for His return and coming kingdom.

WILL WE BE READY?

Up to this point I have deliberately made no mention of tribulation and rapture theology, as it can be so divisive among us. While most believers have their own opinions about these times, including myself, I am not sure if we are really supposed to know for certain until it actually happens. While I believe that we will be raptured at some point, whether in the beginning or the middle or at the end of the tribulation, and that there are some really good scriptural debates on each theory, we should ensure that we are as ready as we can be for this time. G-d forbid that we should be surprised or even disappointed if He does not call us up at the beginning of the tribulation period.

One of my concerns for those of us who are "pre-tribbers" in our doctrines of belief, is how the enemy could dramatically use this against us if we end up having to go through the tribulation and are not prepared for it, firmly believing we will escape this time in history. How disappointed we may become in thinking our G-d has let us down during this very crucial time on the earth.

Please do not get me wrong here: I am not suggesting that this is going to happen, as in my mind only G-d knows the timing here for sure. But I say this so that we would consider it in the event it does not happen the way we have expected. If we were to go through this period before the L-rd returns, would not His grace be sufficient for us and would He not sovereignly protect us like He did with Israel in Egypt (see Exod. 8:22-23)? Israel only endured three of the plagues that were cast upon the Egyptians, and through the remainder of them they were sovereignly protected.

What truly matters here is that whatever the outcome is, we would be ready for it: if He calls me before the tribulation, I would be ready; if He calls me in the middle of it, I would be ready; and if He calls me in the end, I would be ready.

KINGDOM POWER

With our refocus on Israel's gathering and the unity of G-d's family upon the earth to glorify the L-rd, we are further empowering G-d's kingdom to be loosed upon us. This is so the grace and mercy of G-d provides such *dunamis* (explosive power) that the miracles of the first century, that were witnessed and experienced by the founders of the Church, would seem somewhat mild in comparison with what G-d is about to do in all the earth.

This type of kingdom power is awaiting us as we begin to more fully embrace our Ezekiel role and become much more of a praying Church than we presently are. *"For if their rejection is the reconciliation of the world, what will their acceptance be but life from the dead?"* (Rom. 11:15).

Finally, as we come down to the end and the heart of the Church receives the message of reconnection, Jewish believers will come into a period of great favor amongst their Gentile brethren, especially as the family of G-d becomes united. The question I have for you as the book now ends is this: Will you continue to support Israel until the end? Because before it will get better and before the L-rd returns, the time of Jacob's trouble is still to come (see Jer. 30:1-11). This is a time that will finally cause the balance of Israel to find redemption.

But this will not happen in their own strength, but rather through their brokenness. According to the prophet Daniel's response to the question he asked the two angels about the end times, these things will not come to pass until the power of the holy people has been finally broken (see Dan. 12:5-7). For Israel and the Church's dependency must be totally upon the L-rd to bring about the completion.

In light of G-d's mercy, I pray we would carefully think of how to offer ourselves to this work that is holy and pleasing to G-d (see Rom. 12:1). I leave you with the apostle Paul's writing to the Gentile Church:

> *For I tell you that Christ has become a servant of the Jews on behalf of G-d's truth, to confirm the promises made to the patriarchs so that the Gentiles may glorify G-d for His mercy* (Romans 15:8-9).

Are you ready to take on G-d's mercy plan? Are you ready to embrace Ezekiel's call?

Please sign here: _____

ABOUT GRANT BERRY

For more information about *The Ezekiel Generation*, the Father's heart for Israel, and the Church, please visit our website where you can e-mail Grant Berry with any questions or comments, www.reconnectingministries.org.